QUEENS PARK II
Scarlet Oaks
ROCKWOOD BEACH
Creek
WHITE GABLES
Sillery BAY
Mount Pleasant Beach
STOP
Westwood Manor
Rockview Beach
Riviera Isles
Improvement Association
QUEENS PARK I
OUTING PARK
PINE-GROVE VILLAGE
Stoneybrooke Village

The Pasadena Peninsula

The Pasadena Business Association Book Committee would like to say a special thank you to

ISABEL SHIPLEY CUNNINGHAM

and to

EMMA M. SCHRAMM

The Pasadena Peninsula

A CLOSER LOOK AT THE LAND BETWEEN TWO RIVERS

BY

Isabel Shipley Cunningham

2001

PASADENA BUSINESS ASSOCIATION

PBA Acknowledgements

The Pasadena Business Association Book Committee would like to say a special thank you to:

Isabel Shipley Cunningham for the thousands of hours spent researching, interviewing, writing, and indexing text, placing photos and offering of advice. It has been a pleasure to work with Isabel. She has given us all a very valuable gift—the pride and sense of community that comes from the knowledge of our history.

Emma M. Schramm for allowing us to publish her post office history as part of this book. We also thank her for all the advice, and leads.

Richard E. Stearns and The Natural History Society of Maryland, Inc. for all the information on Indian artifacts and for permission to print the pictures of artifacts in this area.

Mary Walsh Johnson for taking many trips out to the White Rocks at all hours of the day to get the best possible shot for the cover of this book.

Laura Wiegmann for taking pictures of all our new sponsors and several other photos we needed.

. . . and last but most importantly, all the **community and business members** who gave of their time for interviews, searched for photos, referred us to the right people and places and supported us as sponsors and patrons and with advice and encouragement.

Cover Photograph

This picture of the White Rocks at the mouth of the Rock Creek River was taken by Mary Walsh Johnson.

Published by Pasadena Business Association, P.O. Box 861, Pasadena, Maryland, 21123-0861
Phone: 410-987-4887

ISBN 0-9674542-1-2

Designed and produced by Fishergate, Inc., Annapolis, Maryland

Printed in the United States of America

Contents

Acknowledgments

I am indebted to many people for sharing their knowledge with me as I researched and wrote *Between Two Rivers: A Panoramic View of the Pasadena Peninsula* and *The Pasadena Peninsula: A Closer Look at the Land Between Two Rivers*. James B. Calvert, Charles H. Calvert, and Emma M. Schramm have answered countless questions patiently and have shared their memories and their collections generously. Jack Kelbaugh has given me file folders containing information about a variety of subjects and photocopies of many newspaper articles, as well as postcards and photographs. I did not cite his collection as a source each time I used his material because his contributions have been constant. He also read and made helpful comments on the text.

It is a pleasure to express my appreciation of the support of the Pasadena Business Association, especially the Editorial Committee, Wendy Harris, Maureen Agro, and George Athas. Their enthusiasm, dedication, and talents have made these two histories possible. I owe a special debt to Dr. James G. Gibb, archaeological consultant, for copyediting the text of both books with precision and offering helpful insights. Throughout this project my son, David W. Cunningham, has guided me patiently through the challenges of word processing.

Once more I thank staff at the Maryland State Archives, Maryland Law Library, Kuethe Library, Enoch Pratt Free Library, the Kuhn Library at the University of Maryland Baltimore Campus, the Maryland Historical Society, and Anne Arundel County public libraries at Annapolis, Riviera Beach, and Mountain Road. I am grateful also to Wayne Olsen at the National Agricultural Library at Beltsville and Ann McIntyre at the National Arboretum branch of the National Agricultural Library for their guidance.

I am indebted especially to those who have shared specialized knowledge with me. Wayne E. Clark, Executive Director of the Office of Museum Services, Maryland Historical Trust, and the Jefferson Patterson

Park and Museum, helped me to understand the pre-history of the Pasadena peninsula. Specific information about this area is not available in reference books. Rev. Edwin C. Schell, Executive Secretary of the Methodist Historical Society, Lovely Lane Museum and Library, gave me copies of his meticulous notes on Methodist Protestant records and church periodicals. His research revealed forgotten information about the White Marsh Church at Lake Shore. Milton O. Duvall's careful study of Civil War records and newspapers from the 1860s shed light on a little-known chapter of local history.

Delegate Joan Cadden, who represents the Pasadena area in the state legislature, and Shirley Murphy, Pasadena's representative on the County Council, have unfailingly answered questions about issues like traffic congestion and preservation of green space. Employees of the Maryland State Highway Administration, the Anne Arundel County Bureau of Highway Administration, the County Health Department, the County Board of Education, and Brian Woodward of the Department of Recreation and Parks have provided important information. Rick Holt, Superintendent of Downs Park, and Deborah Yeater, Superintendent of Lake Waterford Park, have been especially helpful.

Donna Ware, Historic Sites Planner at Anne Arundel County Planning and Code Enforcement; Michael Eismeier of the County Soil Conservation Service; Stephen Bilicki, Maryland Historic Trust Underwater Archaeologist; John Leocha, Assistant County Demographer; and Sherri Marsh, architectural historian, have shared their knowledge generously. I also appreciate the contributions of members of fire departments, clubs, and churches; Carolyn Roeding and Joseph Foran of the Greater Pasadena Council; James R. Morrison of Friends of Hancock's Resolution; and Mark N. Schatz, editor of Anne Arundel County *History Notes.*

The contributions of fifth grade pupils, who wrote community histories in 1952 under the direction of Virginia Dryden Moore, have been especially valuable. They have preserved much information that otherwise would have been lost. Others who provided essential information include Emma Jenkins Wade Sanders, who delved into the early history of the village of Pasadena; Gerald A. Smith, a Baltimore attorney whose father owned the resort called Beachwood; and Clara Dreyer Bomhardt, who shared vivid memories of a waterman's life. Joe Brockmeyer and Tom Owen guided me through the maze of sports organizations that field teams on the peninsula. Joe Brockmeyer also researched the history of many teams.

I thank Marie Angel Durner for sharing her recollections and for citing additional sources of information, Edward T. Calvert for sending me items from his collection, James Quick for his word-pictures of life at Camp Milbur, Clifford Phelps for an explanation of charcoal-making, Charles Hancock Calvert for identifying old automobiles, Willard Mumford for information about farming in Anne Arundel County, Marie Christian for a wealth of information about Green Haven, Jane McWilliams for pointing out avenues for research, Anne Cook Myllo for relating her family's history, and John Mason and Louis Doetsch for their astute observations.

I regret that I can only name many others who added immeasurably to this history:

Harold E. Fink
Samuel G. Kemp
Christopher George
Debbie Smigovsky
Reynolds Bunk
Sarah Tall
Michelle Lohin
Elmer E. Dunn
Diane Holmes
Robert Reyes
Helen Becker
Eileen Zindell
Darlene Schollian Evans
Sandy Anderson
Katie Ellison Holt
Al Grau
Chris Conner
Nancy Quasney
Rosemary Billing-Briggs
Harry Magaha
Robert Bartlett, D.D.S.
William Upton
Charlotte Gleim
Katherine Haines
William G. Rothamel
Tom Caines
Betty Raynor
Dorothy Sands Childs
Ann Jubb Dick
Margaret Ladner
Edwin Chaney, Jr.
Rosie Dailey
Cornelia Anderson Hepinstal
Andrew J. Matusky
Evelyn Reed
Stephanie Zebroski
Sharon Necessary Ranagan
Clara Klug Love
Louis P. Brown
Roger Stitt
Tess Johnson
Charles Manns
Philip Laumann
Albert and Edith Ramsay
John Wilson, Jr.
Robert Baxter
Carroll Babka
Dorothy Parsley

In addition to the contributions of Joe Brockmeyer and Tom Owen, the following people, who give generously of their time and energy to make possible the amazing number of teams that compete in a variety of sports on the peninsula, found time to answer my queries:

Richard Hare
Brent Lounge
Roy Jackson
Tom DeLeonardo
Robert Boyd
Tim Fogle
Lee Espegren
Mark Van Denberghe
Lee Stepp
Mike Breen
Don Bishoff
George Green
Bill Henderson
Gretchen Smith
Ed Vinson
John Warner
Nancy Schrumm
Tracy Crane
Bob Burns
Kathy Le Compte
Kim Salyers
Chip Salyers
Carl Cicchetti
Elmer Hoffman
Cathy Davis
Philip Laumann
Rosemary Billing-Briggs
Debbie Hutchinson
Bruce Warren
Mark Ryer
Chuck Yaruta
Carol Caines
Tom Caines

These people contributed important information that first appeared in the pictorial history of the peninsula:

Orlando Ridout
Jeanne Bohn
Senator Alfred Lipin
Marie Everd Oakie
Esther Groh Webster Williams
Edward C. Seipp
Herbert Sappington
Rayetta Wolle Windsor
Mildred Strobeck
Jack Mellin
Frances Klug Arnold
Virginia Dryden Moore
Robert and Hope Meyer
H. J. Morgereth
Jane Pumphrey Nes
Fran Dickson Koslowski Hasse
Harold E. Slanker, Jr.
John Williams
Helen Neisser
Lois Chairs Jubb
Joan Valenti
Mary Joe Robl
Carol Cross
Debbie Smigovsky
Gerry Strain Hedges
Brian Metzbower
Philip Beigel
Gladys Rowens
Lewis Frazetti
Dolores Klingelhoefer
William Stallings
Randall McLaughlin, M.D.

The following people have provided treasured photographs for this book:

James B. Calvert
Clara Dreyer Bomhardt
Jack Kelbaugh
Tom Feeley
Robert Reyes
Emma Jenkins Wade Sanders
The Schramm family
Ruth Yanky Volkman
Sharon Necessary Ranagan
Laura Wiegmann
Mary Johnson
Clark Elliott
Ann Jubb Dick
George Kelch
Glenda Bullock
John Wilson, Jr.
Ed Vinson
Robert Baxter
Evelyn Wade
Elmer Sims
William E. Harris, Jr.
Ed Vinson

Sources of photographs reprinted from *Between Two Rivers*:

Marion E. Warren
Blue Moon Aerial Photography
James B. Calvert
Jon Armentrout
Jack Kelbaugh
Schramm Collection
Clifford Phelps
Janet R. O'Connell
Anne Cook Myllo
Charles H. Calvert
John Wilson, Jr.
James R. Morrison
Clara Dreyer Bomhardt
Tom Redmond
Jim Anderson
Dale Courville
Dolores Klingelhoefer
Robert Boyd
Brent Lounge
Henry A. Schmidt
Walter Kramme
Drusilla Chairs
Ruth Y. Volkman
John Williams
Joyce Clocker
Elizabeth Williams Schmidl
Riviera Beach Volunteer Fire Company
Rick Holt, Downs Park Collection
Mark N. Schatz, A. A. County Historical Society
Louis Hine, Special Collections, UMBC
Anne Arundel County Division of Planning

Charles Cook photo,
Jacques Kelly Collection

A. Aubrey Bodine photo,
Jacques Kelly Collection

Maryland State Roads Commission,
Jacques Kelly Collection

News-American photos,
Jacques Kelly Collection

Foreword

Between Two Rivers, the remarkable pictorial history of Pasadena published by the Pasadena Business Association, was incredibly successful and embraced by the community. Accolades and praise were heaped on author Isabel Shipley Cunningham for her exploration of the peninsula. The Pasadena Business Association received the gratitude of residents for conceiving and producing the book. Members of the PBA Book Committee were thanked individually and were the happy recipients of hundreds of positive comments.

However, there was still a deep hunger by everyone to know even more about our hometown. Mrs. Cunningham had spent hundreds of hours researching, interviewing and writing about Pasadena, but the first book could contain only a small fraction of all that information. The PBA asked Mrs. Cunningham to expand her material for a second and very different book—an in depth, textbook-type history of Pasadena.

When community residents heard about the second book, they even more generously shared their photos, writings and memories. This second book, *The Pasadena Peninsula: A Closer Look at the Land Between Two Rivers*, is rich in facts and details and tells the whole story of Pasadena that can only make residents even prouder of their home.

While reading this book, remember that Isabel Cunningham traveled the roads of Pasadena visiting the homes of long-time residents, often interviewing them for hours. She reviewed hundreds of photographs, scanned dozens of carnival programs and business ads, and read every piece of research material available to her. She meticulously verified data many times over for accuracy. All of that work was woven into a vibrant and lively account of Pasadena's history, from prehistoric times until now.

This recreation of Pasadena life heretofore unknown to most of us is a gift from Mrs. Cunningham to whom we all owe a debt of gratitude.

The Pasadena Business Association is also grateful to the original Sponsors of *Between Two Rivers.* They believed in the book, and in the Book Committee personally, trusting that this enormous job could be accomplished. Once again, we are proud to have them be a part of our new book along with several new Sponsors who supported this second book even though it is so very different from *Between Two Rivers.* Our Sponsor businesses and the local businesses that generously gave their time and space to display and sell the books deserve the patronage of Pasadena residents.

We are proud that many decided to become Patrons of *The Pasadena Peninsula: A Closer Look at the Land Between Two Rivers.* They will have the pleasure of having their names in a book that will remain in libraries for generations.

Between Two Rivers made a profit, and the Pasadena Business Association has ensured that that money will be used to benefit the community. A trust fund has been established to ensure the future of the four college scholarships awarded to graduates of Northeast and Chesapeake High School each year. Money is also being channeled into support of needy Pasadena families. And part of that profit is being used to fund publication of this current book. The PBA has donated copies of both books to local schools, state archives, historical societies, and community fundraisers.

However, no dollar amount can be attached to the benefit of both books to the community. They have made Pasadena one of the most carefully researched communities in Maryland, and they have given us all a sense of place and pride. Teachers and school children, in particular, will use *The Pasadena Peninsula: A Closer Look at the Land Between Two Rivers.* This history will become a reference book for everyone connected in any way to Pasadena and will be resource tool for writers and historians.

The Pasadena Business Association History Book Project was truly a collaboration of those who shared their memories and photographs; those who supported the Project with money; those who offered positive encouragement and comments; those who sold the books; and those Book Committee members who gave so much of their time.

These books are the legacy of the Pasadena Business Association, and it is hoped that they will inspire even greater discoveries about our past. The PBA remains indebted to all who contributed in anyway to these books, but especially to those who buy the books, read them, treasure them, and then pass them on to the future generations of Pasadena.

Wendy Harris, *Editor*
Paperwork Solutions

Maureen L. Argo, *Assistant Editor*
Cityline Business Park

George Athas
Editorial Committee; New Photos
Legg Mason

James Anderson, *Financial Committee*
Anderson, Davis & Asssociates, CPA

Lois Simpson, *Committee Member*
County National Bank

Debbie Romano, *Committee Member*
Sign-A-Rama

A Message to Readers

When the Pasadena Business Association decided to publish two histories of the Pasadena peninsula, their goal was to give all the people who live in this area a feeling of unity and pride in their shared history. This book aims to reach that goal. Though any attempt to weave together the 350-year history of the farms and villages between the Patapsco and the Magothy will be incomplete, this expanded version of the pictorial history called *Between Two Rivers* describes the region's rich heritage in greater detail than ever before.

Much has changed on the peninsula during the last three centuries, especially during the last fifty years; yet there is a consistent theme: neighborly people living in communities, people who love their homes and families and work hard to give advantages to their children. Despite repeated waves of new residents during this century, basic values remain unchanged. While many people mourn increased traffic and the loss of fertile farms, they welcome access to more products and services, improved medical care, and better schools and libraries.

For the purpose of this book, the Pasadena peninsula is defined according to the 21122 postal zip code boundaries. Though Gibson Island is closely connected to the peninsula historically and geographically, its history has been researched and recorded. In addition, Marianne Taylor's recently published *My River Speaks* covers the north shore of the Magothy River so well that this volume adds little new information about that area.

Names of people and places generally are spelled according to modern usage. Before the first dictionary standardized spelling, words were written as the writer heard them. In old records, the Magothy is spelled Maggothy, Magoty, and Maggotty, and the Patapsco became Patapsico, Pattapscoo, and Potopscoe. In this book Stoney Creek is Stony Creek and Robossons are Robinsons.

References to sources are cited in the notes, except for information that is general knowledge. For information about founding or building recent schools and churches, the Board of Education office or the specific school or church is the source. Listed in the notes are the names of many individuals who have shared information generously.

Churches that were a part of the Methodist Protestant Church (1830-1939) and the Methodist Episcopal Church, South (1845-1939) are clearly identified. Methodist alone refers to the denomination known as the Methodist Episcopal Church from 1784-1939, the Methodist Church from 1939-1970, and the United Methodist Church from 1970 to the present.

Residents of the peninsula have shown pride in their community by providing treasured family photographs and by unfailingly helpful responses to numerous questions and requests. The Pasadena Business Association and the author hope that they, and everyone who is interested in local history, will enjoy this account of a once-neglected part of Anne Arundel County.

The First Inhabitants of the Peninsula

Fourteen thousand years ago the land between what now are the Patapsco and Magothy rivers was covered by a hemlock and spruce forest where mastodons, mammoth, caribou, moose, bison, and giant beavers made their homes. On either side of the cold and wet peninsula were narrow freshwater rivers running through valleys. Because the sea level was 300 feet lower than it is today, what is now the Chesapeake Bay was a river that flowed along the center of a deep valley. The peninsula then extended to that river. Though the first Native Americans arrived during this Paleo-Indian era, the sites of their camps along the streams and rivers are now under water.[1]

Between 9,000 and 6,000 years ago the climate became warmer, and melting glacial ice that covered what is now Canada and the northern United States flooded the valleys that surrounded the peninsula, making them into tidal rivers. Animal life and vegetation became more like the flora and fauna of recent centuries. Deciduous forests of oak, beech, and birch trees offered the Native Americans who lived in transitory camps along the streams more resources than had been available previously.

---

[1]Wayne E. Clark, Executive Director of the Office of Museum Services, Maryland Historical Trust, personal communication; Laurie C. Steponaitis, Maryland Historical Trust Monograph no.1, 1980.

Though the sea remained far below the present level, the rising water increased salinity, and oysters became an important food for the Native Americans who lived by hunting and gathering. Few sites from the Archaic period are known because the rising sea level gradually filled rivers, streams, and the wide river valley that became the Chesapeake. An important Archaic site remains at the western end of the peninsula where early natives came to a massive stone outcropping, now known as Wishing Rock, to make tools and projectile points.[2]

By the Late Archaic period, from about 6,000 to 3,000 years ago, the climate was warm and dry and the water level continued to rise until it was about 35 feet lower than it is today. Oak, hickory, pine, and chestnut trees covered the peninsula. The Native Americans followed wandering seasonal settlement patterns as they used the resources of the peninsula, the forests, and the water. During this period, their pestles, milling stones, and stone bowls are evidence that they used plant sources and hunted and fished for food. Stored hickory nuts and chestnuts were important to their survival during late winter months. With their stone axes, they could make dugout canoes that gave better access to water resources. From 3,000 until 2400 years ago, during the Early Woodland period, the rate of sea level rise was slower, tidal marshes developed, and creeks were fully formed. Animals like bears, bobcats, mountain lions, deer, wild turkey, and beaver were plentiful. A larger population practiced hunting, gathering, and fishing and used low-fired earthen pottery. Base camps tended to be near the water, with smaller camps elsewhere to take advantage of other resources. Numerous family units, probably interrelated, occupied the camps in an increasingly settled pattern of living.[3]

During the next 1200 years, the Middle Woodland period, oysters, rib mussels, snails called periwinkles, turtles, catfish, and sturgeon, as well as waterfowl, beaver, deer, and squirrels offered Native Americans a varied

---

[2]*Ibid.*
[3]*Ibid.*

Artifacts Richard E. Stearns excavated near Fort Smallwood. Projectile points on the top row date from the Archaic Period, 7500 to 4000 B.C.

Proceedings of the Natural History Society of Maryland, no.9, July 1942

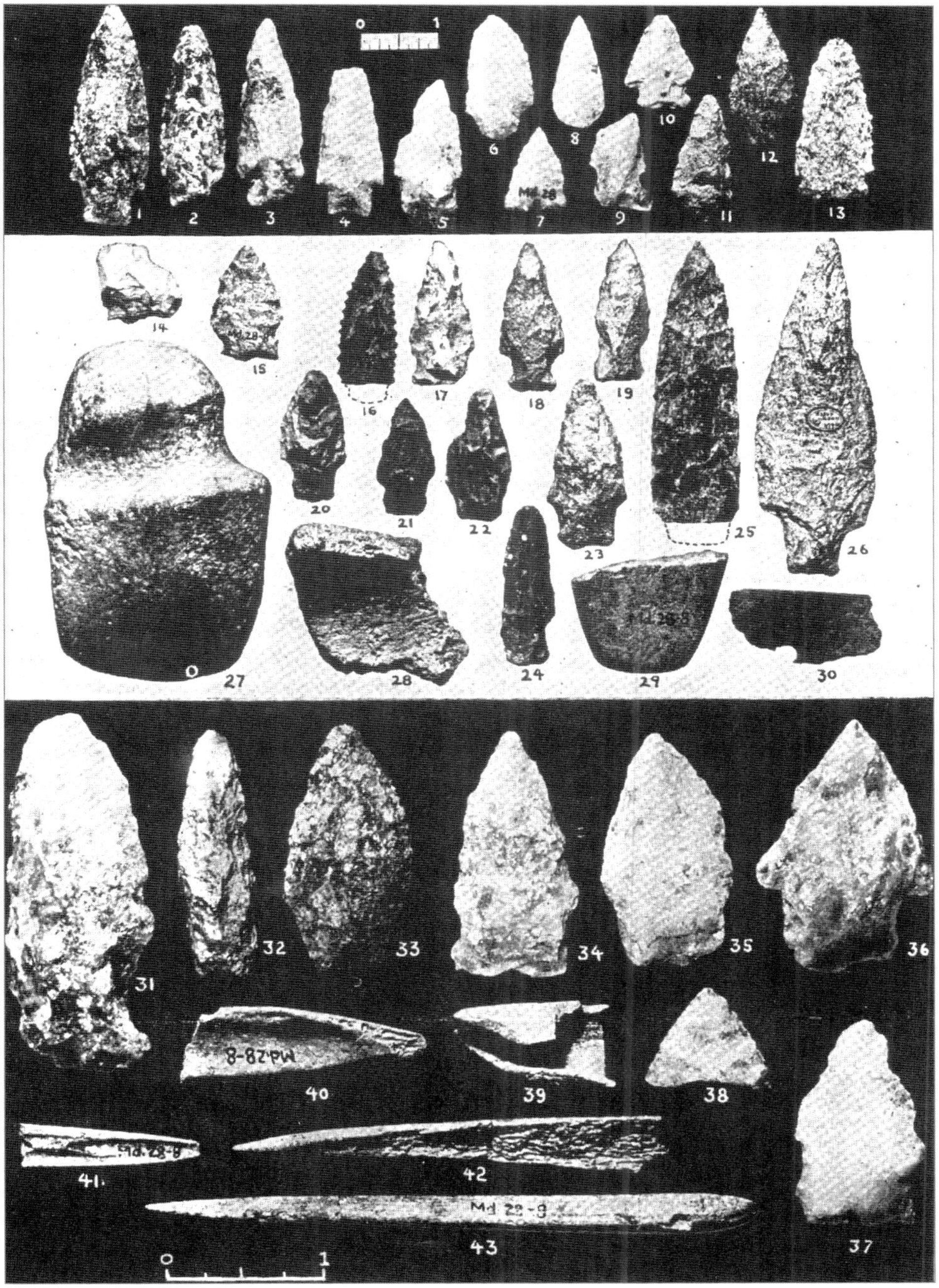

protein diet, while they also carried on limited agriculture. In addition to gathering nuts, they grew goosefoot as a cereal plant, tuckahoe as a root crop, sunflowers, and gourds to use as containers. The Algonquins arrived in this area at this time. Some of their large pottery vessels used to store food have been found near Fort Smallwood Park.

From A.D.800 until about 1600, when English settlers appeared, the Algonquins lived in semi-permanent base camps or villages. They girdled trees to make clearings in the forest, and grew corn, beans, squash, and

Richard E. Stearns excavated these pieces of a Native American pottery vessel, made between 200 and 800, near Fort Smallwood.

Proceedings of the Natural History Society of Maryland, no.9, July 1942 pumpkins. When the land became less fertile after five or six years, they moved on to another area. They not only made a variety of pottery containers but also wove baskets. For centuries, Algonquian tribes lived in seasonal encampments or villages on a peninsula that they knew as a rich hunting and fishing ground. Hunting and gathering parties set out from base camps and returned with deer, ducks, geese, fish, and oysters. Then families gathered to roast the ducks and geese, broil the fish, or steam the oysters.[4]

About a century before English settlers came to the peninsula, the Algonquins were challenged by warlike Susquehannocks. Continued hostilities resulted in the expulsion of the Algonquian tribes by about 1590. When Captain John Smith sailed up the Chesapeake Bay in 1608, he found this region "extreame thicke of small wood as well as trees, and much frequented with wolves, beares, deere, and other wild beasts. We passed many shallow creekes, but the first we found navigable for a ship, we called the Bolus [the Latin word for clay] for that the clay in many places under the clifts by the high water marke, did grow up in red and white knots." The Bolus River "thirty leagues northward" from the Potomac is now called the Patapsco. Captain John Smith "saw not any savages" near the mouth of the river and was surprised that a region so rich in marine life and game was virtually uninhabited.[5]

Though Captain Smith found no inhabitants in 1608, Algonquin tribes and their predecessors had occupied this region for thousands of years. Excavations near the Magothy and the Patapsco have revealed their barbeque pits, thick layers of oyster shells, pieces of pottery vessels, arrowheads, axes, and spearpoints, while farmers have found projectile points and other artifacts throughout the peninsula. When Richard E. Stearns studied a site adjacent to Fort Smallwood, formerly part of the Jenkins farm, he found three large shell deposits (middens) and an axe, arrowpoints, and pottery sherds on or near the surface of the soil. His first

---

[4]Ibid.

[5]John Smith, *The Generall Historie of Virginia, New England, and the Summer Isles* (Richmond, 1819), Vol. I, Third Book, p.176; Vol. I, Second Book, p.118.

excavation revealed a small fireplace, a pit four feet deep filled with oyster shells and animals bones, arrowpoints, and sherds from pottery vessels.

An excavation nearby disclosed a fireplace six feet wide, two pits (probably for roasting oysters) filled with shells, over 1,000 sherds representing twenty pottery vessels, hammerstones, animal bones, and bone objects such as awls. Vessels used at this site were large, the clay tempered with crushed quartz and oyster shell, and the exterior surface showed impressions from coarse fabrics. Stone artifacts were made of rhyolite, quartz, and quartzite. Previously, a member of the Jenkins family had given axes, celts, arrowpoints, gorgets and other artifacts found on this farm to the Maryland Academy of Sciences.[6]

Stearns also examined sites north and south of the mouth of Bodkin Creek where he found pottery sherds bearing the impressions of cords and fabric, their rough surface tempered with crushed quartz and shell. At Tar Cove on the Magothy, members of the Maryland Archaeological Society excavated sherds from three vessels with collared rims, usually found on the Potomac, as well as pieces of cut antler, a small clay pipe, and a bone awl.[7] When farmers on the peninsula plowed their fields, they frequently saw evidence of earlier occupation by Native Americans. A community on the Magothy where many artifacts and layers of oyster shells have been found is called Indian Village in memory of these early occupants of the land between two rivers.

The Algonquins and their native predecessors included the peninsula on their seasonal migrations, not only to hunt and fish, but also to make camp near a towering quartzite formation. This quartzite outcropping, referred to as White Rock Mountain in early documents and later called Rock Hill and Wishing Rock, is a geological oddity. Other known formations of this kind are in New Jersey, Florida, and France. This important archaeological site was well-known to Native Americans 4,000 years ago.

---

[6]Richard E. Stearns, "Some Indian Village Sites of Tidewater Maryland," *Proceedings of the Natural History Society of Maryland*, no. 9 (1942), pp.6-8.
[7]Stearns, *Ibid.*, pp.18, 23.

At that time, the huge mound of quartzite was about 300 feet long by 250 feet wide and possibly 150 feet high,. At least half of it has been mined. The Algonquins would camp nearby and collect material to make tools. Quartzite was perfectly suited for flaking into sharp and durable tools and projectile points. Waste chips from this process can be seen there today.[8]

The White Rocks that stand at the entrance to Rock Creek are part of the same formation as Wishing Rock. This tough, hard quartzite outcropping has been called a geologic mystery. It is unlike any rock found in the surrounding area where reddish-brown sandstone is plentiful. That conglomerate consists of sand and pebbles of the same type of sand found nearby and is held together by iron oxides. Quartzite is composed of sand grains unlike those in surrounding soils and is cemented by white opal and sometimes chalcedony.[9]

To this peninsula, with its ancient and rare white quartzite formations, English settlers came in the mid-1600s. Picture a land bordered by two rivers, a land blessed with many clear creeks abounding in fish, shellfish, and waterfowl, their sandy shores surrounded by dense woods filled with wildlife and birds. Wolves, black bear, elk, deer, wild turkey, and small game roamed forests that were filed with pines, hollies, and giant oak, chestnut, and tulip trees. Rivers and creeks held an abundance of diamondback terrapin, oysters, crabs, herring, shad, rockfish, and many other species of fish. Near the water, the coastal plain was dotted with hills, and the sandy loam soil held red sandstone deposits and traces of various useful minerals. Previously inhabited for thousands of years by Native Americans, the peninsula and its abundant resources soon would support Englishmen and their families.

---

[8]Al Luckenbach, Maryland Historic Trust Archaeological Site Inventory 18AN-760; *The Sun*, October 12, 1990 and February 18, 1997. Jack Kelbaugh first brought this site to the attention of Wayne Clark and Al Luckenbach.

[9]Robert Louis Benson, "Historical Survey of the Natural Resources of Anne Arundel County," *Anne Arundel County History Notes*, vol. 23, no.1 (1991):12-13; John D. Glaser, "Petrology and Origin of Potomac and Magothy Sediments," Maryland Geological Survey Report no.11 (1969), pp.62-64.

Towering ancient quartzite outcroppings, now called Wishing Rock. Native Americans used this extremely hard quartzite for making tools and weapons.
Photo: Marion E. Warren

Englishmen Make Their Homes on the Peninsula

On July 2, 1649, only 42 years after the first English settlement in America at Jamestown and in the year of the first settlement in Anne Arundel County, Thomas Welbourne, a merchant in London, claimed the first land grant on the peninsula between the Patapsco and the Magothy.[10] Doubtless this purchase of a 1200-acre tract on the Magothy at Cape Sable (now North Ferry Point) was an investment. By 1652 the area between Herring Creek to the south and the Patapsco River to the north had been set off as Anne Arundel County.[11] Land-hungry Englishmen soon were patenting land along its waterways.

The name Patapscoe first appeared on a map in 1666 in George Alsop's *Character of the Province of Maryland*, but it was used on land grants as early as 1652. The word is of Algonquian origin, meaning "at the jutting ledge of rock" or "at the rocky point." Researchers believe that the "rocky point" could well be the White Rocks at the mouth of Rock Creek.[12] Centuries ago, before the White Rocks eroded, they would have been taller and the water level would have been lower, making them a clearly visible

---

[10]Gladys P. Nelker, *Town Neck Hundred of Anne Arundel County* (Westminster, Md, 1990), p.7.
[11]Warfield, Joshua D., *The Founders of Anne Arundel and Howard Counties, Maryland* (Baltimore, 1905), p.34.
[12]Hamill Kenny, *The Placenames of Maryland*, (Baltimore, 1984), p.189.

landmark. Rock Creek is shown but not named on Captain John Smith's 1608 map. The first reference to the White Rocks is on a deed dated October 3, 1667, recording George Yates' ownership of *Radnidge*, 160 acres on the Patapsco "opposite the Rocks."[13]

During the 1660s, settlers claimed land on the peninsula slowly, but nineteen deeds were recorded in the 1670s, 27 during the 1680s, and a total of 68 between 1649 and 1700. By that time, relatively little unclaimed land remained. Men who owned property on the peninsula often lived in or near Annapolis while their tenants farmed their land. Charles Carroll held deeds to thousands of acres, and John Gray patented *Gray's Range* (100 acres north of the Magothy) in 1675, *Happy Choice* (400 acres near the head of Rock Creek) in 1684, *Gray's Lott* (239 acres south of Bodkin Creek) in 1685, and *Gray's Adventure* (184 acres southwest of Bodkin Creek) in 1685.[14] During the following decades, these large holdings often were divided into smaller farms.

Tenants needed to clear fields before they could raise tobacco, the chief cash crop at this time, and investors wanted to recover part of the cost of their land by selling lumber. Vast hardwood forests were cleared and the timber transported by barge to Baltimore and beyond. At first, farms were clearings in the forest. Most of the landowners were slave holders, and much of the labor of farming and lumbering was done by slaves and indentured servants. Settlers soon built sawmills and wharves for shipping lumber and tobacco.

The gristmills where wheat and corn were ground into flour for the use of farm families were of vital importance to the community. The "Magoty Mill" (near what is now Lake Waterford) probably operated during the late 1600s. The miller, John Summerland (Sunderland), sold 71 acres including the already existing mill in 1727.[15] By the third decade of the century, two or three mills were operating near the head of the Magothy River.

---

[13]Nelker, *Town Neck Hundred*, p.117, cites A. A. County Land Records, BEG, f.183.
[14]*Ibid.*, 52, 61, 51, 49.
[15]*Ibid.*, p.80.

Land grants in the northwestern quadrant of the peninsula.
Gladys P. Nelker, *Town Neck Hundred of Anne Arundel County*

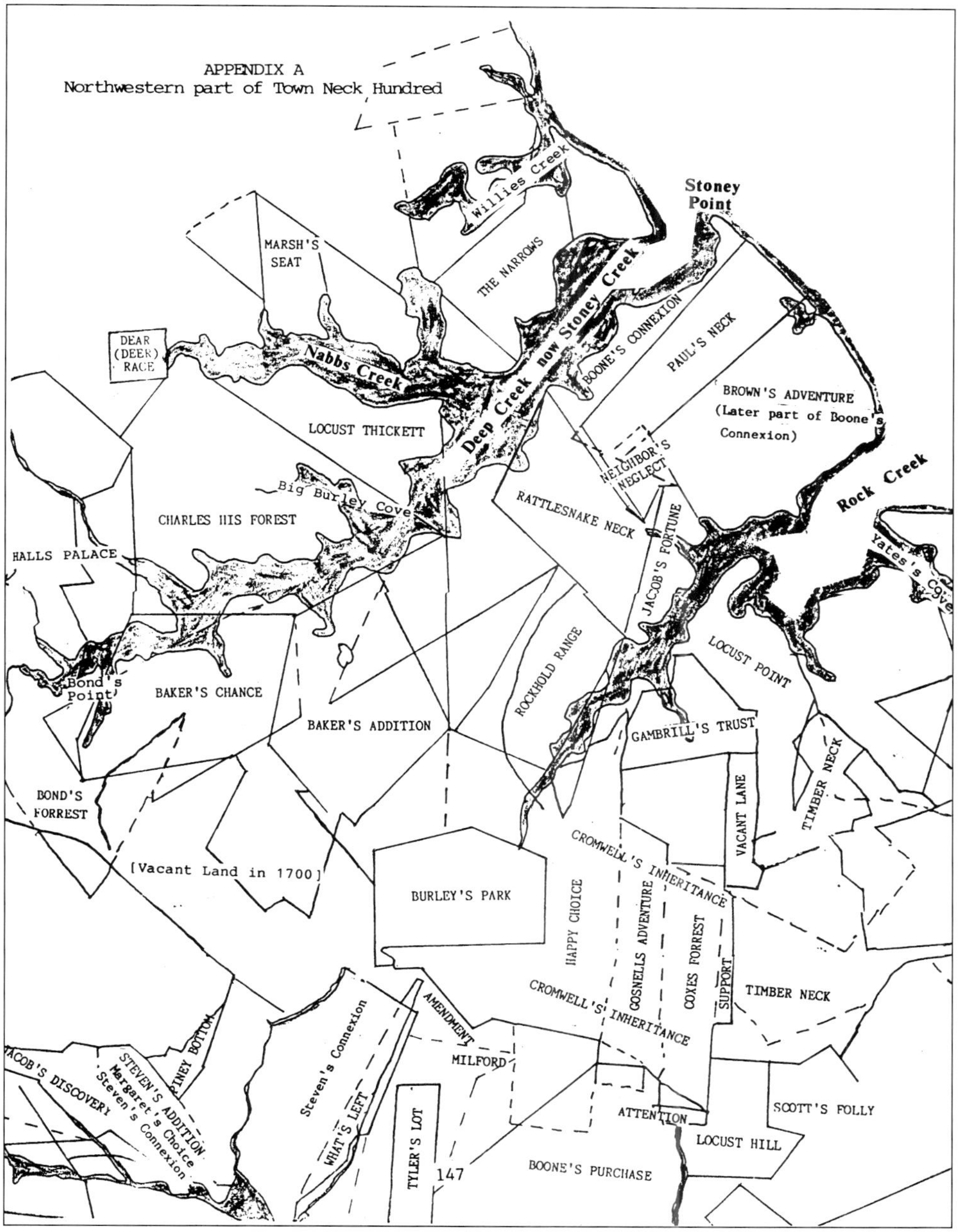

Land grants in the northeastern quadrant of the peninsula.

Gladys P. Nelker, *Town Neck Hundred of Anne Arundel County*

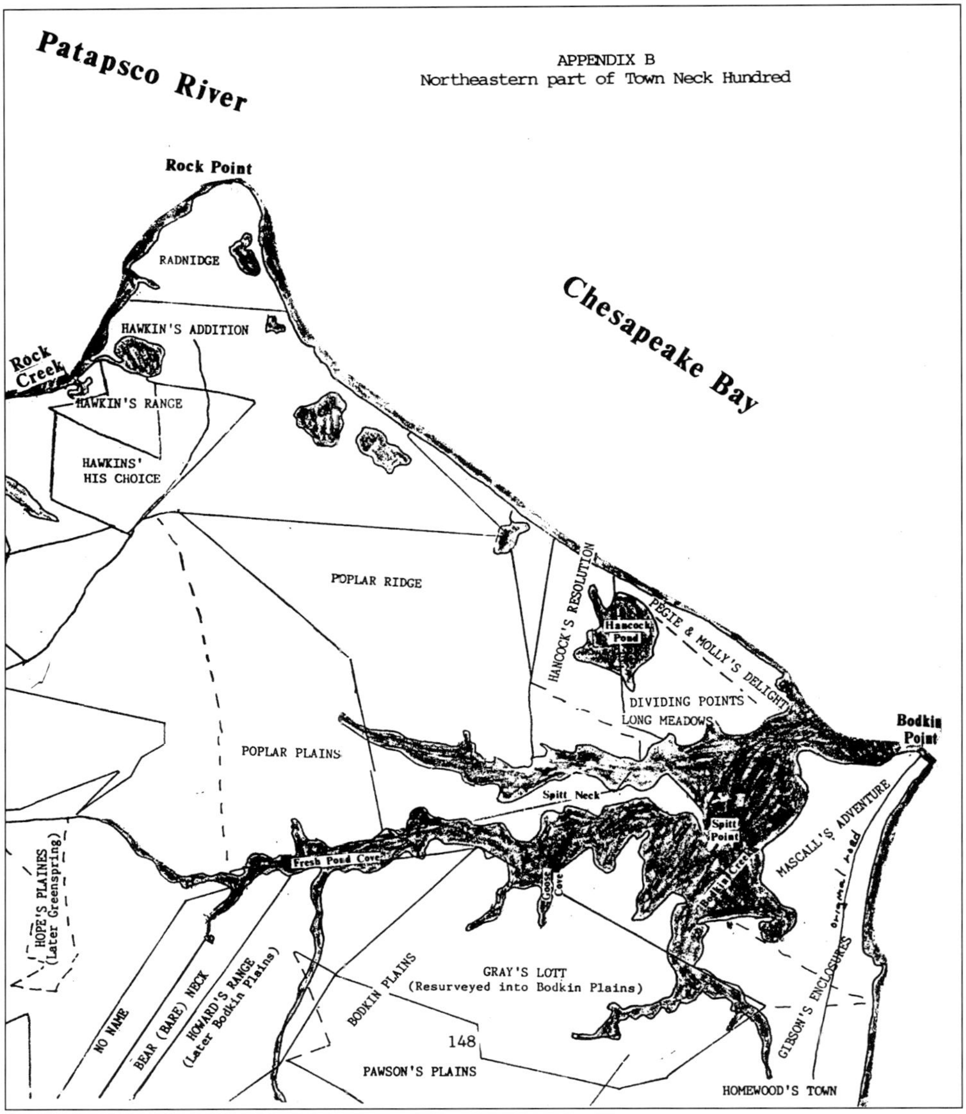

Land grants in the southwestern quadrant of the peninsula.
Gladys P. Nelker, *Town Neck Hundred of Anne Arundel County*

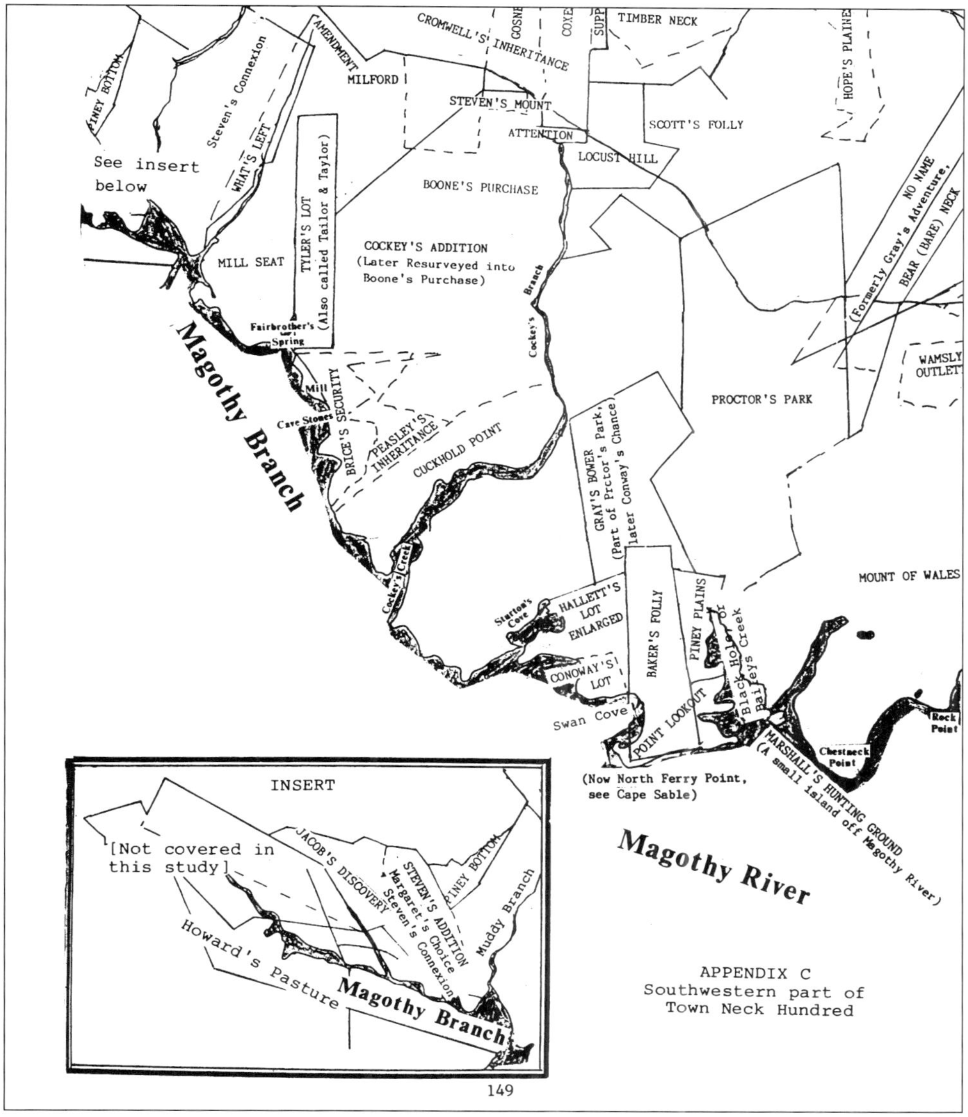

Land grants in the southeastern quadrant of the peninsula.

Gladys P. Nelker, *Town Neck Hundred of Anne Arundel County*

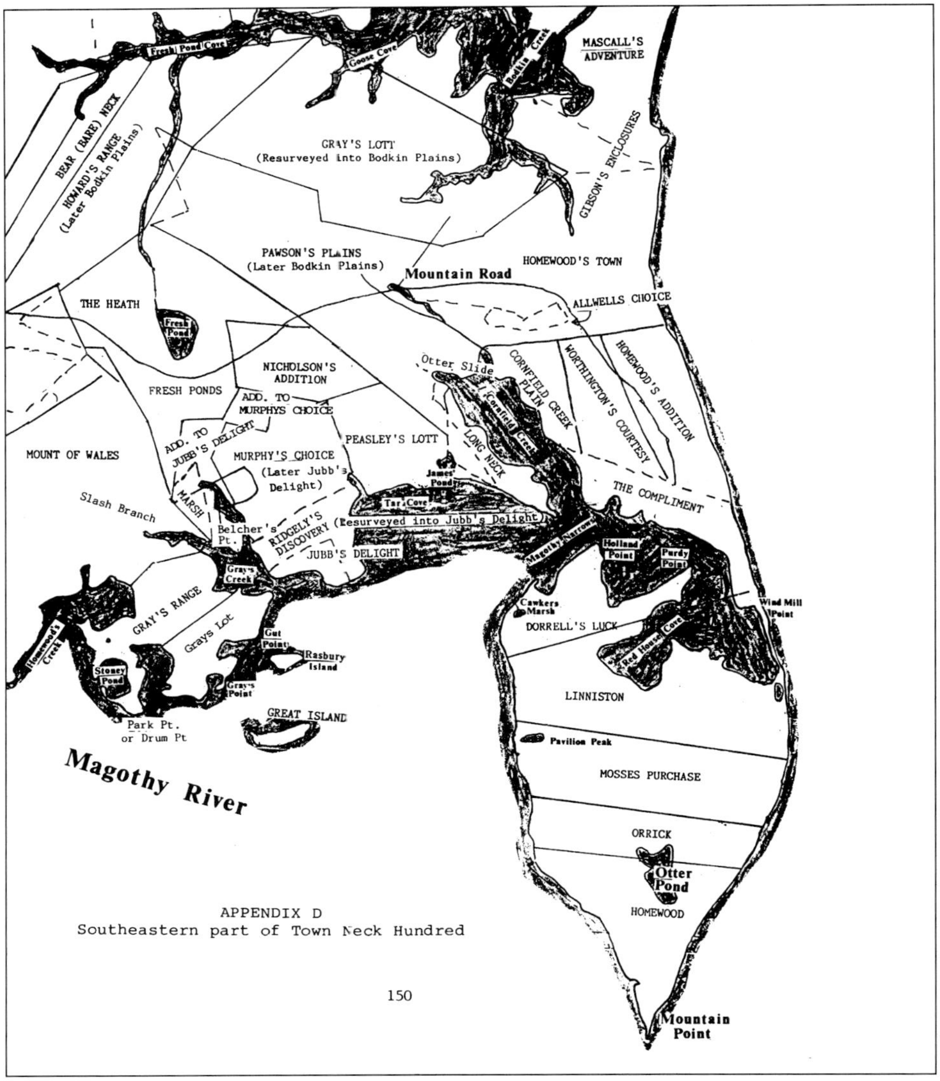

Anne Arundel County's northern boundary changed when Baltimore County was set off in 1659, but the division was not clear until the General Assembly passed an act in 1674 that defined the line as running south from Bodkin Creek across the mountains at the mouth of the Magothy, up the Magothy, then to "the mountain of white stone rock," and west to the ferry over the Patapsco (near where Route 97 now crosses the Patapsco). Inhabitants of growing settlements along the south side of the river petitioned the legislature to return that area to Anne Arundel County, but the House of Delegates voted on October 3, 1694, that the area "remaine still as it is."[16]

In response to continued appeals from residents of the peninsula, in 1696 the legislature appointed a committee to study the boundary line. As a result, the General Assembly passed an act that placed the boundary along a line between the Magothy and the Patapsco, restoring half the peninsula to Anne Arundel. Familiar names of peninsula residents on the Baltimore County tax lists show that John and Humphrey Boone; John, James, Will, and R. Cook; Thomas Hancock and the Widow Hancock; John Robinson; Nathan Stinchcomb; John and Jeremiah Williams; and others had to pay their taxes in Baltimore County at that time.[17]

Though people who lived near the Patapsco continued to insist that they "suffered great Inconveniences" because of the distance to the Baltimore County Court House on Bush River, that boundary remained in effect until 1726. Rain made the trip difficult because travelers had to pass falls that were "utterly unfordable." When people were required to go to the County Court and were unable to make the trip, they were "subject to the Censure of said Court, and very often to grievous fines." This time the people along the south side of the Patapsco convinced the legislature of their plight, and an act restoring the river as the boundary between Baltimore and Anne Arundel Counties passed on July 25, 1726.[18]

---

[16]Maryland Archives, 19:69.
[17]Warfield, *Founders*, pp. 35-36; Baltimore County Tax Lists, 1699-1705.
[18]Warfield, *Founders*, pp.35-36; Edward B. Mathews, "The Counties of Maryland: Their Origin and Boundaries," Maryland Geological Survey, vol.6, part 5 (Baltimore, 1907):437-438.

The rivers and creeks were God-given highways for the early settlers, but they needed roads to get their tobacco and lumber to the waterfront and to travel to sawmills and gristmills. Sometimes neighbors would build a road across their adjoining properties to reach mills or wharves. These roads were narrow muddy lanes that often were impassable in winter, and settlers usually depended on boats for commerce and everyday use. There were no bridges. For these Anglican families, their nearest church was across the Magothy at St. Margarets. Baptismal records there confirm that they made that journey, probably taking a ferry across the river in fair weather. A 1769 land record for a tract called *Point Lookout* refers to Sandy Point, later called North Ferry Point, as a former landing place for the county ferry.[19]

Settlers who cut virgin lumber and grew tobacco did not overlook the area's possible mineral resources. In addition to clay and fine building sand that existed in pits near the Magothy, they found iron deposits. At some locations, the banks of the Patapsco were mined for iron at an early date. The Curtis Creek Furnace and Iron Works was built in 1759; however, there is no evidence of iron mining or smelting on the peninsula.[20] Smelting required large stands of timber to yield charcoal; possibly some of the timber cut on the peninsula was used for that purpose.

Neither state nor county governments provided schools, and most people were unable even to sign their names to legal documents. The first schools were built by groups of parents who hired someone to teach their children. In 1754, on the more populous south shore of the Magothy, Richard Moss's children had walked a mile and a half past a 500-acre forest on their way to school and were opening a gate onto a public road when they saw a bear feeding nearby. After they ran home, Richard Moss and several of his slaves found the bear and killed it.[21] Since an old school on

---

[19]Nelker, *Town Neck Hundred*, p.107.

[20]Jane McWilliams, "Land and People," in James C. Bradford, editor, *Anne Arundel County: A Bicentennial History* (Annapolis, 1977), p.1.

[21]Elihu S. Riley, *A History of Anne Arundel County* (Annapolis, 1905), p.107.

the road to Rock Point was replaced in 1827, parents who lived in that area might have built a one-room school there around the turn of the century.

Events in the wider world affected the peninsula between the Magothy and the Patapsco in the 1770s as people there became aware of increasing tension between the colonies and England. Since Baltimore was a ship-building center where vessels of war and privateers were built, the British fleet attempted to blockade the Chesapeake Bay.

People in the area were alarmed in May of 1776 when the *Otter*, with several other British vessels, anchored at the mouth of the Patapsco near Bodkin Point. The *Otter* captured a ship loaded with wheat and flour, but Captain James Nicholas, commanding the American *Defense*, drove the *Otter* from the Patapsco and captured several smaller British vessels. This was one of the first naval engagements between the American colonists and the British. On August 21, 1777, residents must have watched "a considerable fleet of British men of war, transports, and other vessels" as they sailed past the Magothy and the Patapsco and "stood up the Bay."[22]

The 98 signatures of local men on Maryland's Oath of Fidelity show their support of the war effort. Signers had to appear before the Justice of the Peace, Elijah Robosson (Robinson) and swear "that I do not hold myself bound to any allegiance to the King of Great Britain . . . and that I will be true and faithful to the state of Maryland and will to the utmost of my power support

SOME OF THE MEN FROM THE PENINSULA WHO SIGNED THE OATH OF FIDELITY IN 1778

John Boone	Zachariah Jacobs
John Gray	Richard Jacobs, Sr.
Zachariah Gray	Richard Jacobs, Jr.
Stephen Hancock	Dorsey Jacobs
William Hancock	Samuel Jacobs
Charles Hanshaw, Sr.	Richard Jacobs, son of Joshua
Charles Hanshaw, Jr.	Thomas Robinson*
James Hanshaw	Richard Robinson*
George Johnson	O Neall Robinson*
John Linstid	George Robinson*
Joshua Meek	Vachel Robinson*
Charles Rockhold	and a second George Robinson
Clark Rockhold	
John Rockhold	*Spelled Robosson

[22]*Ibid.* pp.77-78.

Maryland and defend [her] freedom . . . against all enemies." Signing the Oath was a commitment. Unlike neighboring colonies, Maryland required signers to be ready to fight in her defense.[23]

Some of the men who signed the Oath of Fidelity were too old for active service in the military, but local heroes who served in the Continental Army included Charles Robinson, who enlisted for the duration of the war and was wounded in South Carolina; John Boone, a captain in the Maryland Line, 3rd Regiment; Samuel Jacobs, a first lieutenant; James Fowler and John Johnson, privates in the Maryland Line; and Leonard Foreman who served under Captain Frances Cromwell in the Severn Battalion.[24] John and William Hancock were on the list of Continental troops paid by the State of Maryland.[25]

Stephen Hancock, Junior, served as a private with the 1st, 3rd, and 6th companies of the Maryland Line. His grandfather, William Hancock, had leased land near Bodkin Point in 1733, and his father, Stephen Hancock, Senior, had bought that land in 1765, but the family seat remained on the north bank of the Severn River. Stephen Hancock, Junior, added to the Bodkin property and probably built *Hancock's Resolution* about 1785.[26]

Stephen Hancock entered service in the Continental Army on August 1, 1780, at the beginning of the Southern Campaign, and served until November 15, 1783. He and other soldiers from the peninsula who served in the Maryland Line must have seen action at Camden and Cowpens, where Maryland troops were part of John Eager Howard's "warlike thrust," familiar to every Maryland schoolchild, as well as battles at Guilford Court House and at Yorktown.[27] Stephen Hancock received 100 acres of bounty land in Garrett County as a reward for his military service.[28]

After the Revolutionary War ended in victory, Americans, not British colonists, began to guide the destiny of the peninsula between two rivers.

---

[23]Oaths of Fealty 1777-1781, Archives of Maryland, Red Book 22, pp.27, 27.1

[24]DAR Patriot Index, National Society of the Daughters of the American Revolution (Washington, 1966).

[25]Revolutionary Army Accounts, Drawer 50, Maryland State Archives.

[26]Mark Walker, "Plantation in Suburbia: An Integrated Approach to Hancock's Resolution," The Lost Towns of Anne Arundel Project, (Annapolis, Md, 1998):2.

[27]Rieman Steuart, *A History of the Maryland Line* (Towson, Md., 1969), pp.161-165.

[28]Newman, Harry Wright, *Maryland Military Records* (Washington, 1938).

War Again Disturbs Tranquil Life

In the closing years of the 18th century, the community between the Patapsco and the Magothy was ideally situated to take advantage of the growth of Baltimore. Following the Revolutionary War, that small town of 20,000 people quickly developed into a major port. Wheat shipped from Baltimore was in demand in New England, Europe, and the West Indies. Inhabitants of the peninsula took advantage of Baltimore's expanding market for lumber and cereal crops. Wheat and corn replaced tobacco, a labor-intensive crop that never had been suited to the peninsula's sandy loam soil.[29]

As early as 1777, Francis Asbury, father of American Methodism, recorded preaching in July, August, and September in homes "at Magothy where the work of the Lord goes on successfully." The group that met on the north shore of the Magothy soon became a Methodist Society. In 1794 they bought land for a meeting house from Captain Frances Cromwell for "five shillings current money paid to him in hand," and built a one-room log structure on Mountain Road opposite the present Magothy Church.

---

[29] Barbara J. Fields, *Slavery and Freedom on the Middle Ground* (New Haven, 1985), p.5.

(Captain Cromwell, who served in the Severn Battalion during the Revolutionary War, lived in a stone house near the eastern end of Mountain Road.) The first trustees of Magothy Methodist Episcopal Church were Nathan Williams, Henry Ridgely, John Cromwell, William Maccubbin, Zachariah Ashby, Charles Waters, and Richard Boone. The church was served by circuit riders and lay preachers.[30]

Hancock's Resolution, built about 1785, is the sole survivor of the 18th century homes in this area. The 22-by-24-foot, one-and one-half-story, gambrel-roof house was made of native sandstone. Though the Hancocks owned the property, John Hanshaw and his family farmed the property as tenants for several generations. Stephen Hancock, Junior's grandson John was the first Hancock known to have lived there. The dairy is still standing, but the attached kitchen and other outbuildings are gone. Because it is the only surviving stone dwelling of that early date in Anne Arundel County, the Hancock home is of inestimable value to historians.[31]

The first United States census lists about 110 heads of households on the peninsula in 1790. According to the introduction, "Those whose names appear upon the schedule of the First Census were in general the plain citizens who, by their conduct in war and peace, made the Constitution possible and, by their intelligence and self-restraint, put it into successful operation." Among the founders of the Republic who owned land between the Magothy and the Patapsco at that time were familiar names: Waters, Cook, Williams, Johnson, Cromwell, Carroll, Pumphrey, Hammond, Linthicum, Meek, Hawkins, Foreman, Gray, Jacobs, Fowler, Maccubin, Hanshaw, Boone, Robinson, Jubb, Crane, Hancock, Stewart, Linsted, Moss, and Stinchcomb.[32]

Federal tax records for 1798 reveal that many farms still had absentee owners like James Brice, Charles Carroll, John Heselius, Mathias Hammond, and Peregrine Ridgely. These men lived in or near Annapolis,

---

[30]Bertha S. Hein and Ruth E. Bollman, "A Church, Its People, Its Community," (unpublished, 1964), pp.5-6; Virginia A.Pritchett. "A History of Magothy Methodist Church" (unpublished, 1977), p.2.

[31]Donna Ware, *The Historic Properties of Anne Arundel County* (Annapolis, 1990), p.113.

[32]Census of 1790 (Washington, 1907), pp.3, 15-16.

Hancock's Resolution, home of the Hancock family near Bodkin Point.

Collection of Friends of Hancock's Resolution, James R. Morrison, president

and tenants farmed their property. The tenants usually lived in modest two-story frame or log homes, often with separate kitchens and outbuildings including a tobacco barn, cornhouse, and dairy or milkhouse. A dwelling could be as small as a log house 12-by-16 feet with two outbuildings, each 12-by-12 feet. Joseph Maccubbin of *Mount of Wales* occupied one of the largest homes, a 20-by-20-foot brick house with a 16-by-20-foot stone kitchen The typical holding was from 100 to 300 acres, though some were 500 or 600 acres, and a few were more extensive. Many farm owners held from ten to fifteen slaves.[33]

---

[33] 1798 Federal District Tax, Anne Arundel County, Third District.

Community roads near the Magothy and across Tick Neck, Hog Neck, and the Bodkin peninsula were tracks passable only on horseback during much of the year. Waterways remained the best avenues for travel, but better roads were needed. In 1799 residents petitioned the legislature for two new roads because they "labor under great inconvenience" for the lack of a road from Widow Robinson's to intersect "the public road leading from Baltimore-town to the Magothy mountains," as well as a road from Widow Robinson's past Waters' Mill "till it intersects the mountain road leading to Patapsco ferry."[34]

The legislature appointed Richard Cromwell, Dorsey Jacobs, and Richard Merriken to lay out county roads not to exceed thirty feet wide, the expenses to be paid "by the parties therein benefitted."[35] These roads probably led northeast and northwest from the head of the Magothy where Charles Waters owned the old "Magoty Mill" on the property he named *Waterford.* He soon acquired sites for other mills along the Magothy.[36]

The name of Mountain Road has puzzled later generations. British settlers expected a coastal plain to be flat like the Eastern Shore of Maryland. Captain John Smith described the western shore of the Chesapeake as "mountainous," and an early land grant on Gibson Island was called *Seven Mountains*. An English colonist who sailed up the Severn River from Annapolis to Round Bay counted forty "little mountains or eminences" at least 155 feet high.[37] Though the hills on the peninsula are not tall (even Eagle Hill failing to qualify as one of the fifteen highest points in Anne Arundel County), early settlers who were looking up from a boat at sea level called them mountains.[38]

No later than 1810, and possibly as early as 1794, a land owner (probably John Gibson) used slave labor to construct a V-shaped canal that ran east to west in a straight line for 500 yards to connect Locust Cove on

---

[34]An Act Relating to Certain Public Roads in Anne Arundel County, Liber JG, No.3, f.350, Jan. 3, 1800.
[35]*Ibid.*
[36]Nelker, *Town Neck Hundred*, p.80 and Waters deeds dated 1803,1813, 1815, and 1829.
[37]Warfield, *Founders of Anne Arundel and Howard Counties*, p.332.
[38]Michael Eismeier, Anne Arundel County Soil Conservation Service.

Bodkin Creek with a pond that opened onto the Bay. The goal of this ambitious project was to avoid the passage around Bodkin Point. At its widest point near the center, the canal was twenty feet wide at the base, up to sixty feet wide at the top, and twelve feet deep, but generally it was about fifteen feet wide at the base, up to forty feet wide at the top, and ten feet deep. Since extensive forests nearby were logged in the early 1800s, logs may have been floated through the canal to the Bay, where they would have been collected and stacked on ships. Nearby the remains of corduroy roads (roads made of logs) have been found.[39]

Once more war with England disturbed tranquil life on the peninsula, but this time the enemy was a near and present threat. When a British squadron moved up the Chesapeake Bay to blockade the Baltimore harbor during April of 1813, residents of the peninsula could see thirty hostile vessels enter the Patapsco River. Homeowners were alarmed when Admiral Cockburn sent tenders and barges into most navigable inlets, and raiding parties landed in search of fresh water and food.[40]

As the British threatened the area, the local militia was called to defend the shores of the Patapsco and the Bay. Among those who responded to the call during the spring of 1813 were Captain Francis Hancock of the 22th Maryland Regiment and his company of militiamen. Their length of active service varied from one to 21 days between April 14 and May 5. Though some served briefly at Fort Madison on the Severn River, they spent most of the three weeks of the emergency patrolling the Bodkin peninsula and Patapsco River shores.[41]

The British maintained a presence on the upper Chesapeake until the end of the war. Local residents must have been especially apprehensive in August of 1814 when the British commander sent ships to create a diversion near Baltimore while their main force prepared to attack Washington. Sir Peter Porter's men captured some vessels in the Patapsco

---

[39]Al Luckenbach, Maryland Historic Trust Site Inventory 18AN 272; Trevor A. Kiessling, Jr., "Bodkin Neck: The Gateway to the Patapsco" (1979, unpublished), pp.10-11. The canal, fairly intact except for the Pinehurst Road crossing, has been deeded to the Anne Arundel County Department of Recreation and Parks.

[40]William H. Marine, *The British Invasion of Maryland* (Baltimore, 1913), pp.27-29.

[41]F. Edward Wright, *Maryland Militia, War of 1812,* vol.4 (Silver Spring, Md., 1981).

CAPTAIN FRANCIS HANCOCK'S MILITIAMEN

First Lieutenant Zach Cromwell	*Ensign Henry Foreman*
First Sergeant John Atwell	*Second Sergeant Vachel Phillips*
Corporal Charles Boone	*Fifer Joshua Gray*
Private Stephen Hancock	*Private John Hancock*
Private John Williams	*Private Jacob Williams*
Private O Neal Cromwell	*Private Zach Robinson*
Private Benjamin Horner	*Private Henry Dunbar*
Private Cockey Pumphrey	*Private Charles Hanshaw*
Private Lloyd Hanshaw	*Private John Hanshaw*

and, on August 30, 1814, two officers and men in two small boats entered Bodkin Creek and burned a schooner there.[42]

When the British prepared to attack Fort McHenry in September, Captain Francis Hancock and his militiamen stood ready to signal as soon as the British fleet started up the Patapsco. Oral tradition tells that they were to give the alarm from Bodkin Point, using flags by day or burning haystacks by night. Watchers at Steeple House Farm above North Point then took up the signal and relayed it to Fort McHenry. The spyglass Hancock used was treasured by his descendants.[43] Ensign Henry Foreman and Corporal Charles Boone, "from Captain Hancock," were stationed briefly at Fort Madison during this emergency.

Years later, under 1850 and 1855 acts of Congress that gave bounty land to those who served in the War of 1812, local veterans or their widows proved service on the Patapsco and received bounty land. Because this land often was in Western Maryland, the veterans or their widows usually sold it. Those who claimed land in 1851 included Henry Dunbar, who stated that he volunteered and was discharged at Bodkin Point; Rachel

---

[42]Christopher George's study of Sir Peter Parker's Journal of the War of 1812.
[43]Hein and Bollman, "A Church and Its People," pp. 17-18.

Bell Hancock, widow of Captain Francis Hancock; and Mildred Cromwell Pumphrey, widow of Cockey Pumphrey who volunteered at "Magity" in April 1813 and was discharged by death on February 7, 1814. Nancy Hanshaw, widow of Charles Hanshaw, made her claim in 1859.[44]

A war nearby did not stop business interests from beginning a chemical industry where Blackhole Creek empties into the Magothy. At North Ferry Point (Cape Sable), marcasite occurred in compact strata. This mineral, an iron sulfide related to pyrite, was used to produce iron sulfate or copperas. Mining, mineral processing, and shipping began there as early as 1812 when Gerald Troost, a Dutch chemist employed by Dr. Charles Carroll, assisted in founding the Baltimore Iron Works. This was the first plant in the United States that produced alum, a natural resource found near iron deposits. Alum had multiple uses, including a part in making gunpowder. Ore mined along North Ferry Point was taken by barge to Baltimore where the actual manufacture took place.[45]

Recent excavations sponsored by the Maryland Maritime Archaeology Program have disclosed remains of a sandstone foundation for a wooden wharf at Cape Sable. Much slave labor, including the skilled labor of coopers and blacksmiths, was necessary for this enterprise. Between 1813 and 1820, the plant sold $2,000 worth of copperas, used in cleaning outdoor toilets, and alum worth $59,000, a huge sum at that time.[46]

During the decades following the War of 1812, this business prospered because Baltimore was advantageously located at the starting point of both the new National Road leading westward and the first railroad in America. By 1837, enough marcasite was being mined at North Ferry Point to produce copperas in sufficient quantities to supply the entire nation.[47] Baltimore's growing population and its importance as a commercial center would have significant consequences for people living on the adjacent peninsula.

---

[44]Marine, *The British Invasion of Maryland*, p.32.

[45]Robert F. Gould, "Eminent Chemists of Maryland," *Maryland Historical Magazine*, vol.80, no.1 (Spring 1985):19.

[46]Stephen Bilicki, Maryland State Underwater Archaeologist, Maryland Historical Trust.

[47]Robert Louis Benson, *Anne Arundel County History Notes*, vol.23, no.1 (October 1991):13.

Growing with A Young Nation

During the quiet decades that followed the War of 1812, farming and lumbering continued to occupy residents of the peninsula and workboats that sailed the creeks and rivers, the log canoe, bugeye, skipjack, and pungy, were essential to commerce and daily life. A Chancery Court case filed by Richard Caton against Benjamin Hancock in 1820 provides evidence of the value of lumber as a source of income. Caton had sold Hancock 297 acres near Gibson Island for twenty dollars an acre, but the deed stipulated that Hancock could not cut more than 600 cords of wood in any one year until he had paid three $1,000 bonds. But Hancock cut quantities far exceeding 600 cords without making any payments. The court upheld Caton's claim that the land would become less and less valuable as wood was cut, until eventually he would be unable to recover the purchase price.[48]

Some farmers like Henry C. Dunbar owned large tracts of land. In 1822 Dunbar bought Richard Caton's property near Gibson Island (now Pinehurst). He continued to buy land from Caton in 1827 and 1837,

---

[48]Kiessling, Trevor A., Jr., "Bodkin Neck: Gateway to the Patapsco," p.8.

extending his holdings from Bodkin Neck Road (now Bayside Beach Road) to Mountain Road, a total of 623 acres. In 1838 Dunbar added 706 acres near the head of Bodkin Creek and, in 1856, a final 135 acres on Cornfield Creek, a total of about 1500 acres. By that time, he owned twenty slaves. In 1850 his land was valued at $15,000 a huge sum then. He also owned six horses, ten cows, twelve oxen, and fifty swine. His farm produced 1,000 barrels of corn, 500 bushels of oats, 120 bushels of wheat, 150 bushels of potatoes, 500 pounds of butter, $300 worth of orchard produce, and $600 worth of market garden crops. He became the most influential man in the area and served as an Anne Arundel County magistrate.[49]

In 1819 Congress authorized building lighthouses at Bodkin Point, North Point, and Sparrows Point to serve vessels on the way to the port of Baltimore. Ships often grounded on the sandbar near Bodkin Island. Richard Caton sold four acres of the island to the federal government for $600 in August of 1820. William B. Barney, who was in charge of the lighthouse project, signed a contract with Evans and Coppeck on April 10, 1821. By September the firm had completed the keeper's stone dwelling and the 35-foot tower, but the light was not installed and lighted until January 1822. After Captain John Gray was appointed keeper, the lighthouse improved safety for mariners approaching the Baltimore harbor. Though there were earlier lighthouses on the Virginia shores of the Chesapeake, Bodkin lighthouse was the first in Maryland waters. In 1822, Henry C. Dunbar sold the remainder of Bodkin Island to the government for $225.[50]

When John Gray died in August 1822, Barney strongly recommended the appointment of his widow, Araminta Gray, as keeper. President James Monroe allowed her "to continue for the present," but he wrote in January 1823, "If she will get some male friend of hers to accept the appointment nominally, suffer her to do the duties of the keeper." Mrs. Gray's

---

[49]*Ibid.*,12-14; Agricultural schedules of the Federal Census of 1850.

[50]F. Ross Holland, *Maryland Lighthouses of the Chesapeake Bay* (Crownsville and Colton's Point, Md, 1997), pp.4, 6, 8, and 191, note 19.

The 1833 stone lighthouse on Bodkin Point, the first lighthouse in Maryland waters.

Collection of Downs Park, Rick Holt, Superintendent

nephew, Mark W. Foreman, accepted the appointment, while Araminta Gray did the work. According to Barney, she performed "extraordinary well," but she remarried and left the lighthouse at the end of the year. Philip Marshall then served as keeper, beginning January 1, 1824.[51] John Gray is buried in the abandoned Bodkin cemetery.

While John S. Williams represented the Third Election District in the General Assembly, people were aware of the need for schools. Though Richard Caton set aside half an acre for a school near Gibson Island in 1825, the only evidence that the first Bodkin School might have been built then is in the minutes of a Methodist Protestant Church Conference held "in a school near the Bodkin" in June of 1831. According to a deed dated April 18, 1827, another school, possibly a predecessor of Clinton Academy on Tick Neck, replaced an earlier school building "on the county road to Rock Creek."[52]

---

[51]*Ibid.*, p. 143.

[52]Hein and Bollman, "A Church, Its People," p.21; Anne Arundel County Land Records, Liber WG12, f.436.

In 1830 or 1831, local Methodists who wanted greater representation in church affairs left the Magothy Methodist Episcopal Church. The Methodist Conference had denied the appeal of some Methodist Episcopal preachers and laymen, who had protested the denomination's refusal to broaden representation on policy-making bodies. The protesters formed the Methodist Protestant Church in 1830. By June of 1831, a two-day meeting of the Methodist Protestant Church was held in a school near the Bodkin.[53] Soon thereafter the congregation built White Marsh Methodist Protestant Church on Mountain Road where the Lake Shore Fire Department now stands.

In July of 1833, White Marsh Church advertised a camp meeting one mile from Bodkin Creek. Campers could come by boat from Baltimore and the Eastern Shore to the landing on Wharf Creek, and their baggage would be taken to the campground free of charge. The host church offered a boarding tent for those who wanted to take their meals there and "a chapel nearby." A mention of twelve tents at White Marsh Church in August of 1835 suggests that the congregation was holding another camp meeting.[54]

Though schools may have existed on the road to Rock Creek and near the Bodkin by 1827, the Magothy Methodist Church neighborhood apparently felt the need of its own school. Between 1826 and 1845, the church provided a Sabbath School for grades one through five. Classes were held only on Sundays when the circuit riding preacher would have been available. A roll book lists the subjects taught: ABCs and Reading, Spelling, Writing, Ciphering, History, and Geography.[55] Possibly the school that appears on the 1860 Martinet map on Dorsey Jacob's land beside the Methodist Church might have opened in 1846 when the Sabbath School closed. The 1850 census lists Dorsey Jacobs as a teacher.

---

[53]Edwin C. Schell's notes on the Minutes of the Maryland Methodist Protestant Conference, June 10, 1831, p. 180.
[54]*Ibid.*, June 28, 1833, p. 208; August 23, 1835, p. 124.
[55]Edwin T. Calvert, "Hancock's Resolution" (Historic Annapolis brochure, 1965), p.5.

The 1850 federal census for the Third Election District, which included the peninsula, shows a population of 2,107 people in 430 households, 69 per cent white and 29.7 per cent black. Of the black population, 18 per cent were free. Only 51 people were born elsewhere, 17 in Ireland and 13 in Germany. There were 158 farmers, 56 laborers, nine carpenters, two merchants, two doctors, one blacksmith, and one miller. Captain John A. Boone was the captain of a vessel, and Dorsey Jacobs was the only schoolmaster. Of the 486 white children in the district, only 72 attended school. Of the 182 black children, only one attended school.[56]

Slaveholders on the peninsula owned an average of four slaves, fewer than in 1790, reflecting the abandonment of tobacco culture. Those who held slaves included the Lynch, Johnson, Pumphrey, Robinson, Chairs, Gray, Foreman, Hancock, Boone, Dunbar, Linstid, and Williams families.[57] Dorsey Jacobs had freed his nine slaves in accordance with Methodist principles. Addison Johnson, the storekeeper, also freed his two slaves, Wesley and Prissy Henson, and gave them several acres of land where they built a two-room home.[58] Only two people in the Third District died of old age in 1850. More than a third of those who died were under twenty and most were under ten years of age. Scarlet fever and dysentery were major causes of death.[59]

According to the agricultural schedules of the Federal Census of 1850, Henry C. Dunbar of Bodkin Farm was still the largest landholder on the peninsula. Most other farms varied from 75 to 300 improved acres, valued at about ten dollars an acre. Their livestock included from one to six horses, one to ten cows, and fifteen to fifty swine. A few farmers had mules, oxen, or sheep. No one grew tobacco. Perhaps one-third of the farmers grew wheat, usually only ten to thirty bushels, suggesting that it was for their own use rather than for market. About half grew from 300 to 1,000 barrels of corn as a major crop, while Dunbar, Landy Linstid, and

---

[56]1850 Census, Third District, Anne Arundel County (Pasadena, Maryland, 1991), pp. 97, 111-129.
[57]*Ibid.*, p.380.
[58]Pritchett, "History of Magothy Methodist Church," p.8; "Discovering Our School Communities," Pasadena Elementary School History, 1952.
[59]1850 Census, Third District, Anne Arundel County, p.436.

William Williams led in orchard produce and market gardens. Mary Linstid, Archibald Robinson, John Johnson, and John Jacobs also grew fruits and vegetables, pointing the way toward future use of farm land on the peninsula.[60]

By 1850 Anne Arundel County was the most important strawberry producing district in the South. On June 9, 1852, *The Sun* reported that an average of 50,000 quarts of strawberries were shipped from Baltimore to Philadelphia daily during the growing season, nearly all from Anne Arundel. Two years later, one-third of the acreage planted in strawberries in the United States and Canada was in Anne Arundel County.[61] Surely, a large percentage of those acres was on the peninsula.

As Baltimore became an important port, the locally maintained lighthouses on the Chesapeake became obsolete. After the appointment of a federal Lighthouse Board in 1852, the General Assembly passed a resolution asking for "a floating light vessel" to replace the stone lighthouse near the mouth of the Patapsco because many vessels had run aground on the shoals there. Since this light would be a principal guide for foreign ships on one of the busiest shipping lanes in the United States, Congress appropriated $10,000 for the project at Seven Foot Knoll. The final cost was $27,000. Engineers decided to build a screwpile structure, using a new technique developed in England in the 1830s. This eliminated the need for underwater caissons and heavy masonry foundations. Murray and Hazelhurst, Baltimore-based ironfounders, supplied the cast iron parts, and work began in 1854.[62]

The Seven Foot Knoll Lighthouse was a wrought-iron structure that rested on a central leg and eight other cast-iron legs that formed an octagon. Each hollow leg had external threads that were screwed into bedrock below the river. Legs were of varying lengths because of the uneven bedrock. They were filled with concrete, capped, cross-braced, and tied to

---

[60]Agricultural schedules of the Federal Census, 1850.
[61]Willard R. Mumford, *Strawberries, Peas, and Beans* (Arnold, Md., 2000), p.31.
[62]F. Ross Holland, *Maryland Lighthouses*, pp.49-54; Maryland Historic Sites Inventory AA-931, 1987.

the center pole. A set of cast-iron girders ran around the circumference, and another set ran radially from the center to the legs to support the iron plates of the floor.

The house itself was of cast iron, probably the only one ever built. The lighthouse was forty feet in diameter, and its sides were made of 3½-foot-wide cast-iron plates. The first-floor panels were twelve feet high, the second-floor panels were nine feet high, and the lantern chamber panels just under nine feet. The structure stood nine feet above the mean high water mark. When it became operational in January of 1856, the stone Bodkin lighthouse went out of service, though it remained a landmark as it slowly disintegrated over many decades.[63]

During the late 1850s, the village that became Jacobsville clustered around Addison Johnson's store and post office where Old Mill Road (now Armiger Drive) intersected Mountain Road. Johnson's Store gave its name to the entire neighborhood between St. Margaret's and Marley. The rectangular, one-story building with a high gable roof and a low fieldstone foundation still stands at 2601 Mountain Road. The community included a blacksmith shop, the two Methodist churches, Dr. Lynch's home, and other residences.

Martenet's 1860 map shows Clinton Academy on Tick Neck Road and two schools on the south side of Mountain Road, one beside the Methodist Church and the Bodkin School several miles from Gibson Island. Familiar family names appear on the map as landowners—Armiger, Cook, Crane, Chairs, Dunbar, Foreman, Gray, Hanshaw, Hancock, Hines, Jacobs, Jubb, Lark, Linstid, Linthicum, Lynch, Meek, Maccubbbin, Osborne, Pumphrey, Robinson, Welch, Williams, and Lancelot Chard, the owner of the largest property, an extensive tract on the Patapsco.[64]

Black Methodists, who had been members of Magothy Methodist Episcopal Church, built Mt. Zion Methodist Episcopal Church south of

---

[63]*Ibid.*, pp.49-54.
[64]Martinet's map of Anne Arundel County, 1860.

Still standing at Armiger Drive and Mountain Road, this building served the community called Johnson's Store as a general store and as a post office from 1855 until 1872.

Collection of Laura Wiegmann

Part of the Martinet map of Anne Arundel County, 1860.

Collection of the Ann Arrundell County Historical Society

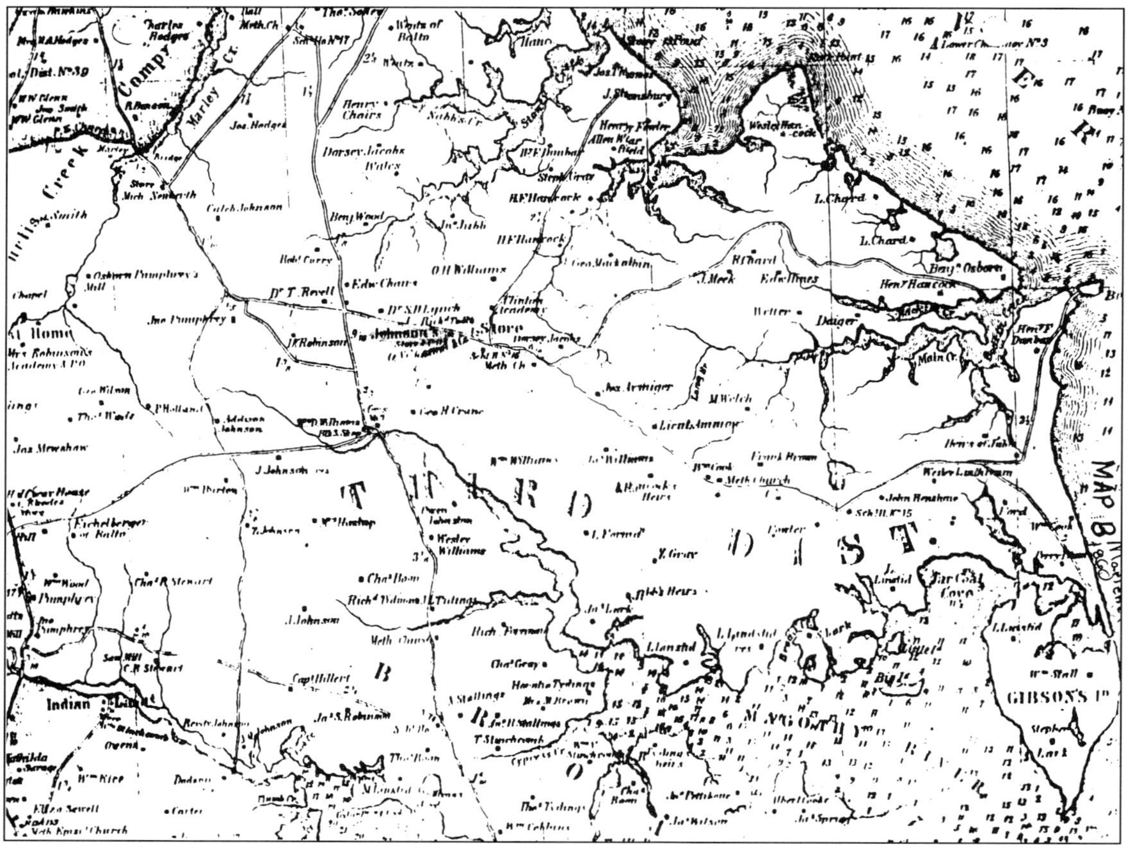

Mountain Road in 1859. James and Elizabeth Williams deeded them one acre of land for a dollar on November 30, 1859. The deed was recorded on January 13, 1860. Previously, as in other Methodist churches founded by Francis Asbury, black members may have worshiped on Sunday afternoon in the Magothy Church. Since black Methodist churches did not have autonomy until 1866, the trustees during this period were Leonard Foreman, Stephen W. Hancock, Joseph Armiger, James E. Williams, and Dorsey Jacobs. As early as 1861, the congregation began the week-long Magothy Camp Meeting that they have held every year since that time. In 1868, Mt. Zion incorporated as an independent church. Theodore W. Kess was lay leader and Sunday School superintendent.[65]

Martenet's 1860 map shows Magothy Methodist Episcopal Church on the south side of Mountain Road. At the same time that the black parishioners built their own church in 1859, Magothy Church rebuilt across Mountain Road from its original location. Dr. George H. Crane and his wife Charlotte deeded the land for the new church on October 15, 1862. The original trustees of the property, who were also the members of the Building Committee, were Leonard Foreman, Josiah Armiger, Dorsey Jacobs, James Williams, and Dr. Samuel Lynch. The new church was larger than the old log church and was lighted by kerosene chandeliers. The cemetery remained on the north side of Mountain Road. Buried in the tree-shaded graveyard are Dorsey Jacobs and his wife Charlotte; their son and daughter; and members of the Dunlap, Armiger, Boone, Cook, Crane, and Hancock families.[66]

The slave schedules of the Federal Census of 1860 show that, although families held fewer slaves than in the early days of tobacco culture, many still depended on slave labor. Only William Stinchcomb, J.E. Williams, Leonard Foreman, Landy Linstid, Stephen Lark, and Oliver Williams held as many as ten to sixteen slaves. Others owned an average of five.

---

[65]"124th Anniversary of Mt. Zion United Methodist Church at Jacobsville, MD, 1859- 1983" (unpublished, 1983).

[66]Hein and Bollman, "A Church, Its People," pp.10-11.

The 1860 federal census valued real estate and personal property in the area known as Johnson's store. Among those who held the largest acreage were George A. Crane, Henry Dunbar, Dr. Samuel Lynch, Stephen and Lemuel Hancock, Lancelot Chard, James Armiger, Mordecai Welch, Henry Joyce, Mary and Landy Linstid, Stephen Lark, Leonard Foreman, and F.W. and J.E. Williams. Dr. Samuel Lynch, J.E. Williams, George A. Crane, Leonard Foremen, Landy Linstid, Stephen Lark, Elizabeth Hancock, Henry Dunbar, and James Armiger held the largest amounts of personal property. Except for a few who listed their occupations as teacher, carpenter, lighthouse keeper, sailor, or physician, all were farmers or farm workers.[67]

But a prosperous and peaceful era was ending as conflict over deeply held beliefs led to a devastating civil war. Soon people who lived on the peninsula would be drawn into the struggle between those loyal to the Union and those sympathetic to the Confederacy.

---

[67] 1860 Census Book 3, Third District, Anne Arundel Co., pp.130-157.

Civil War and Recovery

On April 15, 1861, John Barnes of Baltimore sent a letter to Henry Hancock at Bodkin Point with the startling news that war had begun with an attack on Fort Sumter: "I regret to announce to you that war has actually commenced, and the South Carolinians have bombarded Fort Sumter and taken possession of the fort. The Southern boys have done their work admirably and gained the victory," he wrote. "It was hot work on both sides, but Major Anderson had to surrender the fort to the Southern Confederacy and the Palmetto Flag now proudly waves over the ramparts of Fort Sumter and long may she wave. It is reported and now expected that the Federal Capitol at Washington City will be attacked by the Secessionists."

Barnes urged his friend to "get yourself ready to defend the South. I would not be at all surprised if we don't have civil war in Baltimore before two weeks end. The greatest excitement that I ever witnessed in my life is going on in our city at present." After asking about his friends at Rock Point, Barnes advised them "to pay careful attention to the drill exercises, for I

YOUNG FARMERS CERTIFIED AS UNABLE TO SERVE

Leonard Foreman
Milton Fowler
Dorsey Gray
Edward Hines
James Hancock
Lloyd Hanshaw
John Jubb
John, Charles, George, and Orlando Johnson
John D. Jacobs
Wesley Linthicum
Stephen Lark
George Maccubbin
Thomas, Charles, Columbus, and John Boone
Josiah Armiger
Edward, Henry, Franklin, and William Chairs
William Chard
Joshua, Andrew, and Marcellus Osbourn
Alexander and Alpheus Pumphrey
James Robinson
Charles and William Stinchcomb
Richard, John, and Zachariah Tydings
Joseph Williams
Mordecai Welsh

expect the 'Magothy Home Guards' will soon march either to defend the Government or the South, but I hope they will go South and show their Gallantry and firmness."[68]

Soon after President Abraham Lincoln called on the states to furnish 75,000 volunteers to suppress illegal activities in the South, blood was shed in Baltimore when residents attacked Massachusetts troops that were responding to Lincoln's call. Because the citizens of Anne Arundel County, most of whom were Southern sympathizers, had cast only four votes for the election of Lincoln in 1860, the federal government placed the county under martial law as soon as hostilities began and all civil liberties were suspended.

Raising troops on the peninsula to fight for the Union was a difficult task. In 1862 the Provost Marshall sent an enrollment officer with a small detail of Union cavalry to each home in the area called Johnson's Store to record the names of able-bodied men between the ages of 19 and 45. Any man who claimed to be exempt was examined by the local doctor. Dr. Samuel Lynch, a Southern sympathizer who had cared for local families, certified that many of the young men were "diseased" and unable to serve. Others claimed that they were deaf, had a back injury, a broken arm, crippled fingers, or defective vision. John Edward Jackson Pumphrey told the enrolling officer that "Abe Lincoln only wants to kill all the people," John Robinson compared Lincoln to Herod who slew children, Thomas Tydings refused to accept his notice, and Elijah Tydings had already "left for parts unknown."[69]

---

[68]Edward T. Calvert Collection; James R. Morrison.

[69]Enrollment Record, Anne Arundel County, District 3, John Johnson, Enrollment Officer, 1862. Members of the Johnson family apparently had divided loyalties.

Dr. Samuel Lynch continued to serve the community until his death in 1884. Then his neighbors erected a grave marker inscribed in memory of "his faithful service as family physician for fifty years." Local lore tells that the wheels of the wagon carrying his casket locked and the horses had to drag the wagon from his home (where the Roller Rink now stands) to the cemetery. After the pallbearers removed his casket, the wheels of the empty wagon turned normally.[70]

If the enrollment officer considered men from the peninsula eligible for the draft despite their claims or Dr. Lynch's certification of "disease," they had to report to Camp Bradford in Baltimore. There they were examined to see whether they qualified for exempt status. Thomas Lewin and Richard Magruder qualified because of illness, Joseph Chaney was excused by the War Department, Thomas E. Duvall's broken leg made him exempt until the next draft, and Luther Wood proved to be under the minimum age for service.[71]

Free black men were subject to the draft. Among those from the peninsula who were drafted were Horace Brown of Bodkin Creek and William Snowden, Lloyd Johnson, and Lewis Murray of Rock Creek. Men who were drafted could choose to serve, send a substitute, or pay $300 in lieu of service. Slaves from the peninsula who were sent in place of their masters or their masters' sons included James H. Pack, slave of Henry Dunbar of Magothy; Rezin Jackson, slave of John Yielding of Stony Creek; Jerry Ogle, slave of Thomas Davidson; and Jason Richards, slave of James E. Williams of Magothy.[72]

Refusal to serve in the Union Army did not mean that local men were unwilling to fight. At Camp Bradford, where brokers made a business of supplying substitutes, Rhinegold Blount paid for a substitute and then volunteered and served in the Confederate infantry. John Robinson served as a seaman on a Confederate privateer, the *Tacony*, Edward Heath at the

---

[70]Emma M. Schramm. James G. Gibb, archaeological consultant, explained that wagon wheels will lock when they must support additional weight if the bearings have not been greased.
[71]Milton O. Duvall; *The Sun*, December 22, 1862.
[72]Milton O. Duvall; *The Sun*, October 1864.

Memphis Naval Station, and Elijah Gray with Confederate Marines based in Wilmington, North Carolina. Confederate volunteers included William Armiger, Edelin's Maryland Heavy Artillery; William G. Duvall, Third Maryland Artillery (Chesapeake); Michael Hartman, First Baltimore Infantry; William H. Heath, Maryland American Rifles; and William Rowley, Davis's Maryland Cavalry. Nicholas Fontz, R. Johnson, and Ludwick Wetter simply "went South."[73]

Before January 1, 1863, Confederate volunteers from Maryland usually joined a Maryland command; thereafter, they were assigned wherever they were needed. The name of the unit does not tell where they saw action; Florida commands, for example, defended Richmond. Men from Johnson's Store who served where needed included James Armstrong, Co. K, Third Texas Cavalry; Rinegold Blount, Ninth Florida Infantry; William Davis, First Alabama Artillery; Zachariah Johnson, Co. B, Ninth Virginia Infantry; Richard Lindsey, Co. D, 34th Alabama; Joshua Webster, Co. B, 28th Louisiana Infantry; and Benjamin Wood, 59th Virginia Infantry. The grave of Charles (Buck) Hammond in the Mt. Carmel Methodist Church Cemetery

The grave of Charles (Buck) Hammond, a Confederate soldier, at Mt. Carmel Church cemetery. The symbol at the top was used by Maryland's confederate troops.
Photo: Blue Moon Aerial Photography

[73]Milton O. Duvall's research from contemporary accounts in *The Sun* and Hartzell, *Marylanders in the Confederacy* (Silver Spring, Md., 1986).

proudly bears the name of his unit, Co. C, 2nd Battalion, Maryland Infantry, CSA (Confederate States of America), and a symbol used by Maryland men who served the Confederacy.[74]

Other men stayed at home and helped the cause by sending supplies to the Confederacy in blockade runners that left the peninsula at night. Jefferson Monroe Cook (son of William Henry Cook and Amelia Dunbar Cook, heirs of Henry Dunbar), who owned a large tract from the Magothy to Bodkin Creek, spent large sums sending clothing and supplies.[75] Blockade runners were apprehended on Rock Creek in April of 1862 when the Provost Marshall and his squad arrested 24 men on the charge of intending to go South. They were not local residents but men from the city, some of whom escaped to the schooner that was to take them away. The others were sent on a tug to Fort McHenry, a Union prison at that time.[76]

The federal government called for two 100-day drafts when Confederate troops invaded Maryland in 1864 and 1865. Anyone claiming to be exempt was ordered to appear on or before July 21, 1864, "the only condition to be ACTUAL PHYSICAL DISABILITY."[77] Union recruiters no longer accepted a doctor's statement of poor health as they had in 1862. The men who were drafted did not necessarily serve in the Union Army. Some, like Elijah Gray, were already fighting for the Confederacy.[78]

Little is known of local men who served in the Union Army, with one exception. Joseph Lopez, a native Englishman whose home was on the peninsula, was a

MEN FROM JOHNSON'S STORE DRAFTED IN 1864 AND 1865

The 100-day draft, 1864

John Ellison
George Jubb
Elisha Gray
J.E.J. Pumphrey
Richard Robinson
John H. Stallings
James Turner

The 100-day draft in 1865

James Armiger
Charles Stinchcomb
George Maccubbin
Clarence Johnson
Frank Johnson
Horatio Tydings
Edward Witter
William Fowler,
John Jubb
James Hancock
William Chairs

(*The Sun*, July 1864)

---

[74]*Ibid.*

[75]Anne Cook Myllo. Jefferson M.Cook inherited the land along the Bay from Gibson Island to Pinehurst from his father. His wife, Emma Linsted, inherited the adjoining land on the Magothy side of the peninsula.

[76]*The Sun*, April 7, 1862 and July 1864.

[77]General Order 26, *The Sun*, July 8, 1964.

[78]Milton O. Duvall, research from *The Sun*.

veteran of Co F, 99th New York Volunteers, who lived on the Bodkin peninsula. He had been captured, imprisoned at Andersonville, recaptured after an escape, and eventually released when Sherman marched to the sea. He lamented that he lived, "I am sorry to say, in a part of the United States where a Union soldier is not much thought of. I have had to swallow some pretty hard talk, more so since I received my pension. . . . But, Merciful God, had they suffered for one month as I did for years, they would think that $50 a month were not enough."[79]

Though the community generally favored the Southern cause, Magothy Church remained loyal to the Methodist Episcopal Church that opposed slavery. Dorsey Jacobs, the preacher at Magothy, freed his slaves. Many other Anne Arundel County churches divided or joined the Methodist Episcopal Church, South. Records do not tell whether the war caused conflict within the Magothy congregation. Since families who had been Southern sympathizers attended White Marsh Methodist Protestant Church a generation later, possibly they left Magothy Church, either before or during the war, because of the slavery issue.

The period following the war was difficult for everyone, especially for those who had risked their lives or their resources for the Southern cause. Many former slaves left the farms to find work in Baltimore. These were hard times when labor was scarce and the memory of deep differences divided neighbors. While citizens were "taxed to the utmost," local roads were so bad that they were "notorious," a resident complained, and teachers were not paid at the end of the school year. In addition, farmers were discouraged because plum trees had died as a result of disease and an April frost killed apricot orchards in full bloom.[80]

Despite these problems, the Maryland General Assembly passed a law in 1864 providing for the establishment of a State Board of Education that would oversee public education. The Board's first report lists two schools at

---

[79]Lopez, Joseph O., "Capture, Escape, and Recapture" (unpublished, no date), James B. Calvert Collection.

[80]*Maryland Republican and Advertiser*, April 1, 1871.

Johnson's Store and one at Magothy. The expense of educating each child for one year in 1865 was six dollars. Despite its name, Clinton Academy on Tick Neck Road was not a high school. The courses offered at all the schools on the peninsula in 1868 included reading, arithmetic, spelling, history, geography, and, for advanced students, grammar and philosophy.[81]

In a deed dated November 11, 1865, one acre of land owned by Stephen W. Hancock and later by William Calvert was set aside as the property of the Trustees of Primary Schools.[82] This appears to have been land for Rock Point School number five on what now is Bayside Beach Road about one half-mile from what then was Rock Point Road (now Fort Smallwood Road). The one-room frame building there was 18 feet wide by 24 feet long with a hewed chestnut frame and white pine clapboard siding. Hannah P. Gray taught there in 1869. In 1873, E. W. Maynard was teaching 17 pupils with an average attendance of twelve, normal attendance at a time when helping with farm work took priority over schooling.[83]

After Alfred Stinchcomb gave land for a new Tick Neck School in a deed dated September 18, 1869,[84] possibly the school beside Magothy Church and Clinton Academy merged into school number four, known at different times as Clinton Academy, Magothy School, and Tick Neck School. When Melville Dunlap taught there in 1869, he earned his salary of $437.32 a year with an enrollment of 59 pupils and an average attendance of 30. In 1869 Ella E. Sydnor taught at Bodkin School number six on the south side of Mountain Road not far from Gibson Island. With 39 pupils enrolled and an average attendance of 24, five advanced students were studying philosophy. When E. F. Linthicum was the teacher in 1873, enrollment had dropped to 25 and average attendance to only 12.[85]

---

[81]Report of the Public Schools of Maryland (Annapolis, 1865, 1866, 1868). The 1866 report lists Patapsco Institute near Brooklyn, Anne Arundel Academy at Millersville, and West River Academy at Owensville as the only high schools in the county.

[82]Nelker, *Town Neck Hundred*, p.111.

[83]Calvert, "Hancock's Resolution," p.6; Report of the Public Schools of Maryland, 1869, 1873).

[84]"Discovering Our School Histories," Riviera Beach Elementary School, p.11, quoting Frank Baker of the Board of Education. The school history calls this Rock Point School, but the location "at the junction of the Neidert and Stinchcomb farms" confirms that it is Tick Neck.

[85]Report of the Public Schools, 1869, 1873.

In 1873 a free black man, Greenberry Johnson, who had bought property in 1853 and 1865, offered the Board of School Commissioners land for a Rock Point School for black children. He died before completing this gift, but his children, Mary Johnson, Ann Rebecca Hall, and Mary Elizabeth Richards, carried out his wishes, signing the conveyance on January 23, 1874.[86] This school (number 2, colored) was on what now is Bayside Beach Road at its intersection with what now is Fort Smallwood Road. In 1876, with J.W. Robinson as their teacher, black children on the peninsula attended school for the first time. The following year Alexander Thomas earned $240 a year there with an enrollment of 57 and average attendance of 19.[87]

Despite postwar problems, signs of future prosperity in this agricultural community were apparent. Professor Higgins of the Maryland Agricultural College wrote that the cultivation of fruits and vegetables in Anne Arundel County was giving "greater returns for labor and capital than in any tillage in any other part of the United States."[88] By 1871, the shift from cereal crops to fruits and vegetables on the peninsula was about complete, with farmers growing peas, corn, potatoes, strawberries, and orchard crops like apples, pears, and cherries.

Not only Baltimore but also Philadelphia proved to be such a good market for fruits and vegetables that a commission merchant bought a steamboat to transport produce from Bodkin Creek to Baltimore. The following year he planned to buy a second steamer to serve Rock Creek. Previously, farmers had shipped their crops to market on their own market boats or had paid the owner of a sailing vessel that loaded produce at a county wharf or private wharf. Gradually, faster steamboats replaced sailboats.[89]

Having lost their slaves, local farmers felt a pressing need for reliable laborers, especially for picking strawberries. Changes in federal laws

---

[86]Undated newspaper clipping; oral history related by Johnson's great-great-grandson Charles Manns of Baltimore, who holds a copy of the 1874 conveyance.

[87]Report of the Public Schools, 1876, 1877.

[88]Jane McWilliams, "Land and People," in James C. Bradford, *Anne Arundel County, Maryland: A Bicentennial History*, p.3.

[89]*Maryland Republican*, April 1, 1871.

solved their dilemma when large numbers of Eastern Europeans were allowed to emigrate. By the 1880s, more people entered the United States by way of the Patapsco than at any other place except Ellis Island. Soon Polish and Czechoslovakian (called Bohemian) immigrants were living in "picker shanties" for six or eight weeks each season and picking berries, peas, and beans. By 1894, at least 150 wagons filled with pickers crossed the Long Bridge (Light Street Bridge, abandoned in 1918) in a single day in May. The procession began at daylight and continued until nightfall. Many farmers on the peninsula transported their pickers by boat from Baltimore. Only the Cooks and Calverts used craft like the *Rhoda Virginia* to bring pickers from islands off the Eastern Shore.[90]

Because the farmer did not receive cash for his crop until it reached the market and because the pickers were not comfortable with written records, farmers paid them with brass checks bearing their initials and a numeral to represent the number of quarts or pecks that had been picked. Pickers could use checks to buy items they needed at local stores. The farmer redeemed these checks in cash before the pickers returned to their homes in Baltimore.

In 1872 the post office moved from Johnson's Store to the south side of Mountain Road at Hog Neck Road where Jacobs family members served as postmasters from 1872 until 1888. After September 20, 1872, the village was called Jacobsville.[91] Dorsey Jacobs lived in a three- story house behind the present location of Pastore's. He served the community as lay pastor of Magothy Church and as schoolmaster. He was appointed inspector of Anne Arundel County primary schools and took the oath of office on October 15, 1862.[92]

On October 5, 1872, "in their earnest desire to promote the advancement of the cause of temperance," Dorsey Jacobs and his wife Charlotte deeded one-half acre to the Magothy Division No. 105 of the Sons of

---

[90]*The Sun*, May 17, 1894; Charles H. Calvert.
[91]Emma M. Schramm, "History of the Pasadena Post Office" (unpublished, 1985), p.4.
[92]Nelker, *Town Neck Hundred*, p.73.

LOCAL PATRONS OF THE HOPKINS ATLAS

H.S. Anderson

Joseph Armiger

S.J. Armiger

Thomas A. Brown

Jefferson M. Cook

R.W. Chard

James Ellison

John Ellison

John Hanshaw

Captain W.R. Hales

Thomas S. Jacobs

James Lark

Stephen Lark

H.C. Linstid

Wesley Linthicum

R.C. Smith

Mordecai Welsh

H.F. Williams

J.E. Williams

O.H. Williams

Temperance for a lodge. The trustees of the building were members of the Lynch, Jubb, Hancock, Jacobs, Crane, Linthicum, Lark, Johnson, Williams, and Robinson families.[93]

The Sons of Temperance Lodge, built in 1875, served as the meeting place for the local chapter of a national organization dedicated to abstinence from buying, selling, or using "spirituous or malt liquor, wine, or cider." The Lodge stands just east of the cemetery and across Mountain Road from the Magothy Methodist Church. The one-story, gable-front, frame building rests on a low foundation. The main entrance is in the center of the main block and is protected by a small gable-roofed vestibule.[94] This building later became the Magothy Church Hall and housed the Sunday School and then the overflow from Jacobsville School. It still stands but has been renovated extensively.

The 1878 Hopkins Atlas of Anne Arundel County reflects some growth on the peninsula since the 1860 Martinet map. Four schoolhouses, one on Bodkin Neck, one on Tick Neck, and separate schools for black and white children near Rock Point, served the community, as well as Adam Dash's mill near Waterford, three Methodist churches, the Temperance Hall, a cemetery, four stores, and a blacksmith shop. (Adam Dash's mill was at the site of the early Waters Mill, known as the Wallace Mill in 1866 and as Boyd's Mill at one time.)[95] The Hopkins map shows the first bridge over the Magothy, almost directly south of Jacobsville, downstream from the present bridge.[96]

Both old and new Methodist churches were active at this time. In 1875 Magothy Church at Jacobsville was assigned its

---

[93]*Ibid*. p.73, deed SH7, f.629.
[94]Maryland Historical Trust Historic Sites Inventory AA-2050.
[95]John W. McGrain, "Water Power: The Molinography of Anne Arundel County," (unpublished, no date).
[96] Hopkins Atlas of Anne Arundel County, 1878.

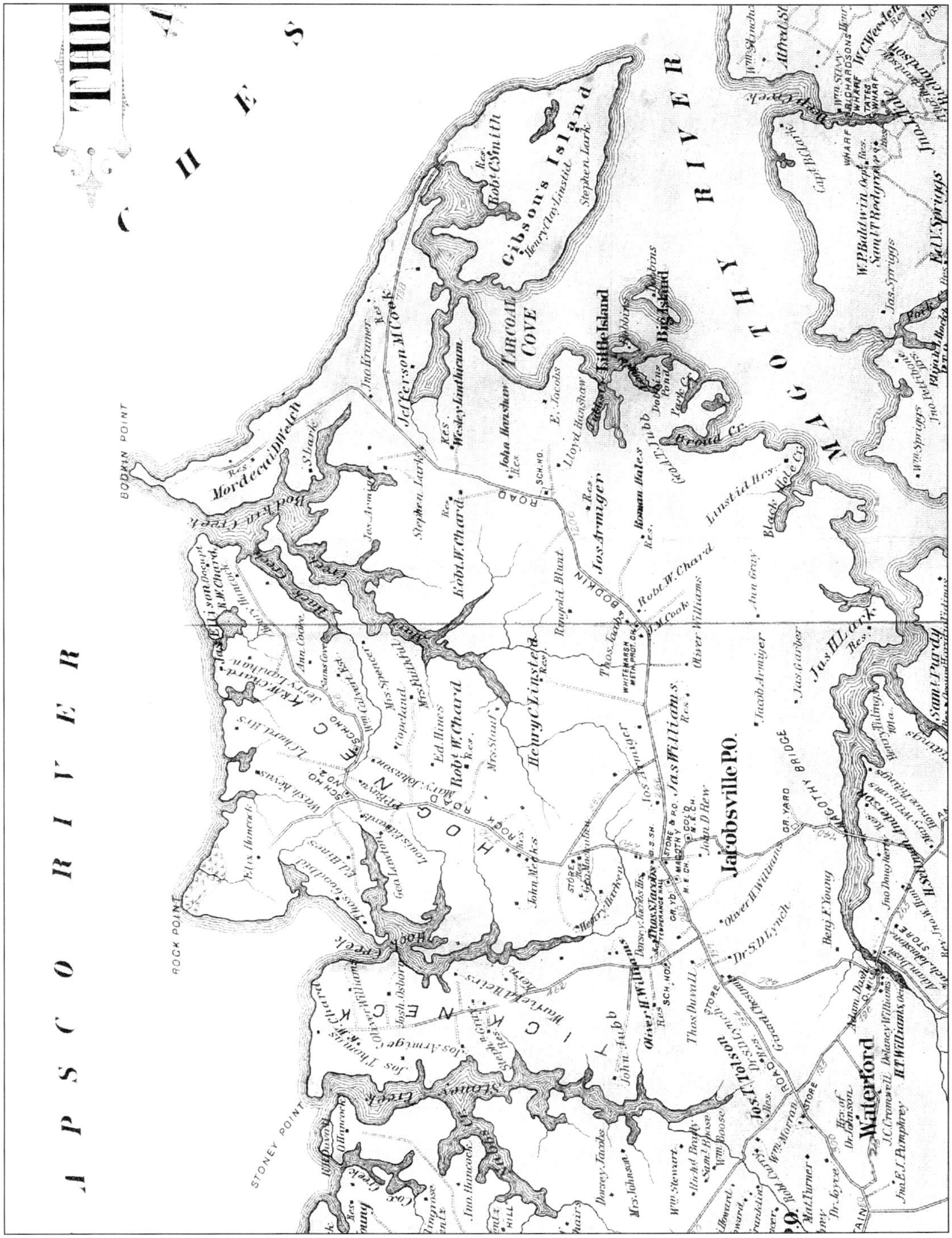

The Pasadena peninsula as shown on the Hopkins map of Anne Arundel County, 1878.

first full-time stationed preacher, John H. Ryland, who received an annual salary of $500. In 1882 Magothy's pastor, J.C. Stewart, built their first parsonage at a cost of $1800 with the help of one carpenter. The congregation bought their first organ in 1883. A fourth Methodist Church joined the three churches already on the peninsula when Virginia Siever sold land for one dollar to the founders of Piney Grove Methodist Church, the predecessor of Pasadena Methodist Church.[97]

Though White Marsh Methodist Protestant Church on Mountain Road at Lake Shore had been active since 1831 and families like the Bottomleys of Gray's Creek and the Chairs, Cooks, Dunlaps, Ellisons, Heaths, Jenkins, Jubbs, Linthicums, and Williams attended services there, the church must have experienced reduced attendance by the late 1870s. In 1877 the pastor was authorized to sell the church, "if he deemed it wise." A search of records revealed that the land never had been deeded to the church; however, on May 5, 1883, T. A. Jacobs executed the necessary deed.[98]

In 1884 some members withdrew from White Marsh Church and met in a tent for three weeks before joining the Methodist Episcopal group that was preparing to build a new church. Others remained loyal to the Methodist Protestant Church, even when the building was abandoned. As late as 1895, they hoped to reopen the church that had been closed for years.[99] The building was used for church and community affairs when services were no longer held there.[100] In 1921 the abandoned building was dismantled and moved to Dundalk to house the Graceland Park Methodist congregation. Later, Herbert Linthicum and Ernest Simms sold the land to the Lake Shore Fire Department for $200.[101]

---

[97]Hein and Bollman, "A Church, Its People," pp.13-14; Hazel Brown and Bettie Heckman, "History of the Pasadena Methodist Church" (unpublished, 1962).

[98]Blodwin Shipley Potee, "The History of Mt. Carmel United Methodist Church (unpublished, 1979); Schell notes, Minutes of the Maryland Methodist Protestant Conference, p.53, deed SH21:406.

[99]Schell, *Baltimore Methodist*, 1-17-1885, p.5; *Methodist Protestant*, 10-9-1895, p.4.

[100]Pritchett, "History of the Magothy Methodist Church," p.17.

[101]Schell notes, Minutes of the Maryland Methodist Protestant Conference, p.127; Potee, "History of Mt. Carmel Church."

The home that Jefferson Monroe Cook built on the Magothy Narrows in 1873. His son and a guest are playing croquet on the lawn in 1926.
Collection of Anne Cook Myllo

In 1884, Wesley Linthicum gave the new congregation an oak grove on a knoll where Jefferson Monroe Cook built Mt. Carmel Methodist Episcopal Church. Other founders were John F. Ellison, James E. Williams, Jr., and Thaddeus H. Williams. The Chairs, Dunlap, Heath, Jenkins, and Jubb families, former members of White Marsh, joined Mt. Carmel at an early date. The new church seated 125 people and was dedicated on August 30, 1885. Three years later, the trustees of Mt. Carmel Church purchased four-and-one-half acres adjoining the church property from Wesley Linthicum for $72.50. On November 9, 1887, they filed articles of incorporation and agreed to lay out and maintain a cemetery.[102]

Jefferson Monroe Cook, builder of Mt. Carmel Church and supporter of the Confederate cause, was a farmer who owned a sawmill and designed

---

[102]Potee, "History of Mt. Carmel Methodist Church"; Schell notes, *Baltimore Methodist*, April 25, 1885, p.5; Jan. 22, 1887, p.5; March 20, 1886, p.4; Anne Arundel County Land Records, SH24:654; incorporation SH21:243.

and constructed Mt. Carmel Church, the architecturally important Bodkin School No. 9, and his house on the Magothy Narrows. His large home with its many gables and wide porch included an office off the living room and a nursery connected to the master bedroom. Only the church survives.[103]

Worshipers often came by boat to the county wharf (at what is now Green Gables) and walked to the church. Jefferson Cook picked up others at their homes and drove them to worship services in his surrey. Whenever the oyster fleet was frozen in Bodkin Creek, oystermen from the Eastern Shore came to Mt. Carmel to worship. Often they were invited to a parishioner's home for dinner.[104]

Mount Zion Church, sometimes called Magothy-Mount Zion, incorporated in 1868 and moved just west of its present site in 1878. Johnsontown nearby was named for the Johnson brothers who hauled logs that were used in building the church. Other founders were the Hall, Brooks, Watts, Kess, Boone, and Kelly families.[105]

That building was destroyed by fire and replaced in 1883 by a gable-front frame building with a steeply pitched roof. The windows were tall and narrow with pointed-arch tops and opaque or colored glazing. At the center of each window was a decorative Biblical motif. The plastered walls were offset by darkly stained wainscot and the paneled balconies were supported by turned posts. Six octagonal Gothic Revival-style metal lanterns suspended from the ceiling provided light. The church played an important role in the religious, social, and cultural development of the local African-American community.[106]

Freetown, a black community that borders the peninsula, existed before the war. Settlement began December 26, 1845, when James Spencer, a free-born black, bought a large tract of land there. William Howard, Nathan Owens, William Turner, Abraham Franklin, and William Hall, all

---

[103]Anne Cook Myllo
[104]Potee, "History of Mt. Carmel Church; Anne Cook Myllo.
[105]"124th Anniversary of Mt. Zion United Methodist Church."
[106]Maryland Historical Sites Inventory AA-1004.

Mount Zion Methodist Church, formed in 1859 and at this site since 1883.
Collection of Anne Arundel County Division of Planning

free men, bought adjoining property in the next two decades. Spencer and Howard served three years in the Union Army, U.S. Colored Troops. By the 1880s, free blacks owned nearly 1,000 acres between Marley and Stony creeks and worshiped at Hall's Methodist Church, built on land given by William Hall. Freetown residents took pride in their first school, built in 1870, and in their independence. Like the black community near Mt. Zion Church, they raised their own hogs, chickens, fruits, and vegetables and helped each other in times of need.[107]

The peninsula would continue its bucolic existence for a few more decades, but the wider world was about to discover its shores.

[107]*The Sun*, February 7, 1999, p.9B.

Peace and Prosperity During the Gay Nineties

If one event dates the beginning of Baltimore's discovery of the peninsula as a place for recreation, that event would be the formation of the Stoney Creek Steamship Company and the Rock Creek Steamship Company in 1883. Initially the Stoney Creek Company operated the *Gazelle* from pier 15 on Light Street. George Efford and Thomas Bottomley were the principal investors in the Rock Creek Company that served Rock Creek and Curtis Creek, the latter primarily a freight route. They bought the *Falcon* and the *George W. Johnson* and chartered the sidewheeler *Chester* that ran from Pier 12, Light Street, and the foot of Broadway. These excursion steamers brought hundreds of people to the beaches each week.[108]

By the late 1880s, one of the landings on Rock Creek was Fair View (later Fairview), a hotel that James Marsh built on his farm overlooking the Patapsco. In an 1890 advertisement, Philip Marsh was listed as proprietor of the summer resort on a beautiful elevation, "one of the finest beaches for bathing in the State. Fine boating and fishing. Positively no intoxicating

---

[108]Robert H. Burgess and H. Graham Wood, *Steamboats Out of Baltimore* (Cambridge, Maryland, 1968), pp.178,180.

Fairview Hotel, a popular destination, now the site of the Maryland Yacht Club.
Collection of Jack Kelbaugh

liquors allowed on boat or grounds."[109] Later the Rock Creek Steamship line owned Fairview, with Thomas Bottomley the principal owner for many years.

The *Chester*, a side-wheeler steamer, stopped at Fairview daily and on Sundays, leaving Baltimore at 8:45 a.m. and 2:45 p.m. Tickets for a round trip cost 25 cents. The *George W. Johnson* left Pier 12 daily at 7 a.m. and 2 p.m. and stopped at various piers on Stony Creek on Monday, Wednesday, and Friday and at docks on Rock Creek on Tuesday, Thursday, and Saturday. On Sundays, stops were made on both creeks. In addition, the steamer could be chartered for moonlight excursions.[110] In the days before air conditioning, Baltimore was hot during the summer, and people gladly paid 25 cents for a ticket to a beautiful beach where cool breezes blew.

---

[109]*The Sun*, July 22, 1890.
[110]*The Sun*, July 22, 1890; July 1, 1890.

The *Severn*, a steamboat built in Baltimore in 1891, bringing vacationers to the beaches.
Photo: Marion E. Warren. Collection of the Maryland State Archives.

By the mid-1890s the Stoney Creek Steamship Company suspended operations; for twenty years, the Rock Creek line handled both routes, with the addition of the *Falcon*. Ads in *The Sun* promised service to Stony Creek twice on Monday, Wednesday, and Friday, and to Rock Creek twice on Tuesday, Thursday, and Saturday. On Sunday the *Johnson* made three trips to both creeks.[111]

Thousands of Baltimoreans enjoyed this opportunity to escape the heat of the city with a loaded picnic basket. Wide white sand beaches, picnic tables, and boats for hire were among the attractions. Men often returned home with baskets filled with rock, perch, and soft crabs. The Rock Creek Steamship Company bought the *Petrol* in 1894, the side-wheeler *Thomas L. Worthley* in 1896, and the *Tourist* in 1899, selling their other vessels

---

[111]Burgess and Wood, *Steamboats*, p.178; *The Sun*, June 17, 1890.

that year.[112] By the turn of the century, steamers were taking excursionists to many small resorts on both creeks.

In addition to boats that carried passengers to and from Baltimore from the creeks along the Patapsco were other boats that picked up and dropped passengers and goods at many landings along the Magothy River. Besides smaller craft, the *Louise*, an excursion steamer with a capacity of 2,500, was a familiar sight there.[113]

Acreage devoted to cereal crops decreased during the 1880s along with a notable increase in growing fruit and truck crops, especially where farmers could easily reach the Baltimore market by water.[114] *The Sun* reported on May 24, 1884, that "vendors always are happy when they can call out Anne Arundel as a prefix to any kind of vegetable or fruit, for that name alone gives assurance that the thing offered is of the very highest attainable excellence." On May 28, the *Evening Capital* described the large number of boats filled with strawberries from the peninsula that arrived at Long Dock on the first day of the market season. The boats, recently painted in bright colors, made a handsome appearance. On their return trip, some took pickers to farms.

Excursions to beaches were summertime entertainment for visitors, but life went on as before for people who lived in the community of Jacobsville. During the winter, music, games, dancing, and "feasting" were typical activities at social gatherings in homes. In 1886 a severe wind storm damaged outbuildings and fences, froze plants in hot beds, and blew three oyster sloops ashore in the mouth of Rock Creek. A steam tug from Baltimore came into Bodkin Creek to free ice-bound oyster boats, but ice from the Patapsco and the Bay filled the mouth of the creek so completely that the tug was unable to move.[115]

In the spring, local farmers journeyed to Baltimore to meet a committee of the legislature to protest being unable to unload their produce at the

---

[112]Burgess and Wood, *Steamboats Out of Baltimore*, p. 181.
[113]Marianne Taylor, *My River Speaks*, (Arnold, Maryland, 1998), pp.172-174.
[114]*Maryland, Its Resources, Industries, and Institutions*, pp.159, 171.
[115]*Evening Capital*, March 4, 1886.

State wharf, and a sheriff's posse stopped a conflict between strikers and non-strikers who were building the Baltimore and Annapolis Short Line Railroad.[116]

In September of 1886, Maryland Lodge No. 1, Knights of the Farm, sponsored a tournament at Rockaway Beach (at the mouth of Rock Creek near what now is Fort Smallwood Park). The first tilting was for the honor of choosing the Queen of Love and Beauty. The Knight of the Patapsco, W.T. Greeves, took twelve rings and chose Mamie Hines to reign over the festivities. The Knight of the Magothy, L.J. Hales, and the Knight of Turkey Hill earned the right to select Gertie Hales and Phenie Linstid as her maids of honor. Some knights, like Joseph Linstead of Eagle Hill and T.H. Hines of the Grove, chose place names as their titles, but W. Linthicum and C.H. Jubb jousted as "Knight of Could if I Would" and "Knight of Would if I Could." At the second tilting, the knights contested for a handsome lap robe, a riding bridle, and a carriage whip. S. Linthicum, the Knight of Turkey Hill, won first prize.

Glass-ball shooting, an early form of trap shooting that began in the late 1860s and continued only until the introduction of clay pigeons in 1887, followed the tournament. J. Jubb won a gunning suit by breaking four of five balls. Everyone then assembled in the dancing pavilion for the coronation ceremony, performed in the presence of the tournament judges, T.S. Jacobs, G.G. Jenkins, and Zachariah Gray. After "a grand oyster supper," festivities continued with a dance "until the wee small hours."[117]

Late in March, the steamer *George W. Johnson* brought fifty Faith Healers to the Marsh farm on Rock Creek where many people had gathered. After Elder Raymond preached a sermon about remarkable cures the Faith Healers had made, Mr. Marsh "brought forward" his valuable horse that the best veterinary surgeons in Baltimore were unable to cure. When Elder Raymond prayed and applied oil to the horse three times, the horse

---

[116]*Ibid.*

[117]*Evening Capital*, September 18, 1886; for glass ball shooting, see Kenneth Ramage, editor, *Lyman Shotshell Handbook* (Middlefield, Connecticut, 1976), p.78.

"was made perfectly sound," and Mr. Marsh declared that he would not sell him for $300. Elder Raymond then led twelve candidates into the creek where they were baptized. He remarked that the shore of Rock Creek was the best place he had seen for submerging in his fifty years as a Baptist preacher. Two weeks later, the *Johnson* returned with sixty Faith Healers who were joined by 300 spectators who gathered to listen to a sermon and to see five candidates baptized.[118]

The following week, the pastor of the Magothy Methodist Church, the Rev. Cyrus N. Robinson, exhibited lantern slides of panoramic scenes from the Bible for the benefit of the Mt. Carmel Sunday School. He planned to attend the Maryland State Temperance Alliance meeting as a delegate and warned that thousands go every Sunday to the city, "that most iniquitous place, worse than Sodom and Gomorrah." There, he said, your sons find "doubtful society, ruin, and moral degradation staring them in the face."[119]

When the Faith Healers returned in late April, a destructive fire was the news of the week. The Faith Healers held a prayer meeting on Saturday night, followed on Sunday by preaching at the Bigood home, testimony of miraculous healings, and baptism of four converts. Later that week, a disastrous fire burned about 200 acres of woodland and 1,000 panels of fencing belonging to R.W. Chard and E.J. Hines. Farmers fought the blaze for eight or nine hours and finally succeeded in stopping its spread by burning woods some distance ahead of the fire.[120]

Despite this loss, the pea crop was promising and strawberries, peach trees, and cherry trees were in bloom, though farmers feared for the raspberry and blackberry crops. By late May, strawberry and pea pickers were arriving in large numbers, and sailboats filled with berries were shipped to Baltimore daily.[121]

---

[118]*Evening Capital*, March 31, 1886; April 15, 1886.
[119]*Evening Capital*, April 22, 1886.
[120]*Evening Capital*, April 22 and 25, 1886.
[121]*Evening Capital*, May 21, 1886.

In August farmers were harvesting quantities of produce, though their families found time for other activities. Landowners shipped tomatoes, peaches, cantaloupes, and watermelons from the peninsula to Baltimore daily, increasingly by steamer, though sailboats still were used. On Sundays, many residents attended a camp meeting at Jackson's Grove near Odenton. Mrs. James Jubb, Miss M.L. Jacobs, Mrs. George R. Jacobs, and "Mrs. Dr." George H. Crane entertained visitors, though Mrs. Dr. Crane fell while boarding the *George W. Johnson* at Light Street and was confined to her room for several days.[122]

A reporter wrote that it was gratifying to record the progress and prosperity of the Third District of Anne Arundel County. Separated by the Magothy River and Bodkin, Rock, Stony, and Curtis creeks, "the inhabitants have been cut off as it were from intercourse with the rest of the world." But a man who returned to the peninsula after thirty years' absence would find it completely changed, he observed. Forests had fallen and "the whole face of the country smiles in one beautiful orchard and garden spot."

Delicious peaches, plums, apricots, strawberries, raspberries, watermelons, and cantaloupes, as well as a variety of vegetables, would cause a man to bless this place where produce has "a more delicate flavor and exquisite richness" than in any other part of the country. Because of local farmers' prudent management, energy, and foresight, he predicted that this soon would be the richest district in Maryland. He found that the people of the peninsula were "liberal and public-spirited, giving freely to everything that advances the public good."[123]

By 1890 the peninsula was producing a large quantity of cabbages, as well as marketing its famous strawberries. Unloaded from sloops, bugeyes, and pungees, Wakefield cabbages from the peninsula were piled on Bowley's wharf in Baltimore where they were trimmed and boxed and

---

[122]*Evening Capital*, August 12, 1886.
[123]*Evening Capital*, August 3, 1886.

sent west or to Philadelphia.[124] In 1888 and 1889 Maryland grew over 23 per cent of the tomatoes canned in the United States,[125] and the local newspaper reported that northern Anne Arundel County produced more strawberries than any other area in the nation. With so many market boats and other craft in use, a boatyard at Tar Cove on Sillery Bay specialized in coating hulls with tar.[126] Tar Cove on Rock Creek probably had a similar history.

Magothy Methodist Church remained the center of this farming community. Just as members had completed extensive renovations and were planning a service of consecration, a wood stove overheated during the night of November 17, 1886, and fire destroyed the building. The pastor, W.M. Hammock, rescued the pulpit from the burning church, and it was still in use 100 years later. After the fire, the congregation met for almost a year in the Temperance Hall. Though this loss was a devastating blow, parishioners laid the cornerstone of a new building on June 11 and dedicated a replica of the renovated church on October 23, 1887. The frame building, lighted by kerosene-burning chandeliers, cost $3,600, but congregational giving reduced the debt to $1,200.[127]

The congregation continued its active schedule in the new building. In the spring the church was decorated with flowers on Missionary Sunday for an afternoon program that included special music and appropriate recitations. In May viewers watched stereopticon slides and enjoyed strawberries and cream. For the Ladies Aid Society's lawn party in June, the church grounds were lighted with Chinese lanterns. In addition, the church hall was the setting for a banquet, a formal tea, and an entertainment.[128]

An excellent example of late-19th century Methodist church architecture derived from the Gothic Revival style, the Magothy Church features two steeply-pitched gable-roofed sections perpendicular to each other, with a bell tower and steeple where they intersect. The steeple and bell

---

[124]*Evening Capital*, September 2, 1887; May 29, 1889.

[125]Maryland Agricultural Experiment Station Bulletin A-E, 1888-1891, p.5.

[126]Taylor, *My River Speaks*, p.91.

[127]Hein and Bollman, "A Church, Its People," p.14; Pritchett, "A History of Magothy Church," p.8; Schell Notes, *Baltimore Methodist*, June 4, 1887, p.5; October 22, 1887, p.5; Nov. 5, 1887, p.5.

[128]*Evening Capital*, May 14 and June 24, 1888.

Historic Magothy Methodist Church, founded in 1777 and at this site since 1859.
Collection of Anne Arundel County Division of Planning

tower are covered with the original wooden fish-scale shingles. The building is nearly identical to plan 18A in an 1889 Methodist Church Building Plan catalogue. Relieving the simplicity of the plan are the lancet window frames, stained glass rose window, ornamental truss on the gable end, and decorative woodwork on the bell tower. The windows contain opaque and variegated shades of stained glass.[129]

Teachers at the four schools on the peninsula continued to educate children, despite an average attendance that was only half the enrollment. During the eighties, William H. Davies and E. Atwell taught classes at Bodkin School that averaged 11 pupils, though 28 to 36 were enrolled. Melville Dunlap (son-in-law of Dorsey Jacobs and Sunday School superintendent at Magothy Church), T. B. Hanna, and Clara Mc Kechney taught at Rock Point School number five between 1881 and 1891. Attendance averaged 10 or 11 with 20 to 30 on the rolls. At the school for black children at Rock Point, Daniel Scott and Levin Conquest enrolled about 45 children with an average attendance of 20.[130]

Daisy H. Robinson, H.F. McNeal, and Mary McCauley taught from 8 to 28 pupils on Tick Neck while from 16 to 36 were listed on the rolls. In November of 1886, students at Clinton Academy gave an entertainment that filled the Temperance Hall to capacity. After a hymn and a prayer, Miss Mollie McCauley presented Becky Jacobs at the piano, Carol Dunlap at the organ, and Miss McCauley, Emma Jacobs, Charles Williams, and Dr. E. Williams singing a quartet. In April examinations were held for two weeks, ending with a test on philosophy. Joseph Robinson's 9.7 average gave him top honors.

In June the students celebrated the end of the school year with an all-day picnic and dancing at Rockaway Beach. Since attendance at the Academy had tripled, the trustees met to discuss enlarging the building. Three young ladies, Carrie Dunlap, Viletta Phelps, and Rebecca Jacobs,

---

[129]Maryland Historical Trust Historical Sites Inventory AA-1043.
[130]Report of the Public Schools, 1881, 1884, 1886, 1888.

were expected to graduate in 1889 and to apply for positions as teachers. Carrie Dunlap taught at Rock Point in 1891 and Viletta Phelps returned to Clinton Academy as a teacher in 1892.[131]

The inauguration of the Baltimore and Annapolis Steam Short Line in 1887 had a major effect on much of Anne Arundel County, but the railroad touched the peninsula only at its western end. Doubtless it led to laying out streets and lots in the village of Pasadena,[132] and at other railway stations along its route. The railway brought the benefits of convenient access to Baltimore to the inland border of the peninsula, and some farmers along the Short Line used it to transport produce to the city. For most of the region, however, the creeks and the Patapsco remained the best route to market.[133]

When the Jacobsville Post Office closed in 1888, post offices at Armiger, Maynard, and Lake Shore replaced it. James Armiger became postmaster at the same location as the earlier Johnson's Store (now Armiger Plaza); Edward Maynard was postmaster at Maynard on Fairview Beach Road; and the Lake Shore post office was in a store next door to the present Lake Shore Fire Department. Neighboring Elvaton became a separate post office in 1889.[134]

At about this time, the Seven Foot Knoll Lighthouse was renovated, though the substructure remained unchanged. The original square lighthouse was replaced by a circular house, composed of rolled-iron plates riveted together to form a self-supporting shell. Three horizontal bands of three-by-six-foot plates formed the exterior wall, with a narrow soffit band connecting the wall plates to the roof plates. The first story, 51 feet in diameter including a five-foot exterior platform, provided living quarters for the keeper, a kitchen, living room, and two bedrooms. Tongue and groove flooring laid on iron plate, interior wood paneling, four-paneled doors, and double-hung windows made the interior home-like. The

---

[131]*Maryland Republican*, November 17, 1886; *Evening Capital*, April 12 and June 24, 1888; Report of the Public Schools, 1881, 1884, 1888, 1891, 1892.

[132]Anne Arundel County Plat No. B-14, Book No.12, folio 11.

[133]Jack Kelbaugh, "By Water, Road, and Rail," *Anne Arundel Co. History Notes*, vol.23, no.3, p.10. The Short Line referred to the shorter route and shorter time spent commuting, compared to the previous route that required transferring at Annapolis Junction.

[134]Emma M. Schramm, "History of the Pasadena Post Office," 1985, pp.4-9.

Seven Foot Knoll lighthouse at Bodkin Point in 1944. The lighthouse was moved to Baltimore Harbor in 1968.
Collection of James B. Calvert

second story, much smaller than the original at fifteen feet in diameter, housed oil tanks and a mechanism for the light. Rising from the roof, a six-foot-wide chamber surrounded by an iron railing held the light.[135]

The area that now is the village of Pasadena was farmland until the 1880s. Addison Johnson, owner of Johnson's store, and the Tydings, Robinson, and Stewart families once owned large farms there. Addison Johnson's son, Clarence Johnson, was the community doctor. His office was in his home on Light Street, and he visited his patients on horseback, carrying his supplies in saddlebags and using a scale to weigh the powders he prescribed. The town of Elvaton was named for his wife, Elva Johnson.[136]

In 1890 the Southern Land and Silk Association, incorporated in Baltimore, bought 100 acres that originally had been part of the tract called *Waterford*. These people came from California to grow mulberry trees and raise silkworms, though they had originally intended to operate a vineyard.[137] After first investing in property at Round Bay, where they named

---

[135]Holland, *Maryland Lighthouses*, p. 54; Maryland Historical Trust Historical Sites Inventory AA-931.

[136]"Discovering Our Communities," Pasadena Elementary School, 1952.

[137]Joani Guhne, "In 1890 McBee House Was One of Four in Pasadena," *Times-Voice Newspapers*, November 20, 1980, p.16B.

streets Pasadena, Alameda, and Los Angeles, the Association bought land in what became the village of Pasadena. There they built five houses along the present Railroad Avenue, Light Street, and Hamburg Street. Oral tradition tells that the woman who lived north of the former railway station named her new home Pasadena after her former home in California.[138] Hope Road was the name of what now is Pasadena Road. The group's hopes were not fulfilled, but the name that they gave their little community now identifies the entire peninsula.

One of the original five homes in the village of Pasadena burned, but the others still stand, though they have been extensively remodeled. According to the Pasadena School history, the families that occupied them in 1952 were the McBees, Ways, Oaks, Taylors, and Dietmillers. The tall white McBee house just north of Pasadena Road (earlier the home of Mrs. Kenny, a midwife) once was accessible from Railroad Avenue, but now can be reached only from Ritchie Highway. The Way home on Light Street, occupied formerly by the Jenkins family, burned, but the Taylor home nearby at the northwest corner of Hamburg and Light Street, once occupied by the Styers, has been converted into a duplex.

The other two houses, the former Oaks' home on the southeast corner of Ritchie Highway and Hamburg and the Dietmiller house on the southeast corner of Hamburg and Catalpa, were their close neighbors before the Ritchie Highway separated them. The Oaks family home once was the home of John Appleton, a contractor who laid the first water system in Pasadena. When the state acquired land for the Ritchie Highway, the village of Pasadena was divided and the Appleton property lost large old shade trees.[139]

Another small group came to the peninsula in 1893. They were Baltimoreans who formed the Patapsco Club for family recreation. A steamboat captain sold them five acres on Rock Creek, accessible only by

---

[138]"Discovering Our Communities," Pasadena School. The plat the Association filed at the Court House in Annapolis for their Round Bay property provides evidence that they used California place names for their land in the county. Pasadena Street in Round Bay survives.

[139]Research by Emma Wade Jenkins Sanders. The building of the East-West Boulevard in 2000 is dividing what was the village of Pasadena once more.

steamer. Later Club Road provided access from Fort Smallwood Road. During the early decades, families lived in Baltimore but they vacationed during the summer in screened tents on wooden platforms. By the 1920s they built cabins, and the next generation lived in summer cottages. Membership was limited to 25 families who owned their cottages, though the club owned the land. Members recall contests and oyster and shad roasts. The Patapsco Club has survived for over a century, but permanent homes on the grounds have replaced summer cottages.[140]

By 1895 Baltimore had become the largest distribution center for fruits and vegetables in the United States. The main source of that produce was "a small section of territory adjacent to Baltimore City" that included the peninsula. In 1894 daily shipments of great quantities of strawberries and other fruits and vegetables were sent to Boston, Montreal, Chicago, "and intermediate points."[141] Though local farmers no longer grew cereal crops for market, as late as 1895 one grist mill on the peninsula was still grinding corn for use by farm families.[142]

An award given by the Patapsco Boating Association for the best fishing yarn, 1897.
Photo: Robert Reyes

A public wharf at Joy Harbor and the Magothy Steam Railroad helped farmers to transport produce to the market in Baltimore. In 1898 the County Commissioners bought land for a wharf at the head of Stony Creek and a thirty-foot-wide right of way leading to Mountain Road.[143] The 1878 Hopkins map

[140]Robert Reyes.
[141]Maryland Agricultural College Experiment Station Bulletin #33, pp.117, 118, 126.
[142]Taylor, *My River Speaks*, p.151.
[143]Green Haven Carnival brochure, July 1940, the Schramm Collection.

The Patapsco Boating Association in the 1890s.
Photo: Robert Reyes

The Patapsco Club's pier on Rock Creek where the ferry stopped, 1941.
Photo: Robert Reyes

shows that Tick Neck Road and lanes that led to farms were the only roads on the peninsula at that time. Probably soon after the wharf was ready for use, investors built a steam railroad from Mountain Road down what is now Catherine Avenue to Shore Road and Outing Avenue. The Magothy Steam Railroad moved produce from Mountain Road to the public wharf. The only written records of this venture are a brief mention in the Jacobsville School history saying that the railroad served the community for fourteen years and an item in the September 1937 issue of *The Green Haven Hash* quoting John Risk as saying that "a railroad ran on Catherine Avenue over twenty years ago."

About 1895 the Chairs family opened a general store at their home opposite Mt. Carmel Church. This was the first store east of Hog Neck Road. Among the items they sold were flour and sugar in barrels, big wheels of cheese, and penny candy. Pickers paid for their purchases with brass checks that the farmers would redeem. Around the turn of the century, Harry and Mamie Hancock adapted a stone outbuilding adjacent to their home near Bodkin Point for use as a store. They sold produce, eggs, and salt meat from their farm, as well as box cheese, soda crackers in barrels, ginger snaps, rock candy, and chewing tobacco brought by boat from Baltimore. Their customers were farmhands, pickers, the lighthouse keeper, and watermen, including oyster dredgers. Later they built a frame building to house their store.[144]

Not far from the Hancock farm, Rock Point was to become the site of preparations for the Spanish-American War. In 1895 the U.S. Army Chief Engineer identified Rock Point as one of three sites necessary to the defense of Baltimore. Flavius W. Hancock and Cassie and Oliver Owens refused to sell their land to the government; however, in condemnation proceedings on June 2, 1896, a United States District Court jury awarded the Corps of

---

[144]Katie Ellison Hyde; Edward T. Calvert, "Hancock's Resolution," p.7.

The William Chairs home and store (right of fence) opposite Mt. Carmel Church.
Collection of Drusilla Chairs

Engineers 100 acres at Rock Point at a cost of $27,500. On July 21, 1896, Flavius Hancock deeded the land to the United States government.

Though Baltimore was not threatened during the Spanish-American War, the Army Engineers completed a powerful coastal artillery battery emplacement in 1900, a concrete structure with a raised platform that housed the guns behind a parapet wall. A T-shaped frame barracks building with a slate gable roof and clapboard siding stood southwest of the defenses. The fort was named in honor of Major General William Smallwood, commander of the famous Maryland Line during the Revolutionary War. Guns for Battery Hartshorne were in place by 1902; guns for a secondary battery were ready in 1905.[145]

The peacetime garrison consisted of eight officers, fifteen sergeants, 63 privates, and three musicians. Two full companies would be needed in

[145]Lt. Col. Merle Cole, "Fort Smallwood's Military Mission," *Anne Arundel County History Notes*, vol.25, no.3, pp.6, 10; Hancock deed, Liber G.W., no.3, f.316; Maryland Historical Trust Historic Sites Inventory AA-897.

wartime, but normally only caretaker detachments were stationed there. The Coast Artillery Corps also planned for landward defenses in case of an amphibious attack. These plans, including an infantry trench to be dug from the head of Wall Cove to a fortified knoll, were not realized, although the project must have been the subject of much discussion as residents of the peninsula looked forward to a new century.[146]

Battery Hartshorne at Fort Smallwood, activated 1902, abandoned 1927.
Collection of the Ann Arundell County Historical Society

[146]*Ibid.*, p.8.

Dawn of A New Century

Most land on the peninsula was owned by descendants of the early settlers until about 1900 when German immigrants, who had come to Baltimore in large numbers, began to buy property there. By 1911 industrious immigrants owned 13 per cent of Anne Arundel County farms.[147] German families with names like Schramm, Klug, Schmidt, Klingelhoefer, Heintzman, and Schultz are among those who became successful farmers and businessmen in a strange country.

Louis Schramm, who was born in Kurhesse, Germany, bought the 236-acre Richard B. Phelps farm on Mountain Road between Waterford Road and Old Mill in 1909. His doctor had warned him that he must give up his work as manager of the Maryland Lime and Cement Company because his lungs needed to breathe clean country air. He moved to the peninsula in 1910 with his wife Fredericka and five of their children. Since farming was new to him, he asked Oliver Duvall to be his foreman and teach the Schramms to farm. They learned quickly and soon were

---

[147] McWilliams in Bradford, *Anne Arundel County: A Bicentennial History*, pp.2-4.

taking care of cows, horses, pigs, and chickens and growing strawberries, dewberries, apples, peaches, pears, beans, peas, tomatoes, cucumbers, squash, peppers, cantaloupes, watermelons, sweet potatoes, and field corn. They sent their produce to market by horse and wagon or by boat from the county wharf at Green Haven.[148]

The Klugs and Schmidts also succeeded as farmers. Benjamin and Phillipina Klug bought 29 acres at the corner of Mountain Road and Waterford Road in 1902, and their farmhouse became a store, a post office from 1907 until 1909, and the Rock Creek and Marley Telephone Company until 1914. His son William bought an additional ten acres across Waterford Road. Augustus Schmidt emigrated from Germany and, in 1887, began to work on a rented farm near Pinehurst. Eventually he saved enough money to buy land that became Clearwater Village and the western half of what is now Riviera Beach.[149]

Sam Hillman came to the area as a peddler who sold useful items from a pack he carried on his back. After renting a store on Rock Creek, in 1908 he and his wife opened a one-room shingled store at the corner of Mountain Road and Hog Neck Road. Since it was the only store for miles around, the Hillmans sold everything people needed: kerosene, clothing, medicine, and groceries including molasses from a barrel. Sam Hillman died a short time later, but Ida Hillman managed the store, made many of the foods that she sold, and took care of her three children under six years old.[150] Hillman's Corner, a landmark for decades, now is Pastore's.

Though lumbering had been a profitable business from the time that colonists first came to the peninsula until the 1860s, only isolated hardwood forests remained in 1902 when Wilmer Johnson bought a huge tract of chestnut and oak trees near Blackhole Creek. His son, J. Fred Johnson, supervised cutting lumber there, using an existing sawmill. In 1904 he married Mabel Jubb, whose family owned a large farm on Cape Sable.

---

[148]Emma M. Schramm, "Sixty Years in Anne Arundel County: The Schramm Farm."
[149]Pasadena Guide Book, 1993 supplement to the *Maryland Gazette*, p.4; Henry Schmidt.
[150]Emma M. Schramm; *Maryland Gazette*, September 19, 1987.

Between 1918 and 1921, Johnson returned to the area to cut hardwood and operate a sawmill near Blackhole Creek. Some of this timber was used to make four-by-six-inch railroad ties.

After he founded the Johnson Lumber Company, J. Fred Johnson used a landing at Chest Neck Point on the Magothy to ship timber to Baltimore by barge. Throughout the 1920s, farmers sold him hardwood from isolated parcels of uncultivated land. Instead of using a local sawmill, this timber was taken by truck to the Johnson Lumber Company headquarters in Glen Burnie. The Jarvis Lumber Company did some of the logging and then sold to Johnson.[151]

At the turn of the century, Anne Arundel County expected public-spirited members of the community to give land for schools and often to build schoolhouses. In June of 1899, trustees of the Mt. Carmel Church Cemetery deeded land to the Board of Education for Bodkin School

Bodkin School, built beside Mt. Carmel Church before 1895 by Jefferson Monroe Cook.

Collection of Anne Cook Myllo

[151] Slanker, Harold E., Jr., "The J.F. Johnson Lumber Co," *Anne Arundel County History Notes*, vol.24, no.4, p.2, and personal communication.

number nine to replace the old Bodkin School on the opposite side of Mountain Road (shown on the Martinet map in 1860 as number fifteen and on the Hopkins map when it was number six).

On May 4, 1898, the trustees of Rock Point School were Henry A. Hancock, E.W. Maynard, and George Washington Calvert. When the old Rock Point School was abandoned around the turn of the century, George W. Calvert built the new school. The county gave him the old building as payment, and he moved it to his home to use as a summer kitchen. For the next decade, enrollment at Rock Point continued to be about 30 to 35 with 15 to 18 pupils present.[152]

Ida E. Wheatley taught at the school for black children at Rock Point through most of the nineties. Both enrollment and attendance increased until the small school overflowed in 1912 with an average attendance of 55. Their teacher received a salary of $170 a year, compared to $304 for the teacher of the school for white children at Rock Point.[153]

At the school on Tick Neck Road, Maria E. Welch taught before and after the turn of the century. In 1903 pupils observed Arbor Day and the birthday of Washington Irving with a program including recitations and songs, followed by planting trees. Parents and children heard a lecture on Maryland history, and the teacher awarded prizes to Elva and Theodore Stinchcomb for regular attendance.[154] According to the Report on Public Schools, enrollment at Tick Neck increased to 52 by 1908 and 63 by 1916, requiring two teachers. During the 1920s, Mildred Collison, Margaret Hamilton, Hilda Coombs, and Margaret Hall taught there.[155]

James S. Billingslea became the community's family doctor in 1904 when he was 22 years old. He rode horseback to visit his patients before he had an automobile. Daily house calls cost two dollars or less. His home, where Maryland Route 100 now merges into Mountain Road, was a two-story, L-shaped, frame farmhouse that had been owned by the

---

[152]Hein and Bollman, "A Church, Its People," pp.21,23; James B. Calvert.
[153]Report of the Public Schools, 1892, 1896, 1912.
[154]*Maryland Gazette*, April 1903.
[155]Report of the Public Schools, 1908, 1916, 1920.

Interior of Tick Neck School, called Magothy School in 1904.
Collection of Emma Jenkins Wade Sanders

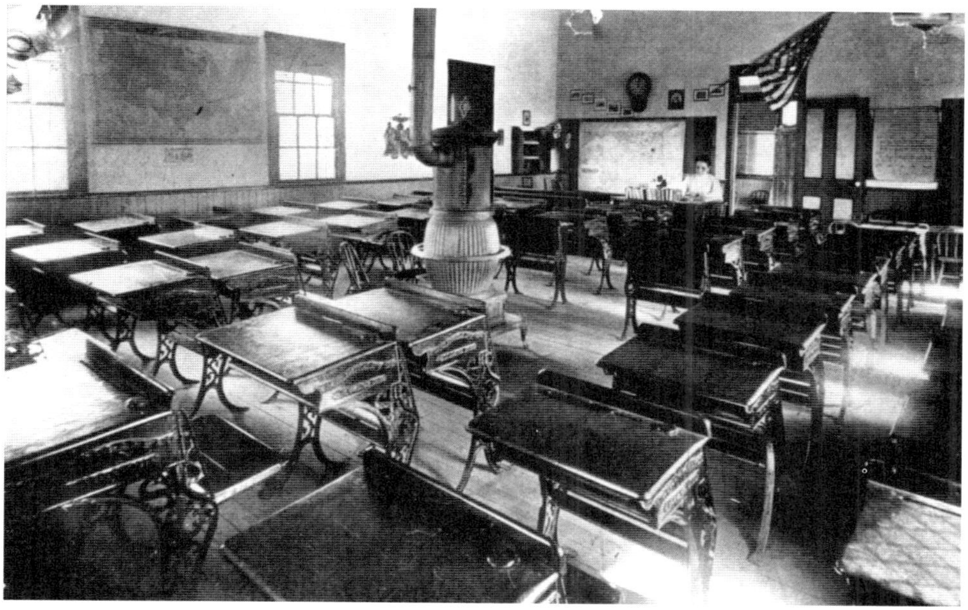

Williams family for several generations. After Dr. Billingslea moved to Glen Burnie in 1919, he continued to care for many families on the peninsula for decades. He also served Anne Arundel County for seventeen years as a member and as president of the Board of Education and twelve years as a member of the Board of Police Examiners.[156]

The whistle of the steamboat continued to announce the arrival of hordes of excursionists at resorts like Colonial Beach and Fairview Park. By 1905, the Rock Creek Steamship Company had sold the *Tourist* and the *Thomas L. Worthley*, which had sunk in winter quarters in Stony Creek. It was raised and the Maryland Seafood Commission converted the

---

[156]*Maryland Gazette*, March 29, 1962; *The Sun*, February 1963, from the Schramm Collection; Maryland Historical Trust Historic Sites Inventory AA-21.

hull into a houseboat that was used by surveyors charting the Chesapeake Bay. The Steamship Company then purchased the twin-screw *Rock Creek*, the 77-foot propeller-driven *Severn*, and, in 1908, the *Clio*. With a capacity of 300 and a bar on board, the *Severn* was a popular excursion steamer. On the Magothy, the steamer *William Linthicum* brought families to a pavilion at North Ferry Point for a day of picnicking and swimming.[157]

The oyster dredges that came from the Eastern Shore were a familiar sight along the Bodkin peninsula until the late 1930s. In 1905 the revenue cutter *Windsor* carrying a U.S. Marshall inspected dredge boats off the Magothy in response to word that some members of the crews had

The steamship *Clio* at Clearview on the Patapsco.
Collection of Jack Kelbaugh

[157]Burgess and Wood, *Steamboats,* p.181; Taylor, *My River Speaks*, pp. 173-174.

been "shanghaied." Men who were questioned said that they had been shanghaied, but they refused to be rescued because they were glad to have a job with regular pay. Bodkin Creek remained the base for the Maryland Marine Police, called the "Oyster Navy" because of their efforts to keep "pirates" away from oyster beds.[158]

Buy boats and market boats had special functions. Buy boats anchored in deep water, and watermen could sell their catch immediately to buyers waiting nearby. Produce buyers anchored off shore because they needed a good wind for their sailboats. A farmer could load produce on a scow, stand at one end, and use a long pole to push the scow to the buy boat. He might choose instead to contract with a boat owner to market his crops, or he might take his produce to Baltimore on his market boat. Alfred Cook's market boat, the *Rhoda Virginia*, was a sixty-foot pungee

Henry Alfred Cook's market boat, the *Rhoda Virginia*, named for his wife.
Collection of Henry Alfred Schmidt, their grandson.

[158]Kerry R. Muse in Bradford, *Anne Arundel County: A Bicentennial History*, p.76. Kelbaugh, "By Water, Road, and Rail," *Anne Arundel Co. History Notes*, vol.23, no.4, p.9.

built in 1902; George W. Calvert's later market boat, a motor freighter called the *Calvert*, had a swinging boom, one mast, and a pilot house.[159]

Workboats continued to carry produce from the farmers' wharves or from the two county wharves at Green Haven and the mouth of Wharf Creek (now Green Gables). At Green Haven, farmers hauled produce along Outing Avenue to the wharf. Sailboats usually were loaded in the afternoon to sail to Baltimore at dusk. In the winter, barges and motor freighters like the *Blandford* hauled manure from dairies, streetcar barns, and street cleaning to provide farmers with fertilizer that was necessary for growing fine fruits and vegetables.[160]

Blacksmiths were as essential in the days of horse-drawn vehicles as service stations are today. William Thomas Stallings, who farmed at Pinehurst until his children were grown, built a blacksmith shop on Mountain Road at Lake Shore Road in 1912. He had learned his trade from Edward J. Hines, the local blacksmith for several decades, and he was known for his fine craftsmanship. Tom Stallings enjoyed shoeing horses, making farm wagons, and repairing farm equipment. He would build a 16-foot boat for fifteen dollars plus materials. He also made coffins without charge for poor families. When he built a wagon, he made every part and forged the iron wheel rims.[161] Robert Gray had a blacksmith shop at the entrance of what is now Chesterfield, and Charles Brown was the blacksmith at Pasadena. Farmers like Henry Alfred Cook and George H. Calvert had their own blacksmith shops on their nearly self-sufficient farms.

Merton Waite, a resident of Anne Arundel County and Chief of Plant Pathology for the U.S. Department of Agriculture, wrote in 1904, "Fruit growing has always been more or less high-class farming. It has largely been undertaken by bright and observing men, who as a rule are more interested in their profession than the ordinary farmer. . . . [They are] above the average in energy and intelligence."[162] Farmers on the peninsula who

---

[159]Charles Hancock Calvert.
[160]Charles Hancock Calvert.
[161]Marie Angel Durner, "Tom Stalling's Blacksmith Shop," *Anne Arundel County History Notes,* vol.8, no.2 (January 1977):3, based on recollections of his son, William C. Stallings.
[162]Yearbook of the Department of Agriculture, 1904, p.171.

grew strawberries, raspberries, peaches, cantaloupes, and watermelons, as well as vegetables, qualified for this praise.

A bulletin of that period reported that Anne Arundel County was one of the three leading counties in the United States for production of fruits and vegetables. By 1907, the Maryland Bureau of Immigration was urging new settlers to come to Maryland and buy acreage in an area noted for growing fine crops. "Land in the neighborhood of Rock Creek sells for not less than $40 an acre," the report stated.[163]

Also in 1907, the Maryland Agricultural Experiment Station reported that "scarcely any branch of horticultural work has increased like growing cantaloupes." No other variety equaled Colorado's "Rocky Ford" for fine texture and flavor.[164] But that was to change soon. As early as 1910, seed catalogues featured the green-meat cantaloupe that Robert Bottomley originated on Hickory Bottom Farm on Fort Smallwood Road. "This is without doubt the best yet. It produces more and better fruit than any

Pickers working on Robert Bottomley's farm, 1909.
Photo: Louis Hine. Special Collections of UMBC

[163]Reynolds Bunk of Millersville recalls that a realtor gave his father this bulletin, probably a Maryland Agricultural Experiment Station bulletin, when he bought his farm in 1908; Annual Report of the State Bureau of Immigration, 1907, p.16.
[164]Maryland Agricultural Experiment Station Bulletin no.116, p.251.

other cantaloupe on the market today and commands a higher price than any other variety," one catalogue claimed.

Large, sweet, resistant to blight, and a fine shipper, the "Bottomley" (along with Anne Arundel's other famous green-meat cantaloupes, Adam Neidert's "Knight" and John Dick Shipley's "Long John") dominated the Baltimore market for decades. The Bottomleys shipped their produce from Tar Cove by sailboat and later by steamboat. About 1918 Louis Schramm developed the slightly larger and earlier "Schramm" cantaloupe, a selection from "Bottomley." The "Schramm" was grown widely around Norfolk. Hundred of thousands of these cantaloupe varieties reached the Baltimore market from the Stinchcomb, Schramm, Schmidt, Cook, Calvert, and Jenkins farms. On one occasion, George Jenkins sent twelve truckloads of melons to market and shipped 2,500 baskets on his scow.[165]

Plowing on William Chairs' farm, 1910.
Collection of Elizabeth Williams Schmidl

[165] Isabel Shipley Cunningham, Anne Arundel's Famous Green-Meat Cantaloupes," *Anne Arundel County History Notes*, vol.27, no.4, pp.3-4, 8-10.

In 1909 Maryland was first in the United States in terms of acreage of strawberries (14,292 acres); first in tomatoes (42,721 acres); third in green peas; and eighth in asparagus, green beans, and bush fruits. From 1880 until 1911, Maryland was either the fourth or fifth leading producer of sweet potatoes in terms of bushels per acre, and in 1912 Maryland was second only to California.[166] Anne Arundel County led all Maryland counties in strawberry and sweet potato production in 1909 and led again in 1910 with 3,937 acres in strawberries.[167] Anne Arundel County was called the strawberry capital of the United States at that time. Since fruits and vegetables were raised mainly in northern Anne Arundel near Baltimore, the peninsula surely contributed to these totals.

In 1909 Anne Arundel County produced 297,514 bushels of sweet potatoes; 152,421 bushels of peaches and nectarines; 42,617 bushels of pears, and 152,421 bushels of other fruits; as well as 5,843,532 quarts of strawberries, 115,855 quarts of raspberries, 340,960 quarts of blackberries, and 6,391,179 quarts of other small fruits. In 1910, the county grew eight million quarts of the finest strawberries, "more than almost any other county in the United States." In addition, Maryland's canning industry was greater than that of any other state, "the Maryland tin can being known wherever civilization reaches." Canning of fruits and vegetables was one of the state's most important and profitable industries.[168]

Though statistics for the peninsula are not available, evidence from a farm on the Patapsco between Swan Creek and Cox Creek shows the productivity of the area. The Hancock brothers, Frank, Lemuel, and Harvey, farmed 325 acres and picked $2,000 (equal to $20,000 today) worth of strawberries in one day in 1902. They made $11,000 on fifty acres of strawberries in one season. They also grew blueberries, dewberries, peaches, apples, potatoes, tomatoes, peas, beans, onions, carrots, cantaloupes, and watermelons. Their farm sales totaled $18,000 a year.

---

[166]Yearbook of Agriculture 1913 and 1915, pp. 375-387.

[167]Report of the Conservation Commission of Md., 1908-09, p.96; Mumford, *Strawberries, Peas, and Beans*, p.32.

[168]Thirteenth Census of the United States, 1910, with Maryland Supplement, p.616; Robert B. Ennis, *Maryland: A Description of Its Lands, Products, and Industries* (Baltimore, 1910), p.138; "The State of Maryland and Its Advantages for Immigrants, State Bureau of Immigration booklet, p.25.

They told a reporter that Anne Arundel County had produced 10 million quarts of strawberries in one season, more than any other county in the United States. Shippers sent their produce as far west as Chicago and as far north as Montreal.[169]

Local produce not only supplied Baltimore and Annapolis, but also Pittsburgh, Denver, New York, Rochester, Buffalo, Boston, and cities in Canada. A *Sun* reporter wrote that "a man who would plant in sandy lands along the Magothy River could in a few years be beyond want and, with attention to business, could become rich." The same reporter described the deep creeks along the Patapsco River, "some of the broadest, noblest, and most beautiful of water courses." Despite his praise of the area's fertility and beauty, he predicted that Baltimore's industrial development would extend along the entire southern side of the Patapsco to Bodkin Point.[170]

Along with agriculture, businesses related to farming also flourished. Instead of marketing produce in Baltimore, corn, beans, and tomatoes were canned on the Schultz and Bottomley farms and at the Adams cannery beside the Pasadena railroad station. Until about 1925, Swift's burlap bag factory made bags that farmers used by the hundreds. Its foundation could be seen in the woods behind the Lake Shore Fire Department for decades thereafter.[171]

Few families seem to have earned their livelihood as watermen or boatbuilders, but farmers often trapped and fished for income during the winter. The Calverts sometimes sent fish by steamer to Freeburger and Sons in Baltimore; later they used their 1921 Model T Ford. Farmers also built their own boats, like George W. Calvert's *Belle*, a 23-foot deadrise with a 6.5 horsepower engine. George Calvert also built a marine railway for launching boats in Back Creek, using a stump puller to drag customers'

---

[169]*The Sun*, June 14, 1910.
[170]*The Sun*, June 13, 1910.
[171]John Williams; Henry Schmidt; Charles H. Calvert.

boats up the ramp. He serviced the *Annie, Florence, Pioneer, No Name,* and others between 1908 and 1913.[172]

Many farms had gasoline-powered boats that held 40 to 75 tons of produce. Before trucks began to carry fruits and vegetables to the market in the 1920s, Long Wharf became so crowded that produce was received there at noon, as well as at 3 a.m. The morning picking could be shipped by "day boat" to reach the Baltimore market at 12:30 p.m., while the afternoon picking would travel by "night boat" at dusk to reach Baltimore by 11 p.m., and wait four hours for the market to open.[173] After many farmers bought trucks in the early 1920s, Long Wharf was not so crowded and all boats set out for Baltimore in the evening.

Electrification of the Baltimore and Annapolis Railroad in 1907 and completion of Maryland Route 648, the Baltimore and Annapolis Boulevard, in 1912, gave Baltimoreans access to Anne Arundel County but did not have an immediate effect on the peninsula beyond the village of Pasadena; however, a bus from the end of the streetcar line at Brooklyn to Lake Shore did affect residents. The enterprise, probably the earliest bus service in the county, began about 1910 when a black Baltimorean named Kinnear employed Joe Whitaker to drive a bus from Brooklyn to Mt. Zion Church. Previously Kinnear had operated horse-drawn sightseeing carriages in Baltimore. His bus served the black community by taking Baltimoreans to church services at Mt. Zion and church members to events in the city.

About two years later, Kinnear sold to a Mr. Finch of Rock Creek. Finch soon sold the line to Thomas Gordon, who formed the Brooklyn and Lake Shore Transportation Company in 1912. He bought new buses to serve the villages of Pasadena, Armiger, Jacobsville, Lake Shore, and Mt. Carmel. Less than two years later, Gordon sold to a Mr. Grieneisen. In 1914 Charles Cook bought the line and, with local ownership, Cook's

---

[172]Charles H. Calvert; James B. Calvert.

[173]*The Sun*, June 14, 1910.

Transportation Company prospered for decades. Cook's first bus was a converted truck with a long wooden seat along each side. He made one round trip to Baltimore daily and two on weekends. To fill the time between arriving in Brooklyn at nine a.m. and the return trip in the evening, at one time Mr. Cook worked in a store at Patapsco and Hanover streets. Mrs. Cook made the trip to the city weekly to take their daughter to her music lessons at the Peabody Institute. She spent the remainder of the day shopping and visiting relatives.[174]

The trip from Lake Shore to the streetcar line at Brooklyn took almost two hours, at an average speed of eight-and-one-half miles per hour. Removable side-curtains protected riders from dust and rain, but solid rubber tires and wooden seats did not provide a comfortable ride. The driver

The Brooklyn and Lake Shore bus at Mt. Vernon Place Square in Baltimore, 1912.
Photo: Charles Cook. Collection of Jacques Kelly

[174]Roger B. White, "Bus Service to Anne Arundel County.," *Anne Arundel County History Notes*, vol. XI, no.3, pp. 1-3.

carried buckets of sand and sawdust and pieces of carpet to fill mud holes and potholes. Fairly often the bus broke down, and the driver improvised repairs. Sometimes the passengers had to get off the bus and push it past a bad spot. In the winter, they carried heated bricks to keep their feet warm.[175]

But trains and buses did not displace the small steamers, barges, skip-jacks, pungees, bugeyes, and ferry boats that continued to be the main-stay of transportation and commerce within the peninsula and with Baltimore. The steamers that picked up passengers and commodities at the county wharves and private wharves and ran continually to and from Baltimore, as well as to Annapolis and the Eastern Shore, have been called "an early form of rapid transit" and the chief cause of the region's prosperity.[176] This peaceful era continued for most of the next decade.

---

[175]*Ibid.*, pp.1-3.
[176]Kelbaugh, "By Water, Road, and Rail," *Anne Arundel County History Notes*, vol.23, no 4, p.7.

A Tranquil Decade Ends in World War

Community life on the peninsula continued to revolve around Magothy Methodist Church in the second decade of the twentieth century. Preparing an elaborate Easter program with twenty recitations and musical numbers kept the Sunday School teachers and children busy. Melville Dunlap, Sunday School Superintendent for thirty years, resigned in order to teach an adult Bible class, and the trustees changed the hour for classes from three o' clock on Saturday afternoon to ten on Sunday morning. In July, the young people of the church planned a picnic with music, games, guessing contests, potato and peanut races, and ice cream, cake, and confections to be sold for the benefit of the cemetery fund.[177] At Mount Carmel Church, William Landy Cook was beginning 35 years of service as Sunday School Superintendent.

About this time, travel became easier when county road crews unloaded oyster shells that had come from canning houses and spread a deep layer over the main roads. Barges brought the shells to the nearest

---

[177]*Maryland Gazette*, c.1910.

wharves for distribution. Wagon wheels eventually pulverized the shells; in the meantime, the shell fragments were hard on horses' hooves.[178]

About 1910 Melville Dunlap, retired teacher, lay preacher, Justice of the Peace, and son-in-law of Dorsey Jacobs, lost valuable papers when his home burned. Determined that he never would suffer such a loss again, Squire Dunlap built a new house and office on Tick Neck Road entirely of pressed tin, inside and outside. Family members remember the decorated squares that formed the ceilings.[179] After the property was sold to be developed as Turf Valley, the unique house at Tick Neck and Bradley roads was destroyed by the fire department in 1983 or 1984.

William M. Jenkins' family and friends in his Model M 1906 Cadillac, c. 1915.
Collection of Emma Jenkins Wade Sanders

[178]Charles H. Calvert.

[179]Blodwin Shipley Potee, "The Squire's Tin House," *Anne Arundel County History Notes*, vol.6, no.3 (April 1975):1. In 1975 his great-granddaughter, Gladys Dunlap Norris, cherished his Magistrate's docket, a valuable record of life on the peninsula a century ago.

Another fire showed the need for better firefighting equipment and improved telephone service. When the Schramm's barn burned in 1911, one of their sons ran to Klug's store to call the fire department; however, the firefighters' only equipment was a horse-drawn wagon carrying a large barrel of water. Soon afterward, the Chesapeake and Potomac Telephone Company bought the Rock Creek and Marley Telephone Company, and the Armiger exchange moved from Klug's store to one room of the Schramm home. Lewis Schramm's daughters, Frances and Emma, were the telephone operators from 1912 until 1932.[180]

J. Leland Hanna of Baltimore bought 512 acres that later became Green Haven in 1910. He subdivided the property and offered it for sale as small farms without success. He then offered lots 25 feet wide and 100 feet deep for as little as five or ten dollars. Though he sold several waterfront lots, most potential buyers thought that such a low price meant that the land was worthless. In 1915 he sold the property to Charles M. Christian.[181]

In 1914 the county built the first bridge over Stony Creek, a wooden drawbridge with wooden side walls.[182] Richard Phelps tended the drawbridge until his health failed. Then his sixteen-year- old daughter, Mildred Phelps (later Mildred Phelps Hahn) took over his duties from six a.m. until six p.m. Sitting in a small building beside the bridge, she raised and lowered the draw about twenty times a day; on Sundays during the summer, she opened the draw as many as fifty times. An excursion boat that came into the creek twice a day and many market boats, sailboats, and yachts prevented boredom.

Though fewer boats passed and her friends did not spend as much time with her in the winter, she was not lonely because she used her free time to read newspapers and magazines and write and crochet. Her mother visited her often and always stayed with her after dark. Despite long,

---

[180]Schramm. "Sixty Years in Anne Arundel County"
[181]Green Haven Carnival brochure, July 1940, the Schramm Collection.
[182]"Discovering Our School Communities," Riviera Beach Elementary School, p.8.

sometimes lonely, hours in hot sun or bitter cold, young Mildred Phelps insisted that she liked her work.[183]

At the western end of the peninsula, a store and school were community centers. Elzey and Ellen Wade owned the store that served the villages of Pasadena and Elvaton. From 1909 until 1914, this store also housed the Elvaton post office.[184] Children from Pasadena attended school in Elvaton before their gray weatherboard one-room school was built in 1911. Like others on the peninsula, this one-room school had a vestibule for hanging coats, double desks, slates for writing, and drinking water carried from a pump in buckets. When the county replaced this school with a four-room shingled building in 1925, the Schramms bought the old building and added it to their home. Each of the four classrooms in the new school had a stove surrounded by a decorative metal jacket (called a Waterbury heater), but toilets were outdoors until 1933. An auditorium was added to the school in 1927 and later divided to make two classrooms.[185]

Not far away, Cora Spencer Carter and other mothers asked the Board of Education to provide a teacher for black children at Freetown. They persuaded members of the Good Templars Lodge to rent one room in their building for one dollar a month for Freetown's first public school. Mabel Cook told her children about attending first grade when the school opened in 1914.[186] (A community school supported by parents had existed earlier.)

For decades, a source of winter income for farmers along the Magothy was the sale of charcoal made by burning pine wood. Walter J. Phelps would buy land where scrub pines grew, cut the wood, and take it to his farm on Mountain Road in Lake Shore. There he built two charcoal "pits" or ricks with four-foot lengths of pine set in concentric circles almost vertically but leaning toward the center. When the circle was fifteen feet in

---

[183]John Mason; undated clipping from *The Sun*.
[184]Emma Wade Sanders; Emma M. Schramm, "History of the Pasadena Post Office," p.9.
[185]"Discovering Our School Communities," Pasadena Elementary School, 1952.
[186]Freetown School Handbook, 2000.

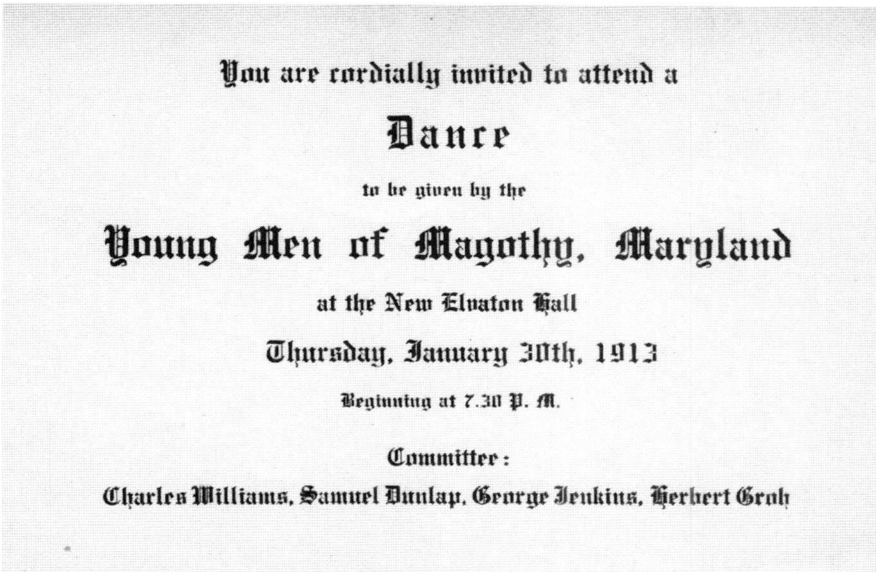

You are cordially invited to attend a

Dance

to be given by the

Young Men of Magothy, Maryland

at the New Elvaton Hall

Thursday, January 30th, 1913

Beginning at 7.30 P. M.

Committee:

Charles Williams, Samuel Dunlap, George Jenkins, Herbert Groh

The Young Men of Magothy's invitation to a dance, 1913.

Collection of Emma Jenkins Wade Sanders

Wade's store served the village of Pasadena from the early 1900s until the 1930s.

Collection of Emma Jenkins Wade Sanders

diameter, he and his son, Clifford A. Phelps, would build two smaller circles on top of the large one. Then they would cover the entire structure with packed sod to make it airtight, except for a hole in the top and air vents in each layer to regulate temperature and rate of burning.

During the next two or three weeks, they checked twice a day to be sure the wood was burning very slowly. If it burned too fast, they blocked some of the holes. When burning was complete after two-and-one-half or three weeks, they blocked all the holes and let the rick cool for a week. After taking the sod off, they made the first draw, removing one foot of charcoal all around the pit. Then they replaced the sod, let the next layer cool, and repeated the process. After filling big burlap bags with charcoal, they sewed the tops closed.

When Walter Phelps received a letter telling him that a firm needed charcoal, he and his son hauled the bags to the Dixie Manufacturing Company or other buyers in Baltimore, using a two-horse wagon. People needed fuel during the coldest winter days, and the horses had a hard time pulling the wagon through snow or on ice. Walter and Clifford A. Phelps remembered the ordeal of getting over Cedar Hill near Brooklyn. When one horse would slip and fall on the ice, they would put a blanket under his feet and get him up again. Then the other horse would go down. In 1920 the Phelps Company bought an old warehouse on Pratt Street for the lumber and hauled boards home every time they took charcoal to Baltimore. With that lumber, they built their home that still stands today. In 1938, Clifford Phelps opened a gas station on Mountain Road.[187]

By 1914 the postal service had closed Armiger and Maynard post offices and replaced Elvaton with the Pasadena post office that had easy access to trains that delivered mail. The Lake Shore post office survived until 1916. From that time, the entire peninsula between the Magothy and Patapsco began to be called the Pasadena peninsula. As late as the

---

[187]Clifford R. Phelps.

1950s, however, a local newspaper made a distinction between "Pasadena Proper" and "Postal Pasadena."

When Albert B. Clark was appointed the first postmaster, he built a tiny addition to his home to serve as the post office. Since he lived only about 500 feet from the railroad station, he was ideally located for receiving and sending canvas bags of mail. When a heavy snow fell, he dug a path through several feet of snow to reach the railroad. Herbert Groh was the rural carrier who served a long route along the peninsula until he entered military service in World War I. He died in a seaplane accident while delivering mail for the Navy off Cape May on October 8, 1918.[188]

Baltimore families who came to the Pasadena peninsula for a day at the beach had glimpsed Utopia. In 1914 Augustus C. Schmidt began to sell lots on the west side of what later became Riviera Beach, part of the 166-acre farm that he had bought in 1903. Baltimoreans at last had an opportunity to fulfill their dream of a place near the water. The initial sale was to Mayor Broening, who built a summer home just twelve miles from City Hall.[189]

At what now is Green Haven, Charles M. Christian formed the Outing Park Development Company and began to sell small lots at a reasonable price in 1915. The son of a doctor, he believed that a family with modest income should be able to live near the waterfront.[190] His enticing ads about "the pride of possession" and "the joys of living" that would result from ownership led families to buy lots at Outing Park where they could pitch a tent and spend the weekend fishing and swimming. With Steven J. Everd as sales manager and builder, Christian advertised 25-by-100-foot lots at $20 to $50 each "with terms to suit any buyer." Every lot owner had access to the reserved waterfront "far away from the noise, smoke, and cares of the city."[191]

---

[188]Schramm, "History of the Pasadena Post Office," pp.11,13; Edward Seipp.

[189]"Discovering Our School Communities," Riviera Beach Elementary School, 1952, pp.6-7, based on an interview with George Schmidt.

[190]Marie Christian.

[191]Outing Park Development Company brochures.

No one was concerned about water pollution when the developer divided former farms into small parcels and encouraged chicken farming there. An ad says that Outing Park was bordered for half a mile by a stream of pure water, and the land adjoining the stream was "porous with abundant shade, making it especially suitable for raising poultry. Hundreds of chickens are raised in the Park each year, and there is an excellent local market for both chickens and eggs." One man made more money in six years by selling poultry products than he had earned in twenty years as a bookkeeper in Baltimore. Many people responded to an invitation to "spend your time caring for your flocks and reaping the profits."[192]

Two years after the Rock Creek Steamship Company bought the *Kitty Knight* from the Tolchester Company and began departures from the foot of Broadway in 1913, Charles and Harry Efford, the sons of George Efford, who had been involved in running the company from its beginning, assumed management of the Rock Creek line and Fairview. Charles Efford, a marine engineer, was in charge of the steamers, and Harry Efford managed Fairview Park. Charles Efford ended service to Stony Creek and sold the *Severn* to the newly-formed Stony Creek Improvement Company. Harry Efford and his sons and nephews rebuilt the Fairview Hotel after a disastrous fire and added bathhouses, a bowling alley, a pool hall, a carousel, a penny arcade, and a dance pavilion, mixing concrete for these structures with sand from the beach and water from the Chesapeake Bay.[193]

Captain Wesley Rowles and Captain Jefferson W. Fields commanded the Rock Creek steamers from the early 1900s until the end of operations in 1941. Stops on Rock Creek included Fairview, Colonial Beach, Gray's, Fox Point, Jenkins, Patapsco Club, and Heintzman's Cottage Grove, while landings on Stony Creek included Kreb's (later Riviera Beach), Summit Grove, Altona Beach (later spelled Altoona), Beauty Beach, Old Glory

---

[192]Ibid.; *The Green Haven Hash*, September 1939.

[193]Burgess and Wood, *Steamboats*, pp.179,183; Roger B. White, "All Ashore for Fairview Park," *Anne Arundel County History Notes*, vol.12, no.2, p.1.

Beach, and Outing Park (later Green Haven). Excursion steamers like the *William Linthicum* stopped at North Ferry Point on the Magothy where there was a picnic pavilion that jutted into the Magothy. Recreational ferry landings on the Magothy were at Pea-patch Point and Windmill Point.[194]

Baltimore's adoption of the peninsula as a playground was not limited to resort hotels and beaches. The Grachur Club, young men and boys from Grace Methodist Church near Bolton Hill in Baltimore, bought property on the north shore of the Magothy at Cockey Creek in 1914. Led by their Sunday School teacher, Claude B. Whitby, they sold Grachur bonds to raise money to buy the land and build a clubhouse with a fireplace. A kitchen followed, but they did not have a dining room until 1921.

To reach their camp, they took the train to Robinson station, walked to the river, and crossed to the north shore of the Magothy by canoe. Though they carried water, chopped wood, and did assigned camp chores, the boys found plenty of time for swimming, canoeing, and games. On Sundays they had an informal worship service in their clubhouse. By the 1920s, families came to the camp from Baltimore by car, but deep sand made driving difficult after they left Mountain Road. In 1928 an electric pump ended dependence on a spring and a well for water. That year the Grachur Club added the Claude B. Whitby Memorial Chapel overlooking the Magothy.[195]

At the western end of the peninsula, Methodists at Pasadena met in private homes and at the Pasadena School until 1917 when they merged with the Piney Grove congregation and built the Pasadena Methodist Episcopal Church, South. While their frame church was being built in 1918, the 54 members held services in a tent nearby, in Albert Listman's home, and in the elementary school.[196]

---

[194]Burgess and Wood, *Steamboats*, pp.179,184; Taylor, *My River Speaks*, pp.99,174-175.
[195]Carl Behm, "The Grachur Story, 1912-1992"; "The Grachur Club," 1972.
[196]Brown and Heckman, "History of Pasadena Methodist Church."

Methodists at Rock Point did not need to make the journey to Magothy Church every Sunday because Henry Alfred Cook conducted Sunday School at *Hancock's Resolution* or at the Rock Point School House. Mamie Hancock played the organ when they met in her home. On the first Sunday of the month, the Magothy preacher held a service of worship at the schoolhouse.[197]

For those who came to the peninsula by car, Lipin's Corner was the landmark where they left the main road to Annapolis and started down Mountain Road to the resorts they had been dreaming of all week. John Lipin opened a gas station there in 1918, advertising gasoline, tires, and accessories. His business grew to include the sale of food and drinks, and motorists often stopped there for gasoline or refreshments. Later, Lipin's Corner was the location of massive traffic jams on Sunday evenings when everyone tried to return home from the beach at the same time. While long lines of cars waited to enter the Baltimore and Annapolis Boulevard, passengers (and sometimes even drivers) could go into the store and buy a cold drink while the cars in line would move only a few cars' length. On Sunday evening, July 12, 1937, traffic stood still from Lipin's Corner to Lake Shore and Fort Smallwood.[198]

The conflict in Europe seemed far away when the United States declared war on April 6, 1917. During a year spent preparing an army to fight to make the world safe for democracy, the United States provided loans and food for the Allies. In May of 1917, Governor Emerson C. Harrington rallied Maryland farmers at a meeting at the State House, telling them that, by increasing productivity, "you are helping your country as patriotically as those who are marching." Professor S.C. Richardson of the Maryland College of Agriculture added that the war would be won "by men in the furrows, not by men in the trenches. Let every farmer nail that magnificent old flag to his plow and sing, 'Plant, Plant, Plant, the

---

[197]Pritchett, "History of Magothy Methodist Church," p.12; James B. Calvert.
[198]Senator Alfred Lipin; *Maryland Gazette*, July 15, 1937.

Lipin's Corner, where Mountain Road branched from the Baltimore-Annapolis Boulevard.
Photo: Maryland State Roads Commission. Collection of Jacques Kelly

boys are marching'." Despite low prices in relation to high labor costs, farmers on the peninsula responded to this appeal.[199]

In 1918 the first American troops entered World War I, and many men from the Pasadena peninsula served their country in the trenches in France. Among them were Joseph Groh, Herbert Groh, and Louis Schramm, Jr. from the western end of the peninsula and Edwin Cook and William Schmidt from the eastern end. At home, the terrible flu epidemic in 1919 forced the closing of five county schools, including the Pasadena and Jacobsville elementary schools.[200]

---

[199]Mumford, *Strawberries, Peas, and Beans*, p.72.
[200]*Evening Capital*, January 21, 1919.

Louis Schramm, Jr., wearing his World War I uniform. His car is a 1918 Standard Eight, made for just two years by the Standard Motor Company in Ohio.
The Schramm Collection

Also in 1919, Baltimore City attempted to dispose of its garbage by establishing a piggery on 160 acres of the Jubb farm at Graveyard Point, now the site of a marina at Ventnor. The plan was to take garbage there by barge and feed it to 15,000 pigs. Forty local residents filed a lawsuit against the city, but the City Solicitor ruled that a piggery did not constitute a nuisance and would not depreciate property values. Before residents could file an appeal, the pigs became ill and some died, the manager of the piggery absconded with $15,000 that belonged to the city, and Baltimore returned to incineration and landfill to dispose of garbage.[201]

---

[201]Robert C. Keith, *Baltimore Harbor: A Picture History,* (Baltimore, 1991); undated photo from *The Sun; Maryland Gazette* clipping, 1919.

Not discouraged by the failure of the piggery, in 1920 the Sanitary Reduction Company bought the Hines farm on the opposite side of Main Creek and built a plant at Spit Point to process garbage that scows hauled from Baltimore. When garbage was cooked in vats to extract oil and grease for making soap, it gave off a foul odor. The waste or tankage was hauled away to be used as fertilizer, though it contained broken glass and metal cans. By the mid-twenties, indignant local property owners complained that the effulgent had polluted Main Creek, underwater grasses had disappeared, and crabs and fish were dying. Though Daniel P. Corey and Charles Hancock Calvert filed legal papers, their efforts to save Main and Bodkin creeks from pollution failed. Because the Sanitary Reduction Company lost its contract with Baltimore City in the late twenties, eventually seaweed, crabs, and fish returned to the creeks.[202]

During the war, prejudice against recent German immigrants forced Gustavus A. Lotze to move his florist and nursery business from Glen Burnie, where his greenhouses were repeatedly broken by stones, to Long Hill near Lipin's Corner. For many years, he imported rare bulbs and grew the newest and best varieties of flowers there. Discriminating customers like the owner of the Hendler Ice Cream Company followed him to his new location, which was easily identified by the tall fire observation tower near the entrance.

The Armistice that ended World War I on November 11, 1919, brought a feeling of optimism to America and to the people living between the Magothy and the Patapsco. They faced the 1920s with anticipation and high hopes.

---

[202]Arthur T. Corey, "The Coreys of Bodkin Creek" (Fort Collins, Colorado, 1990). About seventy residents joined in a Bill of Complaint, now in the Henry A. Schmidt Collection.

Baltimoreans Discover the Peninsula

A decade of peace and prosperity during the 1920s was a productive time for farmers, realtors, and builders. Many Baltimoreans who came to beach resorts on weekends were ready to invest their hard-earned dollars in a small piece of land near the water. Others could afford to build comfortable homes in restricted waterfront communities. In either case, developers were eager to accommodate them. German and Polish families from south and east Baltimore saved to make monthly payments on small lots in Outing Park, while well-to-do families could choose a residential community like Pinehurst on the Bay.

Pinehurst on the Bay dates to 1922 when Stewart and Ernest Robinson, sons of Cyrus Robinson, began to develop a summer colony on Bodkin Farm. This land had been part of Henry C. Dunbar's extensive holding, but Dunbar's heirs had sold 353 acres to Cyrus N. and Charles A. Robinson in 1884 for $8,000 ($22.64 an acre). There they grew fruits and berries, but their principal crop was peaches harvested from 6,500 trees. After Cyrus Robinson died in 1920, his sons formed the Pinehurst

Company on February 1, 1922, and began to sell property on the Chesapeake Bay. The first purchasers had to use machetes to clear a path from the gravel road to lots that were fifty feet wide and from 200 to 350 feet deep. Pinehurst was a gated community, and the Pinehurst Company could approve or reject plans for homes. Early residents included eleven doctors and successful businessmen from Baltimore City and Baltimore County.[203]

Pinehurst featured five miles of waterfront and a harbor that could accommodate large yachts. By 1925 bathing facilities, swings, picnic tables, a baseball diamond, a tennis court, and a neighborhood center called the Tea House were built near the centrally located community beach. At the Tea House, residents enjoyed dinners, card parties, and dances. Everyone

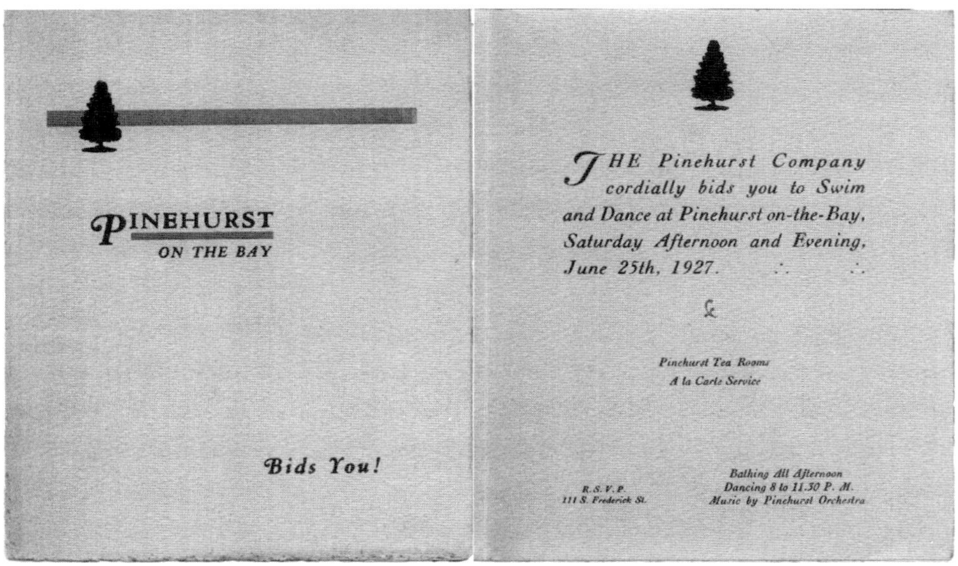

An invitation to swim and dance at Pinehurst on the Bay, 1927.
Collection of Janet Robinson O'Connell

[203]John M. Robinson, "The History of Pinehurst," *Anne Arundel County History Notes*, vol.21, no.2, p.4.

The bathhouse and part of the parking lot at Pinehurst.
Collection of Janet Robinson O'Connell

worked together on projects to improve the community. While adults enjoyed boating and fishing, children played Indians in the woods or rode the long sliding board into the Bay. The Pinehurst Company provided gravel roads, a community water system with a water tower, and sidewalks along main streets. In 1925 the company added a public bathing beach at the southern end of the property. Its 250 feet of wide sandy beach, large bathhouse, and picnic tables under a grove of oak trees attracted many visitors. In 1928 they added a two-story screened pavilion and dance floor.[204]

---

[204]*Ibid.* vol.21, no.4, p.2; Martha Jachowski and John Mogey, "Pinehurst on the Bay/Bodkin," 1994 booklet, p.10.

While other developers were selling larger lots for more money, Charles Merriweather Christian continued to lay out small lots in Outing Park or Green Haven. A journalist as well as a developer, he published newsletters, *The Green Haven Hash* and *The Anne Arundel Advocate*, reminding people that land is the foundation of wealth. "When all things else fail, you will have a place to go . . . free from the regular monthly demand of the landlord." Green Haven, he said, is "joy land," a place where "the sound of the hammer is the song of progress."[205]

Charles Christian promised property owners many amenities: an iceman would deliver at homes four times a week, a laundryman would call twice a week, and the milkman, butcher, baker, and mail carrier came every day. Further reasons to settle in Green Haven included protection of property by the Burns Detective Agency and the encouraging news of good radio reception in a few homes, leading Mr. Christian to conclude that "Green Haven seems to be an ideal location for radio."

Families with limited means realized that a five dollar deposit and a few dollars each week would buy a small lot to enjoy on summer weekends. These were hard-working people who wanted to escape the hot row houses in the city. Their holiday began when they boarded a steamer Friday evening and enjoyed the breeze as they traveled down the Bay. The men arrived wearing suits and the women wore dresses. All the people who owned lots in Green Haven were friends. They stayed in tents or shacks at first, but the entire family was happy as children played on the beach while their parents were swimming, fishing, or crabbing. When they had saved enough money, often they had Steven Everd build them a small summer home.[206]

During late 1924 and 1925, weekly news of Green Haven reported in the *Maryland Gazette* revealed events of interest in the 712-acre community. Harrison's Red Line Bus ran from Green Haven to Baltimore daily at

---

[205]Undated brochure; *Anne Arundel Advocate*, vol.2, no.3.
[206]Marie Everd Oakie.

6 a.m. and returned each evening at six p.m. George Harrison carried not only passengers but also stock for his store, as well as any items that residents could not get in Green Haven. In November Harrison's bus took residents to the polling house to vote, while owners of radios entertained friends who wanted to hear the results of the election. Also in November, Mr. and Mrs. Alfred Stinchcomb "installed a running water system in their home and an electric light plant, saving many trips to the pump." Throughout the year, the Green Haven Improvement Association (not the current association) met regularly.

In December 1924 both Stevenson's Green Haven Grocery and Harrison's Green Haven General Store were well-stocked for the holiday season, and the Boys' Club Choir prepared to sing at the Christmas service at Green Haven Methodist Church. Despite a snowstorm in January, Harrison's bus maintained its schedule and brought eagerly awaited evening newspapers to Green Haven. Other January highlights were Steven Everd's appointment as Justice of the Peace and the marriage of Peter L. Schramm to Evelyn Nethen under an arch of pink and white roses in the Lutheran Church at Elvaton. Two hundred people attended the reception at the Elvaton Hall.[207]

Spring brought baseball practice at Merriweather Field and, on May 1, Stevenson's store moved from winter quarters to the store building on Outing Avenue at Shore Road. George Harrison's brother Charles took over the bus line in March to enable George to spend his time at his store. Both Novak's Green Line and Harrison's Red Line were building waiting rooms for their patrons. With 159 worshipers crowding Easter service at the Green Haven Methodist Church, the congregation planned to enlarge the church at Catherine Avenue and Seventh Street. With the leadership of Rev. William R.L. Ruths, the church sponsored a strawberry festival in

---

[207]*Maryland Gazette*'s weekly news of Green Haven from September 18, 1924, through January 21, 1926. These clippings are in a scrapbook in the Schramm Collection.

Stevenson's Store in Green Haven.
Collection of Jack Kelbaugh

May and submitted plans for their enlarged building to the Baltimore Conference of the Methodist Church.

By June steamers were bringing 3,000 people to Green Haven on Sundays, but 8,000 visitors arrived on the Fourth of July for swimming, fishing, and a ballgame. Frank's began to sell ice cream and soft drinks at the wharf, and a snowball stand opened nearby. During July the Green Haven Life Saving Corps finished training, and eighty people attended a dance at The Shack. The Ladies Aid Fifth Annual Fair was the main event in August, but the news that George Harrison was building a Public Hall on Outing Avenue was exciting. Steamboats and buses were crowded as Labor Day visitors enjoyed the end of summer.

Fifty-three children in six classes attended Tick Neck School in the fall. The church building fund was growing and plans included space for the Boys Club and the Girls Club that Frances Cosden sponsored. The congregation hosted an oyster supper in October. They dedicated their enlarged sanctuary, Sunday School room, and new organ on November first. Thereafter they held Sunday School at two p.m. and worship service at eight p.m. A Christmas Present Sale and Entertainment helped everyone to prepare for the holiday, though many residents returned from Baltimore on Harrison's bus carrying numerous packages. After the holiday season, Chief Manitowog, a Native American evangelist formerly with

The community gathers for life-saving instruction at Green Haven, c. 1925.
The Schramm Collection

Buffalo Bill's Wild West Show, wore tribal costume and feathered headdress when he spoke at the Green Haven Methodist Church to a standing-room-only congregation.[208]

In addition to Green Haven, during the early 1920s Charles Christian developed High Point nearby on what had been the Armiger farm. He laid out streets, naming some for members of his family. At first buyers built summer cottages there, but gradually they converted their cottages into small but well-kept permanent homes. The owners usually worked in Baltimore, some at Sparrows Point.[209] Steven Everd, a building contractor and Justice of the Peace, developed Clearwater Village.

In 1924, near Bodkin Point, the Bay Side Beach Development Company advertised the view across the Chesapeake, a sandy beach, saltwater bathing, boating, fishing, and cool breezes, "an ideal spot to build your bungalow and make your dreams come true."[210] Charles Rittenhouse managed sales and his partner, Emory Archer Kelbaugh, was the building contractor. Restrictions in deeds enabled them to maintain control over their development. They approved all building plans, including exterior paint color, and prohibited outhouses or swine on the premises. Their sedate community, where alcohol and dancing were prohibited, attracted solid citizens like the Schluderburgs (the S in the Esskay Company) and Swepson Earle, author of *Chesapeake Bay Country*. During the booming twenties, carpenters came to work at Bayside in silk shirts.[211]

Though sale of lots at Riviera Beach had begun before the war, sales accelerated when T.W. and Charles Pumphrey formed the Riviera Beach Development Company in 1924. Their advertisements encouraged buying a home that would offer the entire family an opportunity to enjoy life while making payments that were lower than rent. Options included THE CHESAPEAKE, "for the man who is tired of the congested City and wants to get more out of life," THE RIVIERA, "with a bright kitchen that will

---

[208] *Ibid.*
[209] "Discovering Our Communities," High Point Elementary School, 1952, pp.3-4.
[210] Rittenhouse-Kelbaugh letter to prospective buyers, Jack Kelbaugh Collection.
[211] Advertisement in *The Sun*; Jack Kelbaugh Collection.

Jack and Elizabeth Kelbaugh, grandchildren of the developer, Bayside Beach, 1939.
Collection of Jack Kelbaugh

please any mother," and the modest SUITS US that cost $1,250.00, payable at $25 each month. Three miles of sandy beach, excellent harbors, and a fully equipped playground were additional lures. A few years later, advertisements mentioned tennis and basketball courts, a baseball diamond, and an "environment of refinement." Until the thirties, the community remained almost entirely a summer resort.[212]

Though the western end of the peninsula was not near the water, Pasadena's location on the railroad connecting Baltimore and Annapolis encouraged many people to choose it as their home. Joseph Groh had split wood for railroad ties for one dollar a day before he became an apprentice carpenter for Benjamin Duvall, who was building homes in the village of

---

[212]"Riviera Beach, Maryland's Master Waterfront," an undated leaflet; advertisement in *The Sun*, c.1927.

Remodeled bungalows, originally like this sample, can be found in Riviera Beach today.
Collection of Jack Kelbaugh

"THE RIVIERA"

"The Riviera" is our furnished sample bungalow built at the entrance.

The attractive living and dining-room is 12 x 28 feet; the two bedrooms are large and light; the bath is roomy and conveniently located; the bright cool kitchen will please the eye of any mother.

Be sure you inspect the sample bungalow before leaving and get further information regarding price, terms, etc., these you will find as attractive as the home.

The rapid growth of Riviera Beach has been due largely to its ideal and convenient location. Many of Baltimore's business and professional men have selected Riviera Beach.

YACHTING
CANOEING
SAILING

LAND
LOCKED
HARBOR

Riviera Beach information booth on Mountain Road.
Collection of Evelyn Wade

Pasadena on former farmland. After military service during World War I, Groh became a building contractor. He and John M. Appleton built most of the homes in the growing village during the next several decades.[213]

In 1925 John Appleton founded the Pasadena Water Works with six homes on a line that supplied water for indoor plumbing. Before December 18, 1925, all water came from wells. A private contractor collected garbage for one dollar a month.[214] For children in the community, the event of the year was the annual carnival that temporarily closed Mission Street.

In addition to developments along the northern side of the peninsula, individual purchasers were acquiring property on the Magothy River. To accommodate Dr. Guy Hunner, a new resident who owned fifty acres at

---

[213]Esther Groh Webster Williams.
[214]"Discovering Our School Community," Pasadena Elementary School, 1952.

Pea Patch Point on the Magothy, William H. Rothamel spent the winters of 1920 and 1921 building what is said to be the largest log cabin east of the Mississippi. A farmer who worked as a builder during the winter, he adapted an architect's drawings for the 47-by-110-foot, 17-room, three-story home.

With five helpers, Rothamel felled pine trees on the property and used horses to drag them to the building site. He also cut the largest pines on Eagle Hill and transported them by boat to Pea Patch Point. After the 30-foot logs had been peeled and trimmed, he hewed them to a uniform diameter with a broad ax, notched each log, and secured it in place with eight-inch steel pins. He built the two large fireplaces and the chimney of field stone from the property. When Ralph and Ellen Price bought the cabin in 1952, it was as sturdy as ever.[215] Somewhat enlarged, it remains attractive today.

Further evidence of Baltimore's discovery of the peninsula was the opening of Camp Milbur, originally called Camp Broening, on Cornfield Creek in 1921. The founders were Captain Miller and Captain John Burgess (hence the name, Milbur), whose titles reflected their rank in the Boys Brigade. Captain Burgess met with the Boys Brigade every Friday during the winter in a former fire engine house on Mulberry Street in Baltimore. Brantley Baptist Church sponsored his effort to found a summer camp on the Magothy.

Captain Miller, president of the Fairfield Dairy (later Fairfield-Western Maryland Dairy), contributed generously to the project. Because Camp Milbur helped boys who otherwise could not have enjoyed summer on the Magothy, the Fairfield Dairy donated five gallon cans of milk daily, and Muhly's Bakery truck delivered plenty of baked goods without charge. Even Henry Ford responded to an appeal and gave Camp Milbur a Ford car, a truck, and a station wagon.[216]

---

[215]*The Sun*, 1955.
[216]James Quick.

To reach the camp in the early days, the boys would travel from Baltimore by train and then ferry across the Magothy on motor launches like the *Desdemona* or *Maid of the Mist*. Because the camp aimed to build character through discipline, the boys wore uniforms, marched with a band, took part in military drills, and responded to bugle calls. They lived in barracks, exercised under direction every morning, held ranks in the brigade, and worked off demerits received for being late for formation or for meals. While a boy had demerits, he had no water privileges which meant no swimming or boating.

James Quick, foster son of Captain Burgess and a counselor in later years, recalls a wonderful program at "the greatest place ever." The boys had access to rowboats, sailboats, power boats, canoes, three tennis courts, and fields for playing baseball, soccer, and lacrosse. Though Captain Burgess had been crippled by polio in childhood, he supervised all the activities and took the boys to athletic matches and exhibitions at the Naval Academy. They even had a memorable lunch with the midshipmen. When parents visited on Saturdays, a great treat was to go to Angel's store where they sat at tables on the side porch and enjoyed ice cream.[217]

The decade of the twenties was the era of prohibition and bootleggers. Some residents of the peninsula operated stills and speakeasies, while others were runners who delivered to customers. Stills along the Magothy, on Bodkin Neck, and near Lake Waterford produced the whiskey that moonshiners took to Baltimore or Washington, sometimes in a Packard Club Sedan. Rumors say that runners were protected by well-connected politicians, but federal agents raided stills and destroyed them with dynamite. Stories are told of a boiler that hung from tree branches after a still was blown up and of a narrow escape from agents by rowboat. Local lore relates that the whiskey made on the Pasadena peninsula was so good that demand persisted and stills continued to operate after the repeal of

---

[217]James Quick.

prohibition in 1934.[218] Moonshiners, bootleggers, and speakeasies were part of the picturesque vocabulary of the roaring twenties.

But most local residents ignored stills and speakeasies and devoted their energy to farming, business, and family life. Though trucks replaced wagons in northwestern Anne Arundel County at this time, many farmers on the peninsula continued to send produce to Baltimore by water. The Schramms, who were nearer Baltimore than most farmers on the peninsula, bought their first truck as early as 1920. In 1923 Maryland led the nation in production of tomatoes and was second in 1924 and 1925. Farmers from the peninsula, who made a major contribution to this total, met with other northern Anne Arundel County farmers in 1923 to organize a cooperative called the Farm Bureau.[219] In 1925 Alfred A. Stinch-

Louis Schramm, Sr. with family and friends admiring the Schramm's first truck, 1920.
The Schramm Collection

[218]Herbert Sappington; Charles H. Calvert.
[219]Yearbook of Agriculture, 1925, p.936; *The Sun*, February 8, 1923.

comb of Tick Neck was elected secretary of the Bureau that provided bulk purchase of goods that farmers needed.

The early and mid-twenties were not only a profitable time for white farmers, but also for the few black landowners on the peninsula. Hezekiah Manns (grandson of Greenberry Johnson who gave land near Rock Point for the first black school in the area) farmed on Bayside Beach Road near Fort Smallwood Road. Robert Hall's land was located on Fort Smallwood Road near the entrance to Fairview, and Henry Lane's farm was on Bayside Beach Road at Belhaven Road. Their families attended Mt. Zion Church and the old Magothy School. Since the black population was quite small, they did not have their own grocery store but bought supplies at Jubb's, Hillman's, or Sidle's (later Milstein's). During the Magothy-Mt. Zion Camp Meeting, Jubb's store was crowded with people who were attending the annual week-long gathering.[220]

George Schmidt's home on Mountain Road near the present Lake Shore Plaza, 1926.
Collection of Virginia Schmidt Smith

[220]James B. Calvert.

Girls dodge ball team, Pasadena School, 1917. Emma Jenkins is standing at right.
Collection of Emma Jenkins Wade Sanders

Four generations of the related Jenkins, Neidert, Moore, and Stinchcomb families, c.1925. The wheel and tire tracks on the right are Tick Neck Road, the main road across Tick Neck.
Collection of Emma Jenkins Wade Sanders

Louis F. Schramm and his rocking horse, c. 1927.
The Schramm Collection

George Schmidt's produce stand, 1929.
Collection of Virginia Schmidt Smith

As more people came to the eastern end of the peninsula, stores became profitable. In 1923 Samuel and Marie Angel opened a summertime refreshment stand on Mountain Road at Lake Shore. Samuel Angel and his widowed mother had bought nine acres and a small cottage at this location in 1902. A veteran of the Spanish-American War, Mr. Angel wanted to try farming, but he soon realized that farming was not his calling and returned to Baltimore. However, as people began to build homes in the area, he and his wife decided to try to make a living there as storekeepers.

In an 8-by-15-foot space, the Angels sold home-made bottled drinks, cookies, candy, bread, home-made ginger muffins, snuff, and cigarettes. Ice cream was available only on weekends because the Angels had to carry ice from a straw, burlap, and tin-covered pit several times a day to keep the ice cream frozen. No other local store sold this luxury. The next year the Angels built a larger home that housed an all-year grocery store, but they operated at the roadside stand during the summer.[221]

When Angels opened, the Sidle family's grocery store stood next to the present location of the Lake Shore Fire House (where the Royal Farm store is now). Sidle's store began in the early 1920s, but it became Milstein's when the Sidles moved to Glen Burnie and opened the first department store in northern Anne Arundel County. Charles Williams was the proprietor of a store on Mountain Road near Long Point Road during the early twenties. Ida Lampe Martin owned this business in the late 1920s and 30s. This store became Herbe's in the forties and fifties, and the building still stands.[222]

Another successful business in the neighborhood began modestly when William Schramm (son of Louis, the founder of the family) built a greenhouse and began to raise flowers as a hobby. In 1923 he rented a stall in Cross Street Market to sell his flowers on Saturdays. On Sundays he displayed them on shelves in a truck that he parked on Old Annapolis Road.

---

[221]Marie Angel Durner, "Early Days on Mountain Road," *Anne Arundel County History Notes*, vol.16, no.3, p.1.

[222]Marie Angel Durner; James B. Calvert; Milton O. Duvall.

Selling his field-grown gladiolus and dahlias was so profitable that the Schramms eventually devoted whole fields to floriculture. In 1927 William Schramm completed a correspondence course in arranging flowers and began to sell floral arrangements.[223]

Established older churches and groups that formed new churches were active in the mid-twenties. St. Jane Frances Roman Catholic Church on Church Road at Tick Neck Road in Riviera Beach was completed in 1924, but Saint Rose of Lima Church in Brooklyn had begun a mission there years before when mass was celebrated in a tent.[224]

A Methodist Sunday School had begun in Frances Cosden's home in what became Green Haven as early as 1911, but the Green Haven Methodist Church dates to 1921 when Rev. Charles S. Harrison of Magothy Church encouraged the group to build a place for a Sunday School to meet. Rev. William R.L. Ruths nurtured the congregation there until they enlarged the original building and added a Sunday School room in 1925.[225] In 1924 Magothy and Mt. Carmel churches held successful revival meetings where members reaffirmed their commitment while others joined the church for the first time. Mt. Zion Methodist Church continued its annual camp meetings that attracted thousands.[226]

The church that became the Community Methodist Church of Riviera Beach began when a small group of summer residents of various Protestant denominations met to worship together. In 1923 they decided to organize as Trinity Methodist Episcopal Church. Pastors from neighboring Methodist churches held services on Anne Riley's porch, in the Stadiger's garage, and under a large tent at the corner of Carvel and Main streets for ten Sundays each summer. After more people had become permanent residents of the community, on September 12, 1925, they laid the cornerstone of a frame church on Riviera Beach Drive. The church was painted

---

[223]Schramm, "Sixty Years in Anne Arundel County."
[224]"Discovering Our School Communities," Riviera Beach Elementary School, p.10.
[225]"Discovering Our School Communities," High Point Elementary School; *Maryland Gazette*, September 24 and November 5, 1925.
[226]Schell notes, *Washington Christian Advocate*, December 18, 1924, p.15.

pink and dedicated in 1926. In 1939 the congregation changed its name to Community Methodist Church.[227]

Family doctors served the growing community faithfully. Dr. Billinglea's successor was Dr. Leo Breit, whose father was a Russian official at the court of the Czar. During the Russian Revolution, he and other doctors were held by force and made to serve the Revolutionary faction. After nearly dying of cholera, he escaped from his homeland by stealth. When he came to the Bodkin community, he knew no one there and had no transportation. William Landy Cook would lend his car when Dr. Breit needed to make house calls until neighbors contributed money to enable him to buy a car. Margaret Ladner, his first maternity patient, later assisted him at deliveries.

Dr. Breit took care of residents of the peninsula from the mid-twenties until 1948. He had office hours seven days a week, charging one dollar for an office visit and two dollars for a home visit. He took classes at Johns Hopkins to keep abreast of changes in the practice of medicine and did his own lab work with his microscope. Former patients credit him with saving their lives because he was among the first doctors to use the new sulfa drugs in 1942. His wife Anna and his sister, Lubov Kieffer, taught music at the Peabody Conservatory, and he often relaxed by playing the piano.[228]

After George Fox became Superintendent of Anne Arundel County Schools in 1916, consolidated schools gradually replaced one and two-room schools. In 1926, the county abandoned the old Tick Neck, Rock Point, and Bodkin schools and built the consolidated Jacobsville Elementary School for white children where the Eastern District Police Station now stands. The Dunlap family gave this land to the Board of Education.

Former pupils who attended the old barn-red Rock Point School for white children on Bayside Beach Road remember it fondly. Though it had two rooms, only one room was used for eight grades. A pot-bellied

---

[227] "Discovering Our School Communities, " Riviera Beach Elementary School, p.10; Charlotte Gleim, "History of Community United Methodist Church."

[228] James B. Calvert, Anne Cook Myllo, Marie Angel Durner, Sarah Tall, Margaret Ladner, former patients of Dr. Breit.

wood-burning stove in the middle of the room provided heat. Hilda Combs taught there in 1922-23, then Miss Gilmore, Kitty Welch in 1924-25, Agnes Howie in 1925-26, and then Ida Hillman.[229]

At the consolidated Jacobsville school in 1926, Madeline Gibson (principal), Mildred Johnson, Alice Armiger, and Agnes Howie taught 130 children in four rooms, each heated by a large stove. Older pupils pumped water from a well with a hand pump. The Jacobsville Parents and Teachers Association cleared the stumps and bushes from the playground and sponsored a series of six dental clinics for the schoolchildren. Initially the school had no electric lights, but the community bought an electric generator driven by a gasoline engine in 1927. In 1930 four rooms were added to the school, as well as indoor toilets. The five pupils in the first graduating class were Kate Dreyer, Elizabeth Slater, Ellen Corey, Rose Corey, and Roland Calvert.[230]

Charles Hancock Cook with family and neighbors at Rock Point School, 1918.
Collection of Charles H. Calvert

[229]Arthur T. Corey, "The Coreys of Bodkin Creek."
[230]"Discovering Our School Communities," Jacobsville Elementary School; *Maryland Gazette*, 1927.

The Women's Society of Mt. Carmel Church paid five dollars for the old Bodkin School for use as a church hall in 1926. When they asked for a $30 loan to install electric lights in the hall during 1933, the year of many bank failures, the trustees denied the loan. In 1942 the congregation added a kitchen at the back of the old school building.[231]

At about the same time that the Board of Education consolidated the three white schools in 1926, the county closed Rock Point School for black children. The one-room Magothy School beside Mt. Zion Church in Johnsontown replaced the former school. It was built with some funding from Julius Rosenwald's Rural School Building Program. Mr. Rosenwald, president of Sears Roebuck and Company, wanted to improve educational opportunities for black children in the South. Between 1917 and 1932, his program helped to build 24 schools in Anne Arundel County, including both Magothy and Freetown.

The black community contributed land, some money, and labor, and the county supplied supplementary funding. Upon completion, the schools were given to the county. Magothy and Freetown schools followed the standard Rosenwald pattern with five tall small-paned windows on each side of the entrance. Pupils walked to Freetown from Elvaton, Solley, and Marley because it was the only school for black children in a wide area. The Magothy School building has been incorporated into the present Mt. Zion Church complex. The Freetown School has been altered but still stands.[232]

Despite developments along the waterfront, midway through the roaring twenties life on the peninsula continued much as before. Though residents were aware of jazz, bobbed hair, short skirts, hip flasks, and bathtub gin, life in an agricultural community seems to have been as tranquil as ever.

---

[231]Potee, "The History of Mt. Carmel Church"; Schell notes, Minutes of Maryland Methodist Protestant Conference, January 23, 1933.

[232]*Capital*, February 28, 2000; Sherri Marsh, Architectural Historian.

Resorts and Dance Pavilions Attract Crowds

The beaches, amusement parks, and resort hotels continued to attract many people during the late twenties. In 1927 the Effords bought the Stoney Creek steamship line and merged it with their Rock Creek Line to form the Stony Creek Improvement Company. The *Kitty Knight*, bought in 1913, was abandoned in a cove opposite Fairview in 1924, but other steamers like the *Stony Creek*, renamed *Fairview*, continued to bring crowds from piers on Light Street and Broadway. In 1931 the Effords bought the *Tred Avon* and added a stop at the new Fort Smallwood Park.[233] Other popular destinations included George Cook's Alpine Beach, Heintzman's Cottage Grove, McCoach's Colonial Beach, Efford's Fairview Park, and Grantlin's Maryland Beach. People who arrived at the beaches by steamer did not realize that farms surrounded all these resorts.

Fort Smallwood had not been used since 1917, when a unit of the National Guard was activated there for four months. During World War I, artillery was stripped from coastal forts for use in the field. In 1920

[233]Burgess and Wood, *Steamboats*, pp.179, 182, 183.

the War Department discontinued the Baltimore Coast Artillery District. The guns at both batteries at Fort Smallwood were dismounted in 1927 and transported to Aberdeen Proving Ground. Then the property was turned over to Baltimore City to be used as a waterfront park.[234] During the 1930s, thousands of people came to the resort by steamer and by automobile.

Fairview Park, where excursion steamboats arrived twice a day, became one of the most popular beach resorts. Swimmers could rent a bathing suit and towel for 35 cents and enjoy swimming, diving, and a toboggan slide into the water. Young men liked the bowling alley and pool hall with five pool tables, while children patronized the penny arcade and ice cream parlor and slid down the toboggan into the water. Most families brought loaded picnic baskets, but soft crab and ham sandwiches were sold, and Jesse, the cook at the dining room, prepared excellent crab and chicken dinners.

In addition to members of the Efford family, eight or ten employees staffed the resort on weekdays, and as many as twenty were needed on weekends to operate the carousel, manage the bowling alley, rent row-boats, collect fees at the bathhouse and penny arcade, and sell food, ice cream, and soft drinks. When the steamboat's whistle blew, tired, happy, and sunburned picnickers reluctantly gathered at the 350-foot pier and prepared to return home.[235]

Dance pavilions were popular during the prosperous and carefree twenties when young people danced not only the foxtrot but the jitterbug and Big Apple. The largest dance hall on the Pasadena peninsula was the two-story screened pavilion that the Robinsons built on Pinehurst's South End Beach in 1928. Lighted by Japanese lanterns and encircled by tables, the raised maple dancing surface measured 75 by 50 feet. On Wednesday and Saturday nights during the summer, popular bands led by Bob Iula, Jack

---

[234]Cole, "Fort Smallwood's Military Mission," *Anne Arundel History Notes*, vol.25, no,3. pp.1,2, 8-10

[235]Roger B. White, "All Ashore for Fairview Park," *Anne Arundel History Notes*, vol.12, no.2 (January 1981), pp.1-2.

The carousel at Fairview.
Collection of Jack Kelbaugh

Lederer, and Rudy Killian came from Baltimore to play at the dances. The public could enjoy dancing at the pavilion for a modest admission fee. The building, which extended over the water on the Bay front, was surrounded by a screened porch where older people sat in rocking chairs watching boats on the Bay and listening to the music.[236]

The Effords built a dance pavilion at Fairview where bands played in the 1920s, and Charles Heintzman's Cottage Grove offered a partially enclosed and partially screened dance pavilion beside Rock Creek where well-known bands from Baltimore entertained. Residents of Pasadena enjoyed dancing at Chestnut Grove at the intersection of West Pasadena Road and Jumpers Hole Road, and a few recall a pavilion on the hill above the north bank of Lake Waterford near the Baltimore and Annapolis Boulevard.[237]

---

[236]Robinson, "The History of Pinehurst," *Anne Arundel History Notes*, vol.21, no.4, p.7.
[237]Roger B. White, "Saturday Night at the Dance Hall," *Anne Arundel History Notes*, vol.20, no.4, pp.7-8; vol. XXI, no.1, pp.5-6.

The pavilion that the Robinsons built at Pinehurst in 1928.
Collection of Janet Robison O'Connell

In 1933 Gustav and Samuel Kurtz opened Kurtz Pleasure Beach and built an octagonal screened dance pavilion, later enclosed, near the waterfront. They were bakers like their father, who had emigrated from Austria. They had bakery stalls in six markets in Baltimore and had saved enough money to buy 65 acres on the water during the depression. So many of their friends came from Baltimore to visit them that they decided to open a resort. Soon it became their only business. To reach Kurtz's Beach, patrons could take a steamer to Fairview and transfer to Cook's bus, or they could come by Cook's bus from Curtis Bay to Riviera Beach and ride to Kurtz's in a horse-drawn vehicle, or later, in a station wagon. The Kurtz pavilion, now open only to groups for catered dinner-dances, weddings, and other celebrations, is the sole survivor of the dance halls of the thirties.[238]

---

[238]John Mason.

Having fun in the water at Kurtz Pleasure Beach.
Collection of Jack Kelbaugh

Brown's Grove, on Rock Creek near the end of Colony Road, was the only black resort to have its own steamer. Beginning with refreshment stands, a picnic grove, and bathhouses, Captain George Brown added a merry-go-round, a racerdip (roller coaster) ride, a midway, and eventually a dancing pavilion with a good band. He had come to Baltimore in 1893 as a young man "with enough baggage to fill a cigar box." He became the first black member of the Master Mates and Pilots Association and the prosperous owner of three excursion boats, *Starlight*, *Avalon*, and *Newbill*. Local residents remember the steamer *Starlight*, easily recognized by the star on the top, as she made repeated trips up and down the Patapsco to Brown's Grove on weekends.

After midnight on July 5, 1938, fire broke out in the racerdip ride. The blaze was spectacular by the time the Riviera Beach and Orchard Beach Fire Companies arrived. By morning, all that remained of the resort was smoldering rubble. In the black community in Baltimore, people mourned the loss of the only place comparable to the all-white beaches where they could enjoy bathing, boating, dancing, and a waterfront amusement park [239]

Signs of progress for people who made their homes on the peninsula included a new bridge over the Magothy River. The old wooden bridge collapsed during the twenties and was rebuilt farther upstream. The new bridge had wooden planks and a steel frame. It was called Dougherty's Bridge because John Dougherty, a waterman who took locally grown produce to Baltimore on the *Florence*, was the adjoining land owner.[240]

The paving of Mountain Road, a major advance, was a project done in four segments, first as far as Solley Road, then to Klug's store, then to the Schmidt farm, and finally to Gibson Island in 1928. The road was wide enough for two cars to pass, but it had no shoulders. Workmen used shovels and hoes to pack earth along the raised edges of the paving. Secondary roads remained unpaved, dusty or muddy, according to the season.[241]

In 1927 the Consolidated Gas and Electric Light and Power Company extended their lines to Riviera Beach, ending dependence on oil lamps on Tick Neck. Previously Charles Christian had placed telephone poles along Catherine Avenue to bring telephones to Green Haven. When the Chesapeake and Potomac Telephone Company was ready to extend their service, he sold the poles to the company. At this time, one-armed Mr. Hoeger collected all the garbage from Green Haven with one mule and cart.[242]

During the twenties and thirties, a fleet of small buses ran from the streetcar line at Brooklyn to various points on the Pasadena peninsula. As more comfortable and reliable buses replaced converted trucks with long

---

[239]Gilbert Sandler, "When Brown's Grove Went Up in Smoke," *The Sun*, 1995.
[240]Taylor, *My River Speaks*, pp.114-115.
[241]Charles H. Calvert.
[242]Marie Christian, from Robert Christian's notes.

wooden benches, commuting to Baltimore became practical. Clarence Johnson and Brothers, who were based in the village of Pasadena, operated a bus line from Baltimore to Green Haven in 1927. At the same time two black men, Harvey and Joseph Locklear, offered bus service between Curtis Bay and Riviera Beach. In 1928 Charles L. Cook bought Joseph Lochlear's line and ran a bus from Matuskey's Corner at Fort Smallwood and Riviera Beach roads to the Curtis Bay streetcar line. This service continued for 27 years.

Bus lines like General Cooperative Stores, William F. Schmitz , and the Gibson Island Club Coach Company competed with Charles Cook's Mountain Road service. In 1927, Cook sold the line to his nephew and partner, William B. Chairs, who had been his driver since 1916. Chairs formed the Lake Shore Bus Company that ran from Gibson Island to Baltimore. Employees at the Gibson Island Clubhouse, including Supreme Court Justice Thurgood Marshall's father, took this bus on Friday night and returned to Baltimore on Sunday. Mr. Marshall was a stern taskmaster to the busboys at the Clubhouse.[243]

An airport at this time meant a flying field like the one that existed from 1927 until the late thirties on Charles Pumphrey's farm (now Sunny Village, east of Sun Village Shopping Center) near Lipin's Corner. There daring young pilots, who had learned to fly in the service during World War I, rented and graded a field and offered paying customers a brief flight. Flying in light planes required courage, but many people paid five dollars for the right to boast that they had "gone up" in an airplane. Throughout the thirties, many cars parked along Mountain Road to watch the planes and hope to see a parachute jump. If that happened, the crowd contributed to a collection for the brave jumper.[244]

At Lake Waterford, William Wolle and his sister, Henrietta Wolle Windsor, operated a business on the property that their father had bought in

---

[243]White, "Bus Service to Anne Arundel County," *Anne Arundel History Notes*, vol.11, no.3, pp.1-3.
[244]Senator Alfred Lipin.

Planes at the airfield on Mountain Road east of the present Sun Valley Shopping Plaza.
Collection of Evelyn Wade

Pilot and friends at the airfield on Mountain Road with a 1930 Model A Ford and a 1927 Willys Knight parked nearby.
Collection of Evelyn Wade

1912. The elder William Wolle, director of Druid Hill Park in Baltimore, had searched for a home in the country where he could raise rare goldfish. He chose Lake Waterford, built his home there, planted exotic South American plants around the lake, and eventually stocked the lake with bluegill, bass, and pike. In 1927 his son and daughter added a concession stand and rented boats and log cabins to fishermen and vacationers from May to October. Among their regular patrons were the families of midshipmen who stayed at Lake Waterford during June Week (now Graduation Week) at the Naval Academy.[245]

Several new businesses opened at this time. In 1927 William Schmidt, whose farm extended from Hog Neck Road to the present Lake Shore Plaza, built a roadside stand of canvas supported by poles. A year or two later, he completed a twenty-foot-square stone stand on Mountain Road where he

---

[245]Rayetta Wolle Windsor.

sold his produce. During the 1920s, Charles Williams owned a gas station at the corner of Mountain Road and Long Point Road. Later Herbert Linthicum became the proprietor. At the head of Bodkin Creek, Captain Henry Wickert owned a store and ice plant. He brought supplies from Baltimore for his store and the Hancock store in his boat called *No Name*.[246]

When Mountain Road was paved and relocated in 1928, the Angels were forced to buy more land and rebuild. Their store became a landmark for people traveling to their summer homes. The Angel family enjoyed meeting many professional people who stopped at their store on their way to homes on Gibson Island. Children especially looked forward to seeing Mr. Angel's animals, including a monkey and a bear that he later gave to Druid Hill Park. Though he had little formal education, he was self-educated and a skilled taxidermist. He had begun to collect coins as a boy and assembled a fine collection later in his life.[247]

With an increasing population to serve, other businesses expanded. William Klug had bought ten acres on the southwest corner of Mountain Road at Waterford Road opposite his father's store and had been selling vegetables from his farm at a roadside stand. In 1929 he and his wife Elsie opened a Shell gas station and general store where Elsie Klug's pies attracted customers. At the western end of the peninsula, Lett's Whitford Inn on Annapolis Boulevard sold refreshments, and Wade's general store continued to serve Pasadena until Elzey Wade's death in the mid-thirties. By the mid-twenties, James Jubb owned a store east of Hillman's where his wife Effie was in charge later.[248]

Though community life continued to be centered in churches and schools, an organization called the Magnolia Democratic Club formed on July 5, 1928. Charles Herpel served as the first president. Located on Eli Cove near the head of Stony Creek, the members worked for the civic, social, and political welfare of the community.[249]

---

[246]Henry Schmidt; James B. Calvert.
[247]Marie Angel Durner.
[248]Pasadena Guide Book, supplement to the *Maryland Gazette*, 1993.
[249]Green Haven Carnival brochure, 1940, Schramm Collection.

Early view of Angel's store on Mountain Road.

Collection of Tom Richmond

Despite the rebuilding of Stony Creek bridge in 1925, many farmers on the peninsula sent their produce to Baltimore by boat. Robert Bottomley, Oliver Duvall, and John Neidert shipped from Bottomley's wharf at Tar Cove on Rock Creek. Captain Hudson, who came from the Eastern Shore during the season, sailed the Bottomley's market boat, *The Leader*, to Long Dock in Baltimore. Sam Dunlap's wharf was at the end of Bodkin Avenue, and the Armigers used Armiger Wharf on the Bodkin. Near Windmill Point on the Magothy Narrows was Jefferson Monroe Cook's landing. Warren Cook, George Jenkins, and Charles (Buck) Jubb used the county wharf at the end of Ventnor Road. George Jenkins' market boat, the *Fanny Hayward*, was not a bugeye but a freight boat with a pilot house and a freight boom.

Captain Ed Deale's bugeye, the *John R. Benton*, with its two masts and sharply tapered hull, stopped at the county wharf on Wharf Creek and at

Cook's wharf for produce that James, George, and Jefferson Cook, Henry Hancock, James and Charles Calvert, John Shipley, and Hezekiah Mann shipped from Bodkin Neck. The Calverts sent their loaded market boat from the Calvert wharf on Back Creek, and Milton Fick on Cornfield Creek sent his produce to market from Jefferson Cook's wharf in a pungee.[250]

James B. Calvert remembers that when he and his brother Charles sailed the *John R. Benton* to Long Dock in Baltimore, the present site of Harborplace, it was not a quiet trip. He recalls listening to the creaking and crying of the ropes in the deadeyes of the rigging. Even the hull groaned as the bugeye hit swells when they passed the large ship that left Baltimore

The *John R. Benton*, Captain Deale's market boat, on Back Creek.
Collection of Charles Hancock Calvert

[250]Blodwin Shipley Potee, "Bugeyes, Docks, and Wharves," *Anne Arundel County History Notes*, vol. 16, no.2, p.1; Charles H. Calvert.

harbor for Norfolk. Sailing home from Baltimore in a dense fog, the crew carried a smooth iron weight attached to a rope. Before the days of more sophisticated depth finders, to judge the depth of the water they threw the weight ahead of the boat and then took it in. They counted the creeks they passed and knew that, after Rock Creek, the next would be Bodkin. From there, finding their familiar landing on Back Creek was easy.

John Dougherty's schooner-rigged bugeye, the *Florence*, which was designed for carrying cargo and freight as well as passengers, stopped at landings on Pea Patch Point, Cornfield Creek, and Blackhole Creek on the Magothy to pick up fruits and vegetables for the Baltimore and Annapolis markets.[251] The Schramms sometimes shipped from the county wharf at Green Haven, but they were closer to the Baltimore market by road than farmers at the eastern end of the peninsula and often used wagons or trucks to take their produce to market.

Not only the Grachur Club and Camp Milbur brought young people to camps on the Magothy River; in 1928 the Girl Scouts of Baltimore established Camp Whippoorwill on nineteen acres on Cockey Creek that had been part of Captain Robinson's farm. His three-story former home with wide porches became their headquarters. Previously this site had been used briefly as a boys' camp called Whippoorwill Hill. Girl Scouts would travel by train from Baltimore to Jones Station, then by cart to South Ferry Point, and by ferry across the Magothy on the *Diana*. They wore white middie blouses, bloomers, black ties, and knee stockings. Swimming, canoeing, sailing, crafts, and singing around a campfire were among their favorite activities. Before 1930, the 75 or 80 girls who came to the camp for two-week sessions lived in Army tents. Until 1932, they had to carry water from a spring for drinking and cooking.[252]

Perhaps the Depression prevented carrying out the elaborate plans developers made for the Long Point Country Club on the Magothy. In

---

[251]Taylor, *My River Speaks*, pp.176, 178.
[252]Gail R. Blaisdell, "Bloomer Girls Have Vanished," *Maryland Living* (July 7, 1968), p.4; "History of Camp Whippoorwill" (1928-1951), William G. Rothamel Collection.

addition to the usual attractions, their brochure promised archery, croquet, tennis, baseball, basketball, football, a gymnasium, and even an airport.[253] All the resorts and developments on the water at that time were restricted to white Gentiles. Black people could not own waterfront property before 1950.

By the end of the 1920s, new homeowners lived in dozens of small developments and in individual homes along the Magothy, the Bay, the Patapsco, and their many tributaries. Sillery Bay was one of the earliest developments, laid out in 1929. The community improved Long Point Road and gave it to the county in 1935. Most residences were summer homes, but affordable automobiles and better roads would soon enable many people to live near the beautiful creeks and rivers throughout the year.

Girl Scouts sailing on the Magothy River near Camp Whippoorwill.
Collection of Jack Kelbaugh

[253]Schramm Collection.

Girl Scouts relaxing in a tent at Camp Whippoorwill.
Collection of Jack Kelbaugh

Unit meeting at Camp Whippoorwill.
Collection of Jack Kelbaugh

The Great Depression Begins

The period of optimism, silk shirts, and shiny new cars ended with the Great Depression of the 1930s. After the stock market crash of 1929, home sales slowed though building continued at Bayside Beach and elsewhere. When banks closed in 1933 and some did not reopen, everyone knew that the country was facing an economic crisis.

By the mid-thirties, many people who lived on the peninsula not only lost their jobs at a time of widespread unemployment, but some lost their savings as well. Of the 39 families who attended the Methodist Church at Green Haven, only one man had work. Churches and community leaders did as much as they could to help neighbors who had no money and no food. Steven Everd, the local magistrate, gave away quantities of milk and flour and canned goods, and his wife canned food to share, but Judge Everd finally told county officials that he could not feed all the people in his area who were hungry. He offered the county the use of his former dry goods store where social workers distributed food and used clothing.[254]

---

[254]"Discovering Our School Communities," High Point Elementary School; Mildred Everd Oakie.

Despite hard times, the Riviera Beach Volunteer Fire Company, founded by Mac Eschenbach in 1930, became an important part of the community. In September 1931 the company bought a new fire engine with many special features. On a demonstration run on Fort Smallwood Road, which was being graded in preparation for paving, the fire truck overturned and Chief Ellsworth Barton lost his life when a grading machine forced the fire engine driver to move to the sloping shoulder. Mac Eschenbach then served as fire chief. He stored the new engine in a garage behind his Riviera Beach General Store until 1934, when the company built a firehouse on Tick Neck Road on property donated by Pumphrey Brothers, Realtors.

Riviera Beach bought a Buick ambulance in 1937 and began the longest continuous ambulance service in Anne Arundel County. Responding to calls became easier when the county paved local roads in 1937. In 1938 the company built a hall where the Ladies Auxiliary raised funds for a second engine, a second ambulance, and an enlarged firehouse. Riviera Beach firemen began to train at the University of Maryland in 1939. Two years later, the company bought a second pumper and another ambulance.[255]

The Community Methodist Church at Riviera Beach was open only from Memorial Day until Labor Day during the thirties because most people there were summer residents. To supplement his three-month income, the Rev. Charles S. Harrison sold butter, eggs, tea, and coffee at homes in the community where he also invited people to attend church. James Jenkins, who owned a farm on Tick Neck, offered to donate land for a church that would be open all year. When the Methodist Conference was unwilling to appoint a full-time pastor to what they considered a summer colony, Rev. Charles S. Harrison withdrew from the Methodist Church and met with a group on the porch of the Benway home in Riviera

---

[255] "History of the Riviera Beach Volunteer Fire Company."

Beach. There they planned an independent church dedicated to preaching the Gospel to all people.

After meeting in the Benway home for months, in 1931 the congregation built Jenkins Memorial, a church that was open to everyone. Later they added Sunday School rooms. Children remembered a service when Chief Yellow Feather, an ordained Methodist minister and a powerful speaker, preached at the church wearing a feathered headdress and full Native American regalia. Reverend Charles Harrison served faithfully as pastor at Jenkins Memorial until his death in 1954.[256]

Fort Smallwood Road was completed in 1932 and electricity reached the area the same year, but these changes had little effect on people's lives. Elections continued to be held at the local polling house on Mountain

Interior of Jenkins Memorial Church, built in 1931.

Collection of Emma Jenkins Wade Sanders

[256]Leaflet, Emma Jenkins Wade Sanders Collection.

Chief Yellow Feather preached at Jenkins Memorial.
Collection of Emma Jenkins Wade Sanders

Indian Chief To Preach At Bar Harbor Church

CHIEF YELLOW FEATHER

The Rev. Chief Sachem Ousa Mequin, known as Chief Yellow Weather, an ordained minister of the Methodist Church, will speak to the Sunday School and preach the sermon at Jenkins Memorial Church on Sunday, Jan. 29; Sunday School 10 a. m. and preaching at 11 a. m.

Chief Sachem Ousa Mequin is a full blooded Indian and is head of the Wamapanoag Tribe of Rhode Island. He is making his home for the present in Baltimore. He not only speaks frequently in Churches and bfore civic organizations, but he is well known to radio audiences. Since coming to Baltimore he has delivered a number of lectures on the customs, legends and history of the American Indian.

He is known to be a fearless and powerful speaker. He will speak in full regalia for the benefit of the children.

Road between Catherine Avenue and Old Mill Road, now Armiger Drive. Few cars were on the roads, even Mountain Road, and families would sit on their front porches and entertain themselves by identifying the cars and loaded farm trucks that passed. For several decades, William T. Jenkins was foreman in charge of all county roads in the Third District. He had a crew of only six men, but that was enough because few roads existed. When he died in 1959, the county commissioners passed a resolution in memory of his conscientious and devoted service.[257]

In the mid-twenties, the War Department dismounted the guns at Fort Smallwood and sold the land to Baltimore City. At that time, the city employed the Olmstead Brothers, America's foremost landscape planners, who recommended Fort Smallwood's development as a recreational facility. The city appropriated $50,000 for that purpose in 1927 and provided a steamer for access to the park. A 150-foot pier, volleyball courts, horseshoe pits, children's playground, bathhouse complex, and 300 picnic tables attracted visitors when Fort Smallwood Park opened in 1931.

Former barracks became an administration building, while a masonry building with a hip roof, dormers, and a surrounding porch, as well as an octagonal rustic building with an octagonal roof and open sides, served as concession stands.[258] Thousands of people came to the park by steamer and automobile to swim,

---

[257]Emma M. Schramm, Emma Jenkins Wade Sanders.
[258]Maryland Historical Trust Historic Sites Inventory AA-898.

Electioneering at the Third District polling house at Green Haven November 8, 1938.
Collection of Virginia Schmidt Smith

Fort Smallwood Park attracts crowds of people.
Collection of Jacques Kelly

fish, and play badminton or softball. Though the city owned the public park, only white people were admitted.

In 1931 Isadore Hillman rebuilt and enlarged his mother's store, but Hillman's still opened at six a.m. and stayed open until the last customer had been served in the evening. During the thirties, the family added an Amoco filling station. When the terrible hurricane of 1933 struck the area, Gussy Hillman recalls that vacationers from Bayside Beach sought shelter inland at the store and spent the night there. From the 1940s until

NEWER BUSINESSES ON THE PENINSULA IN 1931

S. M. Johnson	Contractors
Herbert R. Linthicum	Contractors
Holmes Brothers	Groceries, meat, and ice—Lake Shore
Barringer's	Beach umbrellas, boats for hire, and sandwiches and refreshments—Fort Smallwood
Charles Williams	General Store—Mountain Road
C.H. McCullough	Butter and eggs—Delivered by auto
Frank Simmons	Meats, groceries, fruits—Tick Neck Road
A.B. Drummond	Groceries, meats, and confectionary—Boulevard Park
A. Reinhardt	Groceries, meats, and provisions—Greenland Beach
V. Vogel	Meats, groceries, fruits, and vegetables
Leroy Williams	Ice, general hauling, groceries, and confectionary
C. Karcher	Meats, groceries, fruits, and vegetables
Walter J. Johnson	Fancy groceries, meats

The last four were in the village of Pasadena.[259]

[259]Fifth Annual Carnival brochure, Jacobsville, July 1931, James B. Calvert Collection.

1968, others managed the store but the Hillmans continued to be the owners until it became Pastore's.[260]

John Wilson, Senior, opened his Amoco service station on Mountain Road in 1934 and moved it a short distance down the road to its present location in 1937. John and May Wilson offered home-grown vegetables, fruit, flowers, and fancy frying chickens in addition to gasoline. Their business became a gathering place for the Lake Shore community.[261] Elsewhere customers depended on familiar stores like Angel's, Chairs' general store opposite Mount Carmel Church, and Joseph and Andy Coach's grocery store on Hog Neck that delivered purchases by horse and wagon.

John Wilson's service station, 1937.
Collection of John Wilson, Jr.

---

[260] *Maryland Gazette*, September 19, 1987.
[261] *Maryland Gazette*, July 18, 1998.

O.A. Fuss's filling station on Mountain Road opposite the flying field near Lipin's Corner.
Collection of Evelyn Wade

A 1929 De Soto or a 1930 Dodge Victory Six at O. A. Fuss's filling station. (Both were made by Chrysler Corporation and were nearly identical.)
Collection of Evelyn Wade

Small neighborhood businesses included Haslup's store and garage and Jubb's store across from Hillman's; Lockermans's store next to Dr. Breit's office beside what is now the Eastern District police station; Brook's store on Mountain Road; and Drummond's at the intersection of Mountain Road and Boulevard Park Road. As early as the twenties, Green Haven had its own small grocery store on the waterfront. Teal's served the community until about 1934 when that site became Christian's real estate office. Shelving from the original store remains in the basement of the building, now a home. Harrison's store on Outing Avenue and Stevenson's store on Outing Avenue and East Shore Road also served Green Haven.[262]

At the eastern end of the peninsula, local residents and men from the oyster fleet patronized the little store at the home of Harry and Mamie

The large building at the top of the photo is Clark's Bayside Inn on Knollwood Drive, 1933.

Collection of Clark Elliott, owner of the inn

[262]Marie Angel Durner; Marie Christian.

Hancock. Young people who lived in summer homes at Bayside Beach remember walking to the Hancock store to buy candy bars from Miss Mamie, who always wore a sunbonnet and ankle-length dresses with long sleeves. She told them that she did not need electricity because she and her brother went to bed at sundown and rose at dawn. The young people also visited the lighthouse keeper and took him candy bars and magazines.[263]

Some new businesses prospered despite the depression. In 1932 Henry F. Stroback bought six boats to rent at his wharf at the end of Lake Drive at Bayside Beach. Soon he was building row boats to rent. In 1936 he opened a small store that carried staples and canned goods for neighbors and oystermen. In addition, he captained three forty-foot fishing boats. His business survived until the early sixties.[264]

Using a local resource, the Arundel Sand and Gravel Company operated near the Pasadena railroad station for many years. The very fine sand dug from their pit was always in demand. Though an extensive supply of building sand existed near the head of the Magothy, this seems to be the only firm that mined sand on a large scale. However, Jefferson Cook dug sand of good quality along Cornfield Creek near the mouth of the Magothy for use in building, and children at the Magothy Elementary School for black pupils recalled that Clarence Hall, a school trustee, sold sand from his sandbank for stucco work. Older residents remember seeing fine hour-glass sand on the cliffside at North Ferry Point and finding amber nearby.[265]

In addition to the bus line that Charles Cook owned from 1928 until 1955, enterprising men drove buses to serve Baltimoreans who wanted to spend a weekend or a Sunday on the beach. Walter Koryto ran a bus between Highlandtown and Outing Avenue at Shore Road, leaving Baltimore at 3 p.m. Saturday and 7:30 a.m. on Sunday and returning Sunday evening. Harrison's Red Line ran on a similar schedule between Fleet and

---

[263]Dorothy Sands Childs.
[264]Mildred Strobeck.
[265]William B. Clark, Maryland Geological Survey (Baltimore, 1917), pp.123-124; "Discovering Our School Communities," Magothy Elementary School; Taylor, *My River Speaks*, p.98.

Bond streets near Fells Point and Harrison's store at Green Haven. John Novak's bus ran only on Sunday between Jefferson and Duncan streets (six blocks east of Johns Hopkins Hospital) and Stevenson's store in Green Haven. Joseph and Francis Gonet also operated a bus from Baltimore to Green Haven from 1934 to 1936. At one time, Charles Christian subsidized Gonet's and Harrison's buses that brought real estate customers to Green Haven along oystershell-paved Outing Avenue.[266]

Farming had been the lifeblood of the Pasadena peninsula for 150 years, but the thirties were a difficult time for farmers. People did not have money to buy luxuries like strawberries, melons, and peaches. Anne Arundel farmers always had received their highest prices for the first of each crop because customers had waited almost a year for garden-fresh peas, beans, tomatoes, and fruit. During the thirties, refrigerated trucks from the Carolinas and Georgia began to bring fruits and vegetables to the Baltimore market before those crops ripened here. Local farmers then received lower prices for their produce. After planting, cultivating, harvesting, and marketing crops, a farmer might find that he had a loss instead of a profit at the end of the year.

Enterprising farmers found other sources of income to supplement dwindling profits. George Schmidt advertised hauling stone, sand, gravel, and wood, as well as grading. Later he had a hardware store. William L. Cook farmed and had extensive peach orchards, but his wife, Urma Cook, owned and operated a dairy with delivery routes on Gibson Island and at Pinehurst.[267] Eckhard Jubb bought and drove a school bus, in addition to selling his produce at a roadside stand.

In 1930 William Schramm, who had discovered that growing flowers was profitable, joined with his brother Peter (both sons of Louis) to become retail florists. They also grew gladiolus for wholesale markets. Soon they were making more money from flowers than from farming. During

---

[266]Mellin, "Green Haven Advertising Brochures," *Anne Arundel History Notes*, vol.22, no.2, p.9. (Bus schedule from the Schramm Collection); White, "Bus Service," *Anne Arundel History Notes*, vol.11, no.3, pp.1-3; Marie Christian, from Robert Christian's notes.

[267]Anne Cook Myllo.

George Schmidt, Moody Schmidt, Vic, Joe, and Pap ready to unload truck that brought tomatoes from the field. Workers who picked the tomatoes are in the background, August 17,1937.

Collection of Virginia Schmidt Smith

George Schmidt with farm workers who are grading potatoes, July 13, 1938.

Collection of Virginia Schmidt Smith

Getting ready to pick strawberries on George Schmidt's farm where Lake Shore Plaza now stands, May 23, 1935.
Collection of Virginia Schmidt Smith

George Schmidt's sandstone produce stand, once a Mountain Road landmark, now Cookie's restaurant, c.1938.
Collection of Virginia Schmidt Smith

Margaret, George, and Vivian Schmidt packing strawberries on the Schmidt farm at the present site of Lake Shore Plaza, c. 1933.
Photo: Marion E. Warren

William Landy Cook packing Long John cantaloupes while others pack tomatoes, 1939.

Photo: A. Aubrey Bodine, *News-American*. Collection of Jacques Kelly

the 1930s, Schramm Brothers planted 700,000 bulbs for successive blooms throughout the season and cut as many as 8,000 blooms in a day and 750,000 in a year, making them one of the largest gladiolus farms in the eastern United States. Throughout the year, they sold flower arrangements, funeral designs, and wedding bouquets locally and raised potted plants in greenhouses to supply two stalls in Cross Street Market with coleus, begonias, geraniums, lilies, tulips, and hyacinths.[268]

When drought threatened their flowers during an exceptionally dry year in the early thirties, the Schramm brothers built a dam across a stream that was fed by springs in their woods just above the place where State Route 100 later crossed their property. Using water from the pond that

Louis and William Schramm among almost endless rows of gladiolus plants.
The Schramm Collection

[268]Schramm, "Sixty Years in Anne Arundel County."

formed above the dam, they built an extensive irrigation system. An electric pump forced water into pipes that they had buried underground. At intervals they erected connecting vertical pipes called risers. Across the risers, they placed horizontal pipes with holes in them. These pipes had to be absolutely level, parallel to the ground. An oscillator at the end of each pipe turned from side to side, sending a spray of water over the rows of plants in the fields. This system watered half an acre at a time. Then the men moved the heavy vertical and horizontal pipes to another field and leveled them, a major undertaking.[269]

On their Bodkin Neck farm at the other end of the peninsula, Daniel P. Corey and his son Arthur installed a sprinkler system during the same dry year. They dug a diversion ditch from a stream at the head of the Bodkin to a sump. At the sump intake, the water passed through a filter to remove debris. A centrifugal pump driven by a five-horsepower electric motor forced water through the sprinkler system, movable lines of pipe with a row of brass nozzles screwed into the pipes at 24-inch intervals. Moving the pipes by hand was difficult, but this system worked.[270]

Though farming was still the main employment on the Pasadena peninsula, a few men worked as watermen. They could catch crabs with a dip net and sell them for two dollars a barrel. Milton Fick, Robert Gray, Buck Kaiser, and Tom and Vince Bailey supplemented their income by fishing and crabbing, selling locally or shipping to Baltimore from Cook's wharf.[271]

Most watermen had winter jobs, but John Dreyer and John Gumpman made a living from the water throughout the year. John Gumpman lived on SilleryBay and used pound nets but not a seine net. John Dreyer and his wife came to Maryland from Austria-Hungary when they were in their teens. He bought land at Hickory Point on Sillery Bay in 1914 and built his own 28-foot rowboats to fish the Magothy and the Chesapeake Bay.

---

[269] Emma M. Schramm.
[270] Corey, "The Coreys of Bodkin Creek."
[271] James B. Calvert; John Williams.

These boats had hand-carved oars but no seats. The Dreyers stood as they rowed and filled the boat with fish to a depth of 18 inches.

The Dreyers also used seven or eight pound nets and a seine net. A pound net was suspended in the water from a long row of poles set in a circle to form a crib. Fish followed a lead net attached to poles leading from the shore into a funnel-like entrance to the crib-shaped net where they were trapped. The Dreyers would tow two boats to the net and go from pole to pole, pulling the net up to hang the crib on the poles. With a huge dip net, they dipped the fish into rowboats and sorted them. Crabs went in one boat and edible fish of legal size in the other, while the remainder of the catch was released into the water.

John Dreyer and George Dreyer sorting a boatload of crabs at Hickory Point, 1926.
Collection of Clara Dreyer Bomhardt

The Dreyer family on their wharf on a Sunday afternoon, 1926. A live box or crab float is in the foreground.
Collection of Clara Dreyer Bomhardt

Mr. Dreyer also used a seine, a large net with one thousand feet of rope attached to each end. From his boat, he dropped rope from the end of the net that was attached to lead weights. Cork floats were attached to the other end. As the net was dropping, the boat made a U-turn in a large semi-circle to surround a school of fish. When the boat approached shore, four to six people on each side of the seine hauled it in at ebb tide and formed a U-shaped pocket so the fish could not escape. Then they used hand nets to drop the fish into rowboats where they were sorted. The Dreyers packed the fish in layers in crushed ice in wooden boxes, loaded a truck with the 100-pound boxes, and sent them to the market in Baltimore. The catch varied, but it usually totaled 500 to 1,000 pounds.[272]

---

[272]Clara Dreyer Bomhardt.

Though Mr. Dreyer often had a hired man or two living in a bunk house, his son and the five Dreyer daughters helped with all the work. The girls hauled the seine net to shore, while their father or brother swam underwater to unhook it from a submerged log or other obstruction. Each girl wore a six-inch wide leather belt called a "becky," which was laced together in front with triple-knotted rope. They looped the ropes they were wearing over the rope of the seine net and leaned back in unison, using their weight to pull the net as they called "Coming up" or "Carry forward." This process took an hour or more and sometimes had to be completed by the light of lanterns. "It was a challenge," Clara Dreyer Bomhardt recalls, "but worth the effort."

The cotton nets required much hard work because grass grew on them after they had been in the water for a month or more. Then Clara and her older sister Kate "wet-scrubbed" the nets before they were dried and cleaned. To prepare for wet-scrubbing, Mr. Dreyer cut two tall poles, stripped the bark, and shellacked the poles. Then he built a 60-by-45-inch platform with holes in the corners for the two poles that he drove into the sand near the shore. As Clara and Kate stood on the platform, pulled the wet cotton net across it, and scrubbed the heavy net, the platform would rise and fall. Wet-scrubbing was back-breaking work.

Their next step was to stretch the net on a rack to dry. When it had dried, Clara and Kate brushed it with scrubbing brushes and examined it for holes. Kate used heavy cotton on fourteen-inch wooden needles to mend any tears. Then they dipped the net in a tub of tar and dried it on a rack. Usually four or five pound nets were in use at a time, while the girls worked on the other three.[273]

Mr. Dreyer bought an old ferry boat and sank it at the shoreline to use as a workshop. When he caught diamondback terrapin, he would pen them and fatten them for market. In the winter, he cut ice from the river

---

[273]Ibid.

The Dreyer's pound net outside the sand bar at Gibson Island, 1926.
Collection of Clara Dreyer Bomhardt

John Dreyer, son George, and daughter Mamie attempting to keep their boat free of ice that damaged their pier, 1926.
Collection of Clara Dreyer Bomhardt

The five Dreyer sisters (Kate, Jennie, Mamie, and Charlotte behind Clara) dry scrubbing a net at Hickory Point, 1928.
Collection of Clara Dreyer Bomhardt

Building a new pier that will have tracks to move a flatbed carrying 100-pound boxes of fish to the shore, 1930. On the left is the scow, a former ferry boat that served as a workshop, and the old pier. A boat with tongs is in the left foreground and the ice house is visible at the far right.
Collection of Clara Dreyer Bomhardt

to fill his icehouse. He built a marine railway from his pier to the ice house, stored fish there, and smoked fish in his smoke house. He sold to Freeburger in the fish market in Baltimore, and they shipped his catch to Philadelphia and New York. His son, George Dreyer, carried on the business after his father's death.

The Dreyer family lived well on the resources of the land and water. During the summer, Elizabeth Dreyer canned fruit, vegetables, and crabmeat for the winter. In the late fall, Mr. Dreyer bought barrels of apples, sugar, flour, and little else to see them through the winter. In the side of a slope, he dug a place for a brick-lined root cellar where he stored vegetables like potatoes and cabbage. He hung herring and eels in a his brick smokehouse where they smoked slowly until they were a delicious treat in the winter. The family also grew peanuts and roasted them. Clara Bomhardt recalls going out early in the morning with a 12-gauge shotgun to shoot ducks for an evening meal. If her mother wanted oysters for dinner, Clara could tong a bucket full in a few minutes. She also set rabbit traps and trapped muskrats to sell for their hides.

Seine hauling, after the net has been pulled in, 1933.
Collection of Clara Dreyer Bomhardt

Clara Dreyer Bomhardt remembers that the Magothy was twelve feet deep at the end of their pier and the water so clear that she could see the bottom. Near the shore, small crabs and fish thrived in the deep and thick seaweed. Multi-colored inch-long minnows swam in the Magothy, and, where Hunter's Harbor is now, salamanders lived in a freshwater spring. Today the Dreyer house and net shed are only memories.

After spending their youth in and near the water at Hickory Point, it is not surprising that all five Bomhardt girls won medals for swimming in competition at Patterson Park. Their brother George held the YMCA East

George Dreyer mending a net at Hickory Point, c. 1938.
Collection of Clara Dreyer Bomhardt

An A. Aubrey Bodine photo of George Dreyer mending a net.
Collection of Clara Dreyer Bomhardt

Coast swimming championship from 1930 through 1935, winning fifty-two gold medals and six silver cups. His family was especially proud of his award for winning a ten-mile competition in the Atlantic Ocean in the days when swimmers were temporarily blinded by salt water because they did not have goggles. Since women could not compete at that time. Clara and Kate Dreyer had to wait for Senior Olympics before winning a total of fifty gold medals. Clara is a Maryland Master Swimmer, holds five state records, and at the age of 75 swims 2,500 yards at six a.m. every day.[274]

Like many people who grew up on the peninsula during the depression, her memories of the those years are of the beauty of the unspoiled waterfront; the bounty of land, water, and sky that provided wonderful food; and happy life in a family that worked hard but worked together.

---

[274]Ibid.

Community Life During the Depression

Despite hard times, during the Great Depression people enjoyed many inexpensive pleasures. For an admission fee of 25 cents each, a family could go to a waterfront resort with a picnic lunch, claim a table under the shade of trees, and spend the whole day on the wide beach. Softball games between Pinehurst and Milbur, a regular Sunday event at the boys' camp, drew large crowds. Most communities supported active Boy and Girl Scout programs. In the village of Pasadena, Henry Benton founded Boy Scout Troop 346 in 1939.[275]

For many people in the community, strawberry festivals, crab feasts, and oyster roasts added zest to life. In cold weather, men hunted quail and shot ducks, while young people looked forward to skating parties on Cook's Pond near the end of Mountain Road or on Oakley's Pond on Pasadena Road near the school. No one had much money to spend during the thirties, but people were not unhappy. Mildred Everd Oakie recalls

---

[275]Robinson, "Pinehurst," *Anne Arundel History Notes*, vol.21, no.4, p.7; "Discovering Our School Communities," Pasadena Elementary School.

that "neighbors all pulled together. That was all you had—each other." And that was enough.

Churches and schools remained the centers of community life. Families looked forward to annual Sunday School picnics and events like Mt. Carmel's church suppers held on William L. Cook's wide beach. A church founded at Pasadena in 1934 as the J. Selby George Memorial Church survives today, but it has been called the Pasadena Assembly of God since 1938. Pasadena peninsula parents were noted for their support of their schools. When Virginia Moore taught at Jacobsville during the thirties and early forties, Jacobsville School won the P.T.A. banner for the best

Huckleberry Island in Blackhole Creek, playground for the Yanky children, 1934.
Collection of Ruth Yanky Volkman

attendance in the county every month for eleven years, impressive evidence of parental loyalty.[276]

During the thirties and forties, many young people from Baltimore came to the Magothy for fun and character development. Camp Milbur, Grachur, and Camp Whippoorwill continually added to their facilities and expanded their programs. Grachur sponsored a camp for 24 underprivileged boys in 1930, using Army surplus tents and cots. Later they bought adjoining property, built more cabins and a craft house, and added

Seventh grade at Jacobsville Elementary School, Madeline Gibson, principal, 1938. Pupils include Alice Marie Schmidt, Edwin Calvert, Monroe Chairs, Ilene Stallings, Catherine Ellison, Catherine Rothamel, Louis Schramm, and William Schramm.
Collection of Ruth Yanky Volkman

[276]Herb Sappington; Virginia Dryden Moore

Pasadena Methodist Church, 1917 until 1958.
Collection of Emma Jenkins Wade Sanders

a game room to the clubhouse. On Labor Day, families came for sailing, canoe races, diving, softball, volleyball, and ping-pong tournaments. Until Lake Shore Drive was paved in the late forties, cars coming from Baltimore had to drive along a sandy, dusty, and rough road.[277]

Camp Whippoorwill added an infirmary in 1930, a lodge in 1933, and built their Big House in 1940 after the old Robinson home burned in 1939. At this time, they installed a water system, ending dependence on a spring and a well. During the summers of 1934 and 1935, two Senior Scouts, Mary Alice Douty and Margaret McClellan, carved a dead chestnut tree to make a totem pole to tell of camp activities. It became a

[277] Carl Behm, "The Grachur Story."

familiar landmark on a bluff above the Magothy. The Girl Scouts helped to build more cabins by skinning and sawing logs in 1946 and 1947. Camp Whippoorwill added a sea wall and a boathouse in 1949.[278]

During the thirties and forties, motor launches like *Maid of the Mist* or the *Diana* ferried passengers to small beaches, pavilions, and summer camps along the Magothy, and an excursion steamer, the *William Linthicum*, stopped at North Ferry Point. Other ferry launches at that time were the *Lucy H.*, *Emma I*, and *Emma II.*[279]

A long-remembered catastrophe was the terrible hurricane of 1933. A northeaster had been blowing for several days when it became a hurricane on August 23. For 24 hours the water level was so high at Bayside Beach that it lifted a bungalow on the creek side of Southwest Road off its foundation and floated it across land to Harbor Road. The storm took away the wide beach that had extended along Bodkin Creek and revealed an old wooden barge that had been hidden in the depths of the sand. Robert Meyer, whose parents owned Knoll View adjacent to Alpine Beach, was able to take a boat from the Patapsco across what had been land to Boyd's Pond.[280]

At Pinehurst the storm destroyed the bathhouse, wrecked the pier, washed the giant sliding board ashore, felled most of the trees in the picnic grove, and flooded the parking lot with four feet of water. In Baltimore, Pratt Street and Light Street were covered with seven feet of water.[281] On the Magothy, a house floated across Gray's Creek and beached on the opposite shore.

During the night of the hurricane, Thomas J. Steinehise, the lighthouse keeper at Seven Foot Knoll, risked his life to rescue the crew of a sinking tugboat, the *Point Breeze*. At 12:30 a.m. on August 21, the captain of the tugboat fired flares and ordered the crew to abandon ship. Despite waves breaking over the craft, Steinhise lowered the station's motor boat into the

---

[278]Blaisdell, "Bloomer Girls Have Vanished," *Maryland Living*, p.4; "History of Camp Whippoorwill," William Rothamel Collection.
[279]Taylor, *My River Speaks*, pp. 173, 180-181.
[280]*Bayside Beach News*, Liz and Dennis Grimes, editors, issue 3, p.5; Robert Meyer.
[281]Robinson, "Pinehurst," *Anne Arundel History Notes*, vol.21, no.4, p.7.

water and rescued five men, taking them and the body of the tug's chief engineer to the lighthouse where he gave first aid to those who were injured. In 1936 he received the Silver Lifesaving Award for heroism.[282]

People who lived in the Jacobsville and Lake Shore communities participated in many social activities during the depression. Guests attending a gathering at the Phelps home enjoyed music, games, and refreshments served at a late hour, while a party at the home of William and Urma Cook celebrated the 18th birthday of their daughter Anne. Many parishioners gathered for a surprise pantry shower in honor of Rev. and Mrs. Melvin A. Baker on their 18th wedding anniversary. Music, games, recitations, and a large flower arrangement on the refreshment table, a gift from Schramm Brothers, made the occasion festive. For her wedding the following year, Marie Angel chose a navy blue suit with a corsage of gardenias. She and her husband, Samuel Durner, left for a boat trip to Norfolk on the *State of Maryland*. In addition, the Jacobsville School P.T.A.'s Card and Game Party in October 1937 drew a large crowd.[283]

Members of Magothy Methodist Church sponsored a strawberry festival in May, a chicken and crab cake supper in August, a turkey dinner in the fall, and a chicken and oyster supper in January. The Junior Missionary Society arranged an amateur night at the Magothy Hall in January 1937, and the young people of the church presented a play, "Aaron Slick from Punkin Creek," in February 1938. Vacation Bible School attracted forty children in July, and church members enjoyed their annual picnic at Fort Smallwood in August and Homecoming Day in October. A Christmas party on December 28 ended the year with games, singing, and refreshments. Mt. Carmel Methodist Church sponsored a Social with games and homemade ice cream and cakes in January and a fried chicken and crab supper in May.[284]

---

[282]Holland, *Maryland Lighthouses*, p. 154.

[283]*Maryland Gazette*, September 5, 1935; January 14, 1936; March 26, 1936; April 22, 1937; October 14, 1937.

[284]*Maryland Gazette*, May 21, 1936; Aug.11, 1938; May 28, 1936; Jan.7 and 14, 1937; Feb.17, 1938; July 9, 1936; July 15, 1937; Sept.5, 1935; Jan.7, 1937; May 21, 1936;.

Unusual entertainment came to the peninsula in September of 1936 and 1937 when the James Adams Floating Theater docked at Green Haven. This was the same show boat that inspired Edna Ferber to write a popular novel, *So Big.* The boat itself was a barge 128 feet long and 34 feet wide, and the shows were plays performed before appreciative audiences along the Atlantic coastal waterways.[285] The Floating Theater drew large crowds whenever it docked at the county wharf in Green Haven.

On Tick Neck, the Riviera Beach Volunteer Fire Company held a carnival from August 15 through 24 and served a supper at the Magothy Church Hall in October. The 228 members of Jenkins Memorial Church observed Eastern Star Day with a special program, flowers, and musical selections. They also hosted Homecoming in October, with services in the morning, afternoon, and evening and lunch and supper served by the parishioners, as well as a county-wide Democratic Rally and a fried chicken and crab cake supper in August.[286]

During the late thirties, the Stony Creek Whippet Club offered an unusual diversion, a dog race on a track on Fort Smallwood Road. The managers printed a schedule with the names of whippets entered in each race, and the ladies auxiliary of the Riviera Beach Fire Department provided food to raise money for their organization.[287] However, opposition to the track grew throughout Anne Arundel County. Churches members, who were opposed to gambling associated with dog tracks, called for a referendum vote and stopped whippet racing in the county in the early forties.

In the village of Pasadena in May of 1936, the Southern Methodist Church hosted a fried chicken supper and the Pasadena softball team was victorious in a double-header against Orchard Beach. In June the Pasadena Elementary School sponsored an amateur show and dance, and in December the P.T.A. presented a comedy, "The District School at Blueberry Corners," with dancing afterward. Slater Bryant, principal of the

---

[285]C. Richard Gillespie, *The James Adams Floating Theatre*, pp.234-235.
[286]*Maryland Gazette*, July 18, 1935; October 14, 1937; September 16, 1937; May 28, 1936; August 11, 1938.
[287]Brochure in the Schramm Collection.

elementary school, took thirteen boys from Pasadena to New York City for a weekend in May. They stayed at the YMCA and visited Radio City, the top of Empire State Building, the Hayden Planetarium, the Aquarium, and the Statue of Liberty, and then stopped in Philadelphia to see Independence Hall and the Liberty Bell.[288]

The burning of a ship off Bodkin Point on July 27, 1937, was a memorable event because it involved the loss of lives. About 7:20 p.m. that evening, flames suddenly erupted in the hold of the *City of Baltimore* on its way to Norfolk. Although the crew and some of the passengers manned the hoses, no water flowed. With a brisk breeze blowing, in three minutes fire swept across the deck. Captain Brooks directed the ship toward Bodkin Point, but it hit a sandbank and stuck about 500 yards off shore. The ninety passengers and the crew were forced to jump overboard to escape the intense heat. A nearby freighter and other ships sent life boats, and small craft from the peninsula helped with the rescue.[289]

Boats brought some of the passengers to Bayside Beach where residents cared for them until ambulances took them to Baltimore. Among those rescued in a small motorboat was the captain, who later was found guilty of negligence for failure to sound the general alarm quickly. By midnight the ship was a shell, two people were known dead, and another was missing. The following day residents of Pinehurst, Bayside Beach, and Bodkin Point watched as three Navy seaplanes searched for bodies near Seven Foot Knoll.[290]

During the twenties and thirties, one man was a unifying influence throughout the Pasadena peninsula. From 1919 until 1940, Raymond F. Benton had no substitute and took no sick days as he delivered mail along his entire route, then including Gibson Island. On a cold day he stopped to help a stranded motorist and did not realize that he had spilled gasoline on his hand. When he warmed his hands over a fire in his home,

---

[288]*Maryland Gazette*, May 21, 1936; May 26, 1938; May 21, 1936; Dec. 9, 1937; May 27, 1937.

[289]*Bayside Beach News*, issue 4, pp. 5-6; Robinson, "Pinehurst," *Anne Arundel History Notes*, vol.21, no.4, pp.7-8.

[290]*Ibid.*

flames burned his left hand causing permanent injury, but he continued as before with the use of only one hand.

Raymond Benton served as mail carrier until 1961. During the twenties, he drove a horse and buggy. Later, during a sleet storm, his small car slid down a hill into the edge of the Magothy where it hung against a piling. But he always delivered the mail, even in deep snow when he used a horse and sleigh. Through good times and hard times, he completed his daily rounds.[291] As the Great Depression continued, residents depended on his friendly and reassuring presence.

[291]Schramm, "History of the Pasadena Post Office, p.14.

The Depression Ends in World War

During the Depression years, black families in the community had no place to go for medical care. Children at Magothy Elementary School remembered that Annie Kess, a black midwife who lived on Mountain Road not far from Lipin's Corner, offered maternal and infant care monthly at her home. When women who worked for families on Gibson Island told their employers about their need for health care, Mrs. Curt P. Richter and her friends decided to help. She and other women in the community organized on June 30, 1938, and accepted Judge Steven Everd's offer of his empty store on Mountain Road at $2,000, a price far below the value of the property. Dr. William J. French, the County Health Officer, directed the formation of a community health unit there. This was the beginning of the Magothy Health Center.[292]

The group raised money through bake sales, dances, bingo parties, and rummage sales and then asked Joseph Groh, a Pasadena contractor, to renovate the building. He donated materials and charged only his actual cost

---

[292]"Discovering Our School Communities," Magothy Elementary School; "History of the Magothy Health Center."

for labor. Members gave furniture, painted the interior, and asked the local garden club to landscape the grounds. The first clinic for babies and children took place on August 17, 1938, at ten a.m. for white children and at one p.m. for "colored" children. By the following year, members had raised funds to purchase the land and building. Thereafter, with twenty-six doctors available at various times, attendance at children's clinics increased steadily. By 1945 members enlarged and redecorated the Center, and in 1951 supporters and staff celebrated the burning of the mortgage.[293]

Annie Kess served for decades at the Health Center that developed from the maternity clinic she started at her home. Magothy Elementary School pupils wrote that the *Afro-American* newspaper named her to their Honor Roll in 1952 for her "unusual and outstanding record." In 39 years of service to residents of the Pasadena peninsula, she delivered 1,500 babies, almost all of whom were living and in good health.[294]

Despite the continuing depression, a general store opened in Riviera Beach, a community composed largely of summer cottages. John Andrew (Smitty) Matusky started a business there in 1938 that became a neighborhood institution. He aimed to fill the needs of local customers and Baltimoreans who came to summer cottages or nearby beaches. Those visitors needed not only groceries, ice cream, sodas, and beer but also sunglasses, T-shirts, beach towels, and children's buckets and shovels. Matusky worked a sixteen-hour day for six days a week for three decades, with help from his son Andy and other family members. His store remained the only grocery store in Riviera Beach until the 1950s.[295]

On Mountain Road, an old business changed management in 1938 when Marie Angel Durner and her husband, Sam Durner, became the owners of Angel's grocery store. Marie Angel had worked in the store since she was ten years old, but she remembers the war years most vividly because of the challenge of handling rationing stamps.[296] During the

---

[293]*Mary land Gazette*, August 11, 1938; "History of the Magothy Health Center."
[294]"Discovering Our School Communities." Magothy Elementary School, 1952.
[295]Andrew J. Matusky; Tom Caines.
[296]Marie Angel Durner.

same year, Stein's store opened at East Shore Road, and Walter Phelps began to sell Gulf gasoline at his filling station nearby on Mountain Road.

In 1940 John and Marie Schollian bought Stevenson's store in Green Haven but did not change its name. Family members remember two gas pumps in front of the store and a lovely garden behind it. The Schollians built a new store on Fourth Street (now 204th) and Outing Avenue in 1946 and continued in business until 1975. Bill and Martha Connell bought the former Stevenson's store in 1946 and made it a variety store and ice cream parlor. John Novak's store stood on the corner of Catherine Avenue and Sixth (now 206th) Street.

During the early 1940s, Marie Schollian's mother, Mary Truffler, housed the first public lending library on the peninsula in her living room on West Shore Road. The Annapolis and Anne Arundel County Library

Walter Phelps' Gulf filling station on Mountain Road, 1938.
Collection of Clifford Phelps

delivered books to her regularly, and neighbors came to her home to borrow and return them. Her daughter Rita would read to local children on the lawn of their home. Rita Truffer opened the Midget Beauty Shop, the first beauty shop on the peninsula, near her sister's store. Later she owned the Village Salon on Mountain Road.[297]

The Green Haven Hash printed news of the Riviera Beach and Green Haven neighborhoods in 1939. The Riviera Beach community was waiting for a reply to their request for a post office and hoping the Board of Education would decide to build a school in Riviera Beach. Residents organized the Riviera Beach Improvement Association and celebrated Labor Day with refreshments, games, and a softball game between single and married men.

At Green Haven, people were concerned about the need for repair of the bulkhead and piling at the county wharf. Residents redecorated the Green Haven Church and made the Magnolia Democratic Club field into a good baseball park. Green Haven held fourth place in the league, and the Club had agreed to sponsor the team the next year. The community looked forward to the Potapskut Sailing Association's regatta on Rock Creek in September. Anyone could enter the races or view the finish line just off the White Rocks.[298]

The Democratic party was strong on the Tick Neck peninsula where the Magnolia Democratic Club held monthly meetings followed by refreshments and entertainment at their clubhouse. In September of 1939, Senator Louis N. Phipps spoke to the group. Frank Griffin served as president, and John Novak headed the Grounds Committee that cleared the site for their new building on Eli Cove. He advertised their waterfront property on Stony Creek as a "bargain to a quick buyer." When the club sponsored the Green Haven Carnival from July 8-17, 1940, John Novak was president and plans to build a new clubhouse continued.[299]

---

[297]Darlene Schollian Evans.

[298]*The Green Haven Hash*, vol.3, no.1. The Potapskut Sailing Association was based at Wall Cove before members moved to the Magothy River.

[299]*Ibid.*; Green Haven Carnival brochure, Schramm Collection.

The Stoney Creek Democratic Club has been a power in Anne Arundel County politics since its founding in 1938. Though the membership in these clubs was limited to men at first, women became members after World War II. Stoney Creek's 700 members are proud of their well-maintained 100-by-600-foot building on Fort Smallwood Road. Theirs is the largest Democratic club in the state and the only one to meet weekly.[300] In 1941 they supported George Schmidt to represent the Third District in the House of Delegates.

Men from a nearby community formed the Powhatan Beach Fire Company in November of 1940. Edward M. Dunn, Senior, one of the founders, served as Powhatan's Fire Chief for forty years. The Maryland Fire Chief's Association elected him to the Fireman's Hall of Fame.

Private cars and improved roads were making steamboats obsolete in 1939 when the first dual highway in Maryland (the Governor Ritchie Highway) split the village of Pasadena and made travel from Baltimore to the beaches quick and easy. The Effords' Rock Creek Steamship line had bought a steamer called the *Mohawk* in 1936 and had altered it to be an oil burner rather than a coal burner. Because shifting sand made water at the old Fairview pier too shallow for the *Mohawk*, the Effords built a new pier on the opposite side of the park to accommodate their finest steamer. Nevertheless, their business was slow.

When war began in Europe, fuel was scarce for steamers that did not carry mail or freight. The Rock Creek line sold the *Tred Avon* and the *Mohawk* and suspended operations in 1941. In 1945 the Maryland Yacht Club leased Fairview Park. When the Yacht Club bought Fairview, built slips and piers on Wall Cove, made the Fairview Hotel their clubhouse, and leveled adjacent land for a parking lot, an era had ended.[301]

With war clouds threatening in 1941, the Jacobsville community continued their customary activities in support of civic organizations.

---

[300]Lewis Frazetti.
[301]Burgess and Wood, *Steamboats*, p.184.

During February neighbors planned a card and game party for the benefit of the Magothy Health Center, and the Jacobsville P.T.A. sponsored an amateur show that was so popular that some people were turned away. The Magothy YWCA met at the Church Hall each Wednesday evening and planned events including a hot dog roast in March and a Social with games and music in April.[302]

Magothy Girl Scout Troops 24 and 25 and Brownie Pack 23 toured the Green Spring Dairy with their leader, Mary Calvert, in February. In April Girl Scout Troop 24 held an Easter egg hunt at the home of Margaret Brumwell and celebrated their first birthday at a party for troop members, parents, and friends.[303]

Magothy Methodist Church supplemented their religious services with many fund raising and social activities. The ladies of the congregation served a crab cake and chicken salad supper in April, a fried chicken supper in June, and an oyster and baked chicken supper in October. In addition to the Thanksgiving Day dinner, the Men's Bible Class at Magothy sponsored a turkey dinner in January and a Strawberry Festival in May. Adults and children enjoyed a motion picture show in the church hall during the winter, the church picnic at Mago Vista in August, and the young people's fall minstrel show at Magothy Hall, featuring Warner's stars from WCBM Radio Theater of the Air. Homecoming Day in October meant not only services at 10 and 11 a.m. and 3 and 8 p.m., but also shared meals and reunions with friends and relatives.[304]

Farther down Mountain Road, the ladies of Mt. Carmel Church served their fried oyster and turkey suppers in the church hall; the Waterman's Protective Association Auxiliary held a card and game party at Easter's Hall on Long Point; and Nathan Stinchcomb, leader of the Mt. Carmel Boy Scouts, took his troop in July of 1941 to Skyline Drive where some of

---

[302]*Maryland Gazette*, January 30, 1941; February 27, 1941; April 4, 1940.
[303]*Maryland Gazette*, February 20, 1941; April 17, 1941.
[304]*Maryland Gazette*, April 17, June 19, September 18, January 9, May 22, February 20, August 7, November 6, and October 16, all 1941.

the boys spent a week at a camp.[305] Soon gas rationing would make such outings and even trips to Baltimore infrequent.

On the Tick Neck peninsula, the Riviera Beach Girl Scout Troop formed in 1941 and a Boy Scout Troop began in 1942. The Green Haven Improvement Association sponsored a dance on May 24 at the fire hall, and the Women's Democratic Club raffled a homemade quilt as a benefit in October.[306]

The Riviera Beach Fire Company provided many opportunities for neighborhood gatherings, all at the Fire Hall except for the annual carnival held from late June through the Fourth of July each year. The Ladies

Riviera Beach Volunteer Fire Company's equipment in 1935.
Collection of Riviera Beach Volunteer Fire Company

[305] *Maryland Gazette*, November 6, 1941; July 3, 1941.
[306] *Maryland Gazette*, May 22, 1941; October 2, 1941.

Auxiliary served a roast pork and sour beef supper followed by a dance in April and held a game party each Tuesday; the Fire Company held their Anniversary Dance on May 4, 1940; the Junior Ladies Auxiliary sponsored an Amateur Show on October 19; plans featured a Halloween Dance and supper on October 26; and the Ladies Auxiliary entertained all the Anne Arundel County auxiliaries in December.[307]

Jenkins Memorial Church also offered neighborhood diversions. They served a fried chicken and oyster supper in April of 1940 and again early in December of 1941. They also presented a play called "The Old District School" in May, held their Sunday School picnic in July, and their honor class hosted an old-fashioned barn dance in November.[308]

The Woodland Beach clubhouse was remodeled in 1940 in time for an oyster roast. The Woodland Beach Fire Company planned to reorganize in October 1940, and the Woodland Beach Property Owners mourned their past-president, Dr. Thomas W. Ward, who died at his residence in Washington, D.C.[309]

In the village of Pasadena, Henry Benton had founded Boy Scout Troop 346 in 1939. Scout activities continued, and the Third District Democratic Club on Whitney's Landing Road planned a card and game party in March. The Pasadena P.T.A. sponsored a play called "Hillbilly Courtship" in April, a card party on June 3, a Halloween Dance in October, and a dance and one-act play in November.[310]

But the realities of war were about to replace dances and card parties. Earl Williams' gift to the Jacobsville School of a seven-by-ten-foot American flag and a Defense Rally at the Magnolia Democratic Club in Green Haven show that residents were aware of gathering storm clouds. An early warning came to Charles Calvert of Bodkin who received notice that he was among the first to be called into service in the U.S. Army. Sixty-two

---

[307]*Maryland Gazette*, April 18, 1940; July 3, 1941; April 4, 1940; February 7, 1941; May 22, 1941; April 18, 1940; October 3, 1941; December 4, 1941.

[308]*Maryland Gazette*, April 4; October 31; April 18; July 4; and October 3, all 1940.

[309]*Maryland Gazette*, October 10, 1940; January 23, 1941.

[310]*Maryland Gazette*, March 13, 1941; April 18, 1940; June 19, 1941; October 16, 1941; October 30, 1941.

of the young men who had spent carefree days at Grachur saw action in Europe or the Pacific.[311]

Life changed for everyone when the United States entered World War II. This was a time of total dedication to the war effort through military service, employment at defense plants, and support of gas, tire, meat, sugar, and shoe rationing. Our allies and our own country desperately needed tools of war and ships to deliver them. Unemployment had been the worry of the thirties; finding enough people to fill defense contracts was the challenge of the forties.

With Maryland Drydock, Bethleham Steel, Fairfield Shipyard, and other employers just across the Patapsco, families looking for work arrived on the Pasadena peninsula from Virginia, West Virginia, the Carolinas, and Tennessee. They often came with no more than they could carry in an old Ford and moved into former summer cottages where they discovered the wonders of electricity and indoor plumbing. Boats took workmen to defense plants across the Patapsco daily. At the Pasadena Yacht Yard, the remains of a flight of steps leading to a pier show where workmen boarded boats to go to their jobs at Sparrow's Point during World War II.[312]

These newcomers were assimilated into the community just as their predecessors had been because they shared the same basic values as many older residents. They were hard-working, honest, friendly, church-going people. Virginia Moore, who was principal at Riviera Beach during the forties, visited the homes of all her pupils. She feels that the portrayal of newcomers as ignorant mountaineers was unfair. These people were used to a simpler life far from a large city, but they were good parents who were concerned about their children.[313]

While Raymond Benton continued to carry mail to all the residents of the Pasadena peninsula, Edward Seipp had been driving a school bus and a charter bus for Clarence and Benton Johnson after graduating from high

[311] *Maryland Gazette*, March 20, July 17, and July 3, all 1941; Behm, "The Grachur Story."
[312] John Mason; Louis Doetsch.
[313] Virginia Dryden Moore.

school. He wanted to take part of Raymond Benton's route, but he had no car. After he won a car at a carnival, he became a rural carrier on June 1, 1940. Two years later he entered military service, but the Army released him for sixty days to train a substitute rural carrier. While he was in Pasadena, his outfit was ordered abroad. As a result, he spent the war years as an aircraft mechanic in Oklahoma. When he returned home, he and Benton divided the route, Seipp covering the area from Lipin's Corner to Hillman's Corner (now Pastore's) and Benton from Hillman's to Gibson Island. President Truman appointed Edward Seipp postmaster in January 1948, and he served until his retirement in 1972.[314]

Robert Christian's "Letters from Bob" column in the local newspaper told about his military service, but the war seemed close to the peninsula when a single-engine training plane plunged into the Magothy River off Swan Cove in September 1943. An army lieutenant and a private died when the plane sank in eighteen feet of water. People nearby came in rowboats to attempt a rescue, and William G. Rothamel plunged into the cold water and cut the belts that held one man; however, Rothamel was unable to free him because his foot was caught under the crushed fuselage. Police, firemen, and residents pulled the wrecked plane ashore with two 350-foot lines of rope and recovered the bodies of the pilot and co-pilot.[315]

One business that prospered during the war was William Chairs' Lake Shore Bus Company. With the gas shortage, people depended on a bus line that sent station wagons to pick up customers who lived off the regular route at places like Brumwell's Store and Long Branch. During the war, Chairs buses served twenty communities: Fort Smallwood, Sanders Park, Colonial Beach, Fairview Beach, Ventnor, Forest Glen, Pinehurst, Green Gables, Long Point, North Shore, Boulevard Park, Chelsea Beach, Magothy Beach, Beechwood Forest, Indian Village, Bayside Beach, Poplar Ridge, Clearview Village, Brookfield Road, and Tick Neck Road.[316] His buses

---

[314]Edward C. Seipp

[315]*The Sun*, September 26, 1943; William G. Rothamel.

[316]"Discovering Our School Communities," Jacobsville Elementary School, 1952.

transported more than one thousand war workers daily to shipyards and other employers with defense contracts. After 1943, this route ended at a terminal at Redwood and Liberty streets in Baltimore. By the 1950s, Chairs' ten modern buses made fifteen round trips daily along Mountain Road.[317]

Cook's Transportation Company also prospered during the war years because it often was the only way for residents of the Tick Neck peninsula to travel to and from work. Cook also used station wagons to connect off-line communities like Powhatan Beach and Green Haven with the bus line. By 1943 his office in the Esso Station across from Matuskey's store was too small, and he built a bus station and office at Matusky's Corner. Shipyard workers depended on his buses to get to work in Baltimore, Fairfield, and Curtis Bay.

One notable passenger was the beloved singer, Kate Smith, who rode one of Cook's buses from Pennsylvania Station to Fairfield Shipyard to christen a Liberty ship. Former commuters fondly remember Tucker Woods, a native of Riviera Beach, who drove for Cook in the early 1950s. Cook's buses served the community for 27 years, from 1928 until he sold the route to the Baltimore and Annapolis Railroad Company (B&A) in 1955. MTA Route 63 serves the same area today.[318]

On a breezy Easter Monday in 1944, a fire near the Magothy ranged out of control and burned 200 acres, threatening the communities of Sillery Bay, Gray's Creek, North Shore, and Boulevard Park. Residents joined the battle as 500 people fought the blaze for five hours. Despite the efforts of nine volunteer fire departments, Coast Guard units, soldiers from Fort Meade, and a large battalion of German and Italian prisoners of war, the fire burned six dwellings, four garages, a barn, a fish shed, three boats, and several automobiles.[319] Years later Jane Pumphrey Nes attended a dinner party in Salzburg, Austria, and discovered that the white-haired

---

[317]White, "Bus Service," *Anne Arundel History Notes*, 11, no.3, p.2.
[318]White, "Bus Service," *Anne Arundel History Notes*, vol.11, no.3, pp.2-3; "Discovering Our School Communities," Riviera Beach Elementary School History, pp.8-9; Sandy Anderson.
[319]*The Sun*, April 11, 1944.

gentleman seated next to her had been in command of the prisoners of war who fought the fire near her childhood home.

Residents of encircled homes at Boulevard Park had to escape by boat, and at Sillery Bay members of the Earleigh Heights Volunteer Fire Company were completely surrounded by flames for two hours. As they fought to break through, their engine caught fire and the heat was so intense that the paint cracked on the portable tanks the men carried. The Red Cross set up an emergency station with coffee and sandwiches for the men who stayed all night to put out any remaining fires.[320]

A direct result of the fire was the founding of the Lake Shore Volunteer Fire Company in 1945 with Thomas Holmes as president. The organizational meetings were held in Holmes' store, and the group soon bought a second-hand fire engine that they kept in a barn. Since the old White

Lake Shore Volunteer Fire Company's first truck, 1945.
Collection of John Williams

[320]*Ibid*.

Marsh Methodist Protestant Church had been abandoned, the auxiliary raised money from dances, raffles, card parties, and an oyster roast to buy that property. In 1945 Leo Flanigan dug the basement as his contribution, Herb Linthicum built the cinder block building with a brick front, and the ladies auxiliary, with May Wilson as the first president, furnished the kitchen. Firemen attended a training course at Riviera Beach and held a carnival to raise $1,000 for a new engine. By March of 1946, with William Harrington as fire chief, they began 24-hour service in their new white and gold fire engine.[321]

World War II ended at last in 1945. To remind the community of men who gave their lives for their country, a veteran's memorial was placed beside the Green Haven Fire Company. This memorial and the plaque naming the residents of the peninsula who served in both world wars was removed when the Green Haven Fire Company merged into the Armiger Fire Company. However, in 1993 Samuel G. Kemp, a World War II veteran, established a permanent memorial "so we will not forget." Dedicated on July 4, it stands at the intersection of Mountain Road and State Route 100. The text says in part, " Dedicated to the men and women of this community who served and who gave their all so that we can live in this land." Community groups and individuals contribute to maintenance of the memorial and periodic replacement of the flag.[322]

Once more, the peninsula faced a post-war rush to the suburbs, but this time people had cars and a road system that made daily commuting to the city easy.

---

[321]Lake Shore Volunteer Fire Company dedication brochure, John Williams Collection.
[322]Samuel G. Kemp.

Post-War Population Explosion

The rush to the peninsula that began as soon as veterans returned from World War II never has stopped. Peace, prosperity, a growing population, good cars, and good roads encouraged families who were establishing homes to move to the country. Anne Arundel County's population increased 71 per cent between 1940 and 1950, and the population of the Third District that includes the Pasadena peninsula increased at almost twice that rate.[323]

Veterans wanted to buy land, build a house, and start a family. Where else could they go that would be near city employment and near the beautiful waterfront that had been their childhood playground? Because lack of labor during the war had made farming difficult, many farmers were willing to subdivide their land or sell to developers. The stage was set for population growth at a pace far ahead of local government planning, and the struggle to balance an owner's right to develop his land with stability of the environment was about to begin.

---

[323]McWilliams in Bradford, *Anne Arundel County: A Bicentennial History*, p.8.

Sale of properties at some waterfront developments had been slow during the depression years and had stopped during the war when gas was rationed and building materials were scarce; now building resumed at a frantic pace. Robert Christian worked to open new sections in the woods at Green Haven. He used a Willys Jeep to remove stumps of trees he felled to make room for homes. By putting logs together, he made a drag and laid out roads to 15th Street (now 215th Street) and then put a weight on the front of his jeep to grade the streets. When children gathered to watch, he promised them a ride in the jeep if they would stay out of his way while he worked.

After Robert and Marie Christian married in 1946, he built a log cabin on 13th Street where they lived happily for two years without electricity or running water. Marie Christian remembers hearing about one Sunday afternoon when there were only two cars on Outing Avenue, and they managed to run into each other. She also recalls her husband's tales of the young people's A T and L (All Tired and Lazy) Club. Founded by Henry Wittig, who also started the Green Haven baseball team, members served as security police and as lifeguards at the wharf, in addition to planning parties and dances. All the people in Green Haven were friends. When anyone called for help, the entire neighborhood responded. Since Charles Christian was busy as the publisher of the *Southern Maryland Times* and the *Maryland Gazette*, his sons Robert and Thomas L. Christian managed the real estate business at this time.[324]

Rapidly growing Green Haven organized a fire company in 1947 with Milton Behm as president. In 1949 the company built their first fire house and bought an old fire truck. The Ladies Auxiliary sponsored various activities to raise funds for improvements, including the purchase of a pumper in 1952 and an ambulance in 1956. Members of the community formed the present Green Haven Improvement Association in 1955, while

---

[324]Marie Christian.

Young ladies of the Pastime Club that met for sewing, talking, and refreshments, c. 1950. In the background is the Deitmiller home, one of the first five homes in the village of Pasadena.
Collection of Emma Jenkins Wade Sanders

The Green Haven Ladies Club enjoying a trip to New York in 1948.
Collection of George Kelch

the High Point community had organized their Improvement Association in 1952. High Point sponsored an annual Christmas party and worked to get street lights, street signs, and other community improvements.[325]

Though the Green Haven-High Point area grew exceptionally fast, signs of growth and progress were everywhere. Many communities like Venice on the Bay, North Shore, and Rockwood Beach began with a few summer homes before the war. In the post-war years, families built permanent homes. These were neighborly places where people knew and helped each other. Rockwood was named for the white rocks at the mouth of Rock Creek and for Fort Smallwood. Beginning with three beach houses in 1942, this tightly-knit neighborhood of 86 homes is typical of beachfront communities on the peninsula.[326]

A new concrete and steel bridge over Stony Creek that opened for traffic in 1948 made Baltimore seem closer than before. The old one-way drawbridge had been rebuilt in 1925, but it had become a bottleneck, especially whenever a yacht passed through the draw. On Christmas Eve, 1948, the State Roads Commission opened a concrete and steel bridge at a cost of $963,141, including the approach roads.[327]

Many farmers who once had supplied Baltimore with fruits and vegetables had to sell their property for development, pursue other business interests, or find a new use for their land. The ever-resourceful Schramms made this adjustment. In 1944 William Schramm (grandson of Louis) graduated from high school and began to raise turkeys. Two years later, he and his brother Louis started Schramm's Turkey Farm with 5,000 birds. By 1970 they were raising, dressing, and selling 12,000 broad-breasted turkeys each year.

In 1948 the family opened a small roadside stand on Mountain Road to sell vegetables and flowers. When they found that they could make a greater profit from retail sales there than from selling flowers wholesale,

---

[325]"Discovering Our Communities," High Point Elementary School.
[326]H.J. Morgereth.
[327]"Discovering Our School Communities," Riviera Beach Elementary School, pp.8-9.

they built a permanent roadside stand and combined raising turkeys with growing vegetables, fruit, and flowers for retail sale. Emma Schramm (who had taught at Jacobsville School from 1948 until 1965) and her cousin Evelyn Schramm joined Emma's brothers, William and Louis, as full-time partners in the business in 1965.[328]

The Klingelhoefers and some other local farmers adapted to the post-war farming situation in a different way. Alfred Klingelhoefer owned a farm on Fort Smallwood Road, and his brother Walter owned 154 acres on the west side of Mountain Road where Maryland Route 100 now ends. Instead of truck farming, they planted tobacco; however, they did not cut, strip, and market the crop but sold it in the field. Walter Klingelhoefer

The Stony Creek Bridge in November 1946.
Photo: News-American. Collection of Jacques Kelly

[328]Schramm, "Sixty Years in Anne Arundel County."

Schramm's turkey farm in the early fifties.
The Schramm Collection

apparently was the only Anne Arundel County farmer who raised and marketed 51 acres of asparagus. He added a platform to the front of a jeep to transport asparagus from the field to a packing shed where it was trimmed and tied in bunches. Despite the continuing shortage of farm labor, this venture was successful.[329]

Eckhardt Jubb, whose farm later was bisected from Waterford Road to the Schramm property by State Route 100, was one of the farmers who planted tobacco in 1948 when growing vegetables was no longer profitable. He still sold corn, tomatoes, cantaloupes, and watermelons to customers who came to the peninsula for the weekend and patronized his stand on Outing Avenue. Eckhardt Jubb had owned a school bus as early

Asparagus packing shed at the Walter Klingelhoefer farm in the early 1940s near the intersection of Route 100 and Mountain Road.
Collection of Dolores Klingelhoefer

[329]Dolores Klingelhoefer; Charles H. Calvert; James B. Calvert.

as 1937 and had transported soldiers between Fort Meade and Baltimore during World War II. After the death of his wife in 1951, he bought four more school buses. This business proved so successful that he eventually owned thirty buses, and the county bought part of his former farm to use as a school bus terminal.[330]

Robert Bottomley, who had retired from farming, real estate, and other business interests in 1931, sponsored contests in the schools to encourage children to develop skills. In those days of gender stereotypes, he gave a prize to the boy who built the best birdhouse and a prize to the girl whose sewing was judged best. During the 1940s, he visited Jacobsville

William Eckhardt Jubb and Lucy Hancock Jubb's farm in the 1950s. State Route 100 later bisected the farm.
Collection of Ann Jubb Dick

[330]Ann Jubb Dick.

School each year and showed the children some of the 3,000 Native American artifacts that he had collected locally.[331]

With increased population, local communities needed more schools. In 1944 Riviera Beach Elementary School opened, and Charles M. Christian gave land for an athletic field in High Point where the Board of Education was building a school. Completed in 1945 at cost of $74,000, the one-story brick High Point School had eight classrooms. The P.T.A. raised funds to provide a movie projector, duplicator, slide projector, playground equipment, and encyclopedias.[332] Previously children in High Point and Green Haven had attended the overcrowded Jacobsville School.

---

[331]*Maryland Gazette*, 1957; Emma M. Schramm.
[332]"Discovering Our School Communities," High Point Elementary School.

High Point School served as a junior high school for three years until George Fox Junior High opened in 1948. The new school was named for the Superintendent of Schools from 1916 until 1946. During George Fox's tenure, 54 modern buildings had replaced 80 poorly-equipped small schools. Thereafter, the High Point area grew so rapidly that the Board added five classrooms, an office, a cafeteria, and a gymnasium in 1957. In 1946 the Board of Education added a third room to Magothy Elementary School beside Mt. Zion Church, a school attended by black children.[333]

Increasing population led Lutheran and Roman Catholic churches to join the early Methodist churches on the peninsula. A Lutheran congregation in Orchard Beach began when Mrs. Evelyn Brach and five helpers found forty families who were willing to meet in the fire department hall

George Fox Junior High School, the first on the peninsula built as a junior high, 1947.
Photo: Blue Moon Aerial Photography

[333]Katharine M. Kibler in Bradford, *Anne Arundel County: Bicentennial History*, p.118.

Emma Schramm and her 43 second grade pupils at Jacobsville School, 1949. As a new teacher in 1948, she taught 48 children.
The Schramm Collection

for worship services while they raised funds for a building. Members of Emmanuel Lutheran Church of Stony Creek held their first service in their own building on May 29, 1949. During the next five years, they added space for a Sunday School and ten stained glass windows designed by Leonids Linauts, an artist whose studio was in Pennsylvania. In 1982 this congregation became Emmanuel Lutheran at Riviera Beach.[334]

In 1946 St. Jane Frances de Chantel Catholic Church became a parish with Father Raymond Kelly as the first pastor. Just two years later, three sisters of Notre Dame opened a parochial school there. Their school hall seated one thousand people. The Chelsea Community Church, now Lutheran, began with Sunday School classes in the Magothy Beach Community Hall in 1948. Supporters raised funds to build an interdenominational church in 1950 and held their first service in 1951.[335]

---

[334]Nancy Quasney; Emmanuel Church Directory.
[335]"Discovering Our School Communities," Jacobsville Elementary School, p.16; Riviera Beach Elementary School, p.10.

Saint Jane Frances de Chantel Roman Catholic Church
Collection of William E. Harris, Jr.

In the late 1940s, Faith United Methodist Church evolved from an early Sunday School and community church in Green Haven. That congregation organized formally as Green Haven Methodist Church in 1949. In 1952 the Magothy Methodist Church Hall housed not only Sunday School classes and youth and women's groups, but also two Girl Scout troops, a Brownie Scout troop, a Boy Scout troop, and a Sea Scout troop.[336]

In 1945 the Maryland Yacht Club, founded in Baltimore in 1908 and quartered at Broening Park near Hanover Street Bridge after 1925, leased the Fairview property from the Effords with an option to buy. Between 1945 and 1956, the Maryland Yacht Club at Broening Park closed when summer quarters at Fairview opened and reopened in the fall. Six

[336]"Discovering Our School Communities," Riviera Beach Elementary School, p.10.

thousand yachtsmen, friends, and neighbors attended the dedication of the Club's summer quarters on June 16, 1946. In 1948 the club began to sponsor an annual event, the crowning of the Queen of the Chesapeake. Each year princesses representing yacht clubs around the Chesapeake Bay compete for this honor at a colorful ceremony.

By 1956 air and water pollution forced the Maryland Yacht Club to leave Broening Park and buy the Fairview property, where they built slips and piers on Wall Cove and converted the old Fairview Hotel into their clubhouse. As early as 1947, wives of members had formed an organization called the Galley Slaves. Any wife or sweetheart of a member could join this group and wear their yellow cap with a cookpot insignia. In 1956 a Ladies Auxiliary formed to help the Club financially. Their Shipwreck Party and Fashion Show were popular events.[337]

Long before most people were conscious of the importance of the environment, two groups on the peninsula addressed the need for conservation. Charles Pumphrey organized and became the first president of the Magothy River Association in 1946. In June of 1947, a group of men formed the Stoney Creek Fishing and Hunting Club, Incorporated. Their purpose was to encourage and stimulate interest in fishing, boating, and hunting and to engage actively in conservation of fish, game, and other natural resources.[338]

With increasing population, D.C. Strain built homes at Lake Shore and Lyndale, while others began new commercial ventures. By 1947 Florence Gable had opened Gable's grocery store on the corner of Mountain and Brookfield roads, and the Lake Shore Volunteer Fire Company brochure listed forty-four advertisers including restaurants, a bakery, a florist, two beauty parlors, two barbershops, and two hardware stores. The Riviera Pharmacy provided prescriptions, sodas, sundaes, and cigars, while Wirth's New Modern Fountain sold milkshakes, sandwiches, and baby

---

[337]Harold E. Fink, "Our History" (an account of the Maryland Yacht Club), pp.1,9,10,14, 14,17, 20-21.

[338]Jane Pumphrey Nes; Articles of Incorporation, Stoney Creek Fishing and Hunting Club.

and sickroom supplies. Customers needing electrical work or plumbing and heating could find help at D.C. Strain and Son or at Fred Kaatz's Anne Arundel Electrical Service, both at Lake Shore. Combining different types of business, Easter's Pavilion on Long Point sold seafood, beer, and electrical appliances, while Daubert's Marine Railway rented boat slips and repaired motors but was also a restaurant and tavern.[339]

At Riviera Beach in 1942 Elizabeth Frisino transformed the old farmhouse that belonged to the Thomas family into a resort hotel called Locust Lodge. Her endeavor prospered for thirty years. Despite several additions to the original home at Meadow Road and Main Avenue, original details like some fishscale shingling remain. The main part of the building consists of two gable-roofed two-story structures, connected by a flat-roofed section. The columned one-story porch is partially enclosed. Nearby are Thomas family graves dating from 1821 to 1887.[340]

Two other new businesses began at this time and prospered. Louis S. Doetsch, one of the young veterans who came to the Pasadena peninsula in 1945, remembers when the land around his Pasadena Yacht Yard was all woods, and there was much open space near Riviera Beach. More than fifty years later, the Pasadena Yacht Yard is still an active business. William Stallings opened a Betholine station at Mountain Road and Disney Avenue in 1947. After he added hardware, the business became Dunlap and Stallings. He then began to sell insurance at the store and from the home he built across the street. That building housed Nationwide Insurance and later became the Lee Stallings Funeral Home.[341]

When Fran Koslowski Hasse and her husband, Robert Dickson, opened a business called Tall Oaks in 1949, her neighbors were Sanders Park (where Brown's Grove had been), Pat and Bill's Tavern, Danny's grocery store, and the old Colonial Beach Hotel on Rock Creek. Tall Oaks previously had been Reamer's, a grocery store with a beer license, but Fran and

---

[339]Lake Shore Volunteer Fire Companyt brochure, 1947.

[340]"Charles Madden, "Locust Lodge," Riviera Beach Improvement Association Newsletter, November, 1994; Maryland Historical Trust Historic Sites Inventory AA-730.

[341]William Stallings.

Two ladies at Kelch's Confectionery in Green Haven, 1948.
Collection of George Kelch

Aerial view of Pasadena Yacht Yard taken in 1961. The Pasadena Yacht Yard was founded in 1948 by Louis S. Doetsch.
Collection of William E. Harris, Jr.

her husband changed its appearance by removing two of the interior walls the day they bought it. Early days were difficult for a 27-year-old woman starting her own business in a sparsely populated area. "I was scared," she recalls, "because I mortgaged my mother's house and this one to the gills." When people wanted sandwiches with their beer, she drew up a modest menu and began to cook. Her crab cakes sold for 35 cents, but fried chicken cost 95 cents. She continued to sell groceries when she started her restaurant with six tables and 24 chairs.

In 1952 Fran Hasse added 110 seats for her customers. Five of her old oak tables came from the Colonial Beach Hotel. "In order to survive, I had two dollar parties," she remembers. On Friday evenings and Sunday afternoons, the restaurant filled with customers who would bring a guitar and play the piano and sing. Many of these people still visit her and enjoy her famous stuffed softshell crabs. Not only are the customers faithful; most of her employees have stayed for decades. Wayne White, chef for 35 years, says, "It's like a family here. Miss Fran is very good to me." Nancy Loughry, waitress and cook for 25 years, adds, "You start here and you never leave. Everyone cares for one another." Vicky Dickson, Mrs. Hasse's daughter-in-law and co-owner explains, "She's so good to everybody. People just love her. She's a very giving woman." That is the reason that Tall Oaks is a survivor today.[342]

When decorated veteran Ray Kenny returned from World War II, he worked as a refrigeration and air conditioning mechanic at Maryland Drydock for a few years before opening a furniture and appliance store on Fort Smallwood Road in 1950. Four years later, he moved Pasadena Furniture to its present location on Mountain Road. During five decades this business has built a loyal following. Customers who have moved out of the state return to buy furniture there. Though Ray Kenny, Senior, still serves

---

[342]Fran Dickson Koslowski Hasse, *Maryland Gazette*, June 26, 1999.

as president of the company, Ray Kenny, Junior, is general manager and two of his children are active in the family business.

Another post-war venture had unforeseen results. Though slot machines were legal in the United States only in Nevada and four counties of southern Maryland during the 1940s, Anne Arundel County approved eleven licenses for slot machine distributors, including three with addresses on the Pasadena peninsula. By the end of the decade, pinball machines, console slot machines, and "one-arm bandits" were everywhere — at beach resorts, restaurants, drug stores, and even grocery stores. When the machines produced large profits, the license holders began to exert increasing influence on Anne Arundel County officials.[343] In response, citizens' groups organized to work against slot machine interests and for more responsible government

Positive changes in the community at this time included the organization of three service clubs. George Schmidt, a member of the Glen Burnie Rotary Club, proposed forming the Lake Shore Rotary Club in 1947. He, along with Al Corey and Fred Kaatz, began a recruitment drive that led to founding of the chapter on December 2, 1947, and Charter Night on January 28, 1948. With Fred Kaatz as the first president, the club met initially at the Mt. Carmel Church Hall and has continued to meet there for over fifty years. The women of the church serve the Rotary dinners in teams of four. In a short time, the Lake Shore Rotary Club organized Boy Scout Troop 473, added to the Magothy Health Center, and raised money for community service projects. During the fifties, they maintained a loan chest at the Magothy Health Center where people could borrow crutches, walkers, or wheelchairs.[344]

On December 11, 1947, the Riviera Beach Lions Club held their Charter Night at Matusky's Supper Club. The 28 charter members included Louis Bookhultz, president, Doctor J. Brady Smith, vice president, Father

---

[343]Charles F. Kirkley, Report of the Committee to Study the Effects of Legalized Gambling in Anne Arundel County, May 1960, pp.6, 13-14.

[344]"The Rotary Club of Lake Shore: A Celebration of 50 Years of Service, 1947-1997."

Raymond P. Kelly, and Rev. Charles S. Harrison. The Club became the East Anne Arundel County Lions Club in the early fifties. Albert Ramsay, the oldest surviving member, recalls their service to people with limited vision over the decades. In addition to national projects including the Lions Association for Sight and Hearing, the Lions Vision Research Foundation at Johns Hopkins University, and the Leader Dog for the Blind School in Michigan, they contribute locally to the Salvation Army, Goodwill, and Boy Scouts. They also provide Christmas baskets, hearing aids, and eyeglasses to families in need and give annual scholarships to students at Chesapeake and Northeast high schools.[345]

On March 31, 1948, Edward Seipp founded the Pasadena Rotary Club and served as its first president. The club met first at the Pasadena Methodist Church and later at Riverside Restaurant. Membership remained small until the club disbanded about 1975. Most of the members joined the Severna Park Rotary Club.[346]

When Dr. Breit retired in 1948 and Dr. Randall McLaughlin took over his practice, Dr. Brady Smith in Riviera Beach and elderly Dr. Gaalas on Bodkin Neck were the only other medical doctors between Glen Burnie and Annapolis. Dr. McLaughlin bought four second-hand chairs to furnish his waiting room, his wife painted an instrument cabinet that Dr. Breit had left in the basement, and he was ready for patients during morning and evening office hours. In addition, he was available to anyone who knocked on his door at any hour of the day or the night. A stranger to the area, Dr. McLaughlin had to make house calls daily "to every nook and cranny" on Hog Neck and far beyond. To save valuable time when he answered an emergency call, he identified the nearest point that was familiar to him. Then he asked the caller to meet him there.[347]

Though steamers no longer brought excursionists to waterfront resorts, large numbers of people returned to favorite beaches each summer or

---

[345]Albert and Edith Ramsay.

[346]Robert Bartlett; "Discovering Our School Communities," Pasadena Elementary School, p.9.

[347]McLaughlin, "Memories of the Anne Arundel Years," *Anne Arundel History Notes*, 28, no.4, July 1977.

patronized new places like Pasadena Beach, Sunset Beach, and Belhaven Beach. The hotel at Belhaven is a marina now. Five family-owned resorts were close to the mouth of the Patapsco: Alpine, owned by the Milburn family; Knoll View, by Carolyn Meyer; Pasadena, by her son, Robert Meyer; Maryland, by the Grantlin family; and Kurtz's, still owned by the Kurtz family. Young men wearing suits, ties, and straw hats and young women in long dresses and white gloves came there to dance on Saturday evenings. From 1936 until 1950, Kurtz's offered an additional attraction, a two-lane bowling alley.[348]

Local people came to these beaches during the week, but Saturday was the day that churches from Baltimore and as far away as Laurel, Towson, and Mt. Airy brought busloads of people for their annual Sunday School picnics. They arrived with picnic baskets filled with fried chicken, potato salad, and homemade cakes and spent the day swimming, playing games, and socializing. Sometimes a hundred buses would create a terrible traffic jam as they all returned home along narrow county roads at the end of the day.[349]

The Rev. Hiram Smith, a Baptist pastor who opened a resort called Beachwood in 1948, was the most courageous of the new resort owners. Despite the usual restrictive covenants against black ownership, he bought land on the upper Magothy adjoining a small resort called Beechwood Forest and, with the help of his children, cut trees, cleared the land, and advertised Maryland's finest interracial beach and amusement park. His advertisement shocked the community and resulted in attacks in newspapers, many mean-spirited acts, and a lawsuit. While the lawsuit was pending, the Supreme Court ruled that states could not enforce restrictive covenants.

Many black churches hired buses to take their members to Beechwood for recreation and religious services. Among the attractions were picnic

---

[348]Hope Meyer; John Mason.
[349]Hope Meyer.

tables, boating, crabbing, fishing, and a small amusement park with a ferris wheel and a little merry-go-round that children pedaled with their feet. In addition, three motor launches, the *Elsie*, the *Deborah*, and the *Beechwood Park*, took passengers down the Magothy as far as the totem pole at Camp Whippoorwill. Boats anchored along the Magothy to watch whenever Rev. Hiram Smith led a line of white-robed candidates for baptism into the water.[350]

Throughout the fifties, when many beach resorts closed, Beachwood's two parking lots were filled with hundreds of cars and buses. Corporate groups like Black and Decker, Westinghouse, and Waverly Press arranged picnics for their black employees there because it was the only place where white managers were welcome too. Since Hiram Smith was a member of the Neptune Yacht Club, that group held their picnics at Beechwood. Patrons treasure memories of visits from Joe Louis and Jersey Joe Walcott. Across the road was a Girl Scout Camp called Whispering Pines where black Girl Scouts enjoyed a program including swimming and crafts.

After buying Beechwood Forest and two homes on adjoining land, Rev. Hiram Smith owned eighty acres. Later, he sold property to two black doctors from Washington, D.C., Dr. Saunders and Dr. Singleton Hughes. When Franklin Owens bought there, he became the first local black owner of property on the Magothy. Though Beechwood survived later than most resorts, the end came in the early sixties when easy access to the ocean, private pools, and other amusements made local resorts obsolete.[351]

Because many taxpayers could not enjoy the city's fine bathing facilities at Fort Smallwood Park, seven black Baltimoreans filed a segregation suit in the U.S. District Court in 1950. When Judge Calvin Chestnut ruled that the segregation policy was unconstitutional, the city responded by opening the park to black Baltimoreans on the last ten days of each month.

---

[350]Gerald A. Smith, son of Rev. Hiram Smith.
[351]Ibid.

The District Court ruled that this also was unconstitutional. The city then divided the beach into black and white areas, and attendance declined.[352]

During the early fifties, *The Sun* reported that thousands of Baltimoreans were sweltering while a nearby 100-acre resort with a white sand beach, playground, bathhouse facilities, 416 picnic tables, and a 1,152-foot pier were abandoned. The lack of patrons, officials said, was partly the result of confusion "as to the allocation of days for whites and Negroes. This plan has been abandoned, and the park is open to both races seven days a week." The article adds, "Separate bathing facilities are provided for Negroes on the river side of the park." Finally, in 1956, two years after the Brown vs. Board of Education decision, Fort Smallwood Park was integrated.[353] By this time, beach resorts were in decline. Though large numbers of Baltimoreans would move to the peninsula in succeeding decades, the beaches were no longer the magnet that attracted them.

---

[352]Maryland Historical Trust Historic Sites Inventory AA-898.
[353]*The Sun*, July 28, 1953; Maryland Historic Trust Historic Sites Inventory AA-898.

Growth Brings Changes

As more and more people moved to the peninsula during the 1950s, older residents sometimes longed for the days when the entire area had been rural farmland. Dr. Randall McLaughlin recalls many small farms in 1948 when he arrived in the community "before the onslaught of housing developments and mini-malls." Except for families who came there only in summer, residents knew almost everyone who passed by. During the next two decades, trees were felled, roads were widened, and crossroads became shopping centers. The venerable county commissioner form of government was not prepared to solve problems caused by uncontrolled growth. Without zoning laws or other controls, growth was haphazard, and citizens' groups began to demand an adequate water supply, proper sewage disposal, and long-range planning.

Just as the Pasadena peninsula had played a part in earlier wars, the region was called on again during the Cold War. Fear of Soviet long-range bombers led the U.S. Army's Antiaircraft Command to plan a line of defense around Baltimore and Washington that included a large Nike station on the Klingelhoefer farm, formerly Robert Bottomley's land, on Fort Smallwood Road. By 1952 the Army had activated gun batteries there which later were converted to missile batteries, called the ultimate defense. In 1957 the Army Air Defense Command replaced the Antiaircraft Command, and the Maryland National Guard thereafter took over five Nike-Ajax sites including Fort Smallwood. In December 1962 the Fort Smallwood Nike station was deactivated because the Russians were no longer relying on manned bombers and because missiles had proved less deadly than gun batteries in Vietnam.[354]

Despite the Cold War, community life continued as usual. The end of passenger service on the Baltimore and Annapolis Railroad in 1950 marked the triumph of the gasoline engine over the railroad as well as the steamer, but it had little effect on the peninsula beyond the village of Pasadena. Both a Men's Democratic Club and a Women's Democratic Club were active there in the 1950s.[355] In 1952 the Lake Shore Democratic Club organized with women as charter members and full participants. On Cockey Creek, the 191 members of the Grachur Club continued to celebrate Labor Day each year with sailing, canoe races, softball, volleyball, and ping-pong tournaments.

Milton Norris and Murray Sheetenhelm prepared the Kiwanis Club of Mountain Road for Charter Night on January 29, 1952. President Warren G. Eyerly and Vice President Isadore Hillman led the group of 25 members. They sponsored Kids Day at the old Jacobsville School with 1,000 children attending; provided free-loan hospital beds, wheelchairs, canes, and crutches; and arranged for Santa to visit five local schools to give candy canes to the pupils. At first Santa arrived by airplane or helicopter, but members later built a motorized sled to take him from school to school. The Kiwanis Club now sponsors an essay contest in ten elementary

---

[354]Merle T. Cole, "Fort Smallwood's Military Mission," *Anne Arundel History Notes*, 15, no.1, pp.6-7, 9-10.

[355]"Discovering Our School Communities," Pasadena Elementary School.

The causeway at Gibson Island covered by water and rocks during the hurricane of 1952.
Collection of Tom Feeley

The parking lot near the Pinehurst pavilion during the hurricane of 1952.
Collection of Tom Feeley

schools, gives scholarships at Northeast and Chesapeake high schools, and helps families in need, serves disadvantaged children, and assists senior citizens with health problems.[356]

During the fifties activities continued at the Maryland Yacht Club. The old cottages and the picnic tables from Fairfield days were gone, but a new pier, concrete walks, a caretaker's cottage, and a pool replaced them. By 1950 sixteen teams made up the Yacht Club bowling league. The Junior fleet, formed in 1952, enjoyed sailing the Catfish they were given in 1958. The Ladies Auxiliary began to hold their popular International Dinners as a fund raisers in 1956. In 1958 the club charged visitors from $1.75 to $3.25 for dinner, and slips were free unless boats stayed more than two days.[357] By 1957 the Bodkin Yacht Club on Main Creek was operating from a marina, but in 1962 members bought and remodeled a former tavern to use as their clubhouse.

Though teams existed before the fifties, the founding of the Riviera Beach Little League in 1953 increased peninsula residents' enthusiastic support of children's teams. While Don Kerr played for the Baltimore Browns, an Oriole minor league team, he saw boys playing Little League baseball in Pennsylvania where Little League began. When he returned to Riviera Beach, he organized four teams at eight-to-ten age level and four teams from ten to twelve years of age. This was one of the earliest Little Leagues in Maryland and the earliest sports organization still playing on the peninsula. Acting as their equipment manager led John Bartolomeo to start a well-known business called Bart's Sporting Goods.

In 1958 Ed Heaphy, Earl Collison, Ray Oliver, John Reina, Bill McDonald, and D. Logan organized a football club called the George Fox Buccaneers. Their playing fields at High Point Elementary School and George Fox Junior High School were not lighted, but parents circled the fields with their cars at dusk and turned their headlights on to provide

---

[356]John Wilson, Jr.; "Discovering Our School Communities," Jacobsville School.
[357]Fink, "Our History," pp.18-22.

light. Coached by Ed Heaphy, in their second year the Buccaneers won their first county championship with an undefeated record.[358]

Gus Serio, Hoy Clodfelter, and Ray Berger coached baseball teams that played at Lake Shore Elementary School before Vernon Oaks became the first president of the Lake Shore Little League in 1959. He fielded one 12-and-under travel team. Soon Ed Shenks, Gus Serio, and John Fallon were coaching four teams.[359] The Lake Shore Athletic Association formed in 1962.

For the small percentage of residents of the peninsula who were black, the important changes in the fifties were related to the end of segregation in public schools. During the twenties and thirties, the Board of Education had built schools with plumbing and electricity for white children,

The 14-to 16-year-old Green Haven Jets football team in 1949.
Collection of George Kelch

[358]Joe Brockmeyer.
[359]Gretchen Smith

but black children at Magothy and Freetown elementary schools continued to attend classes in old buildings with coal stoves, outdoor toilets, no electricity, and no janitorial service. Those who wanted to attend high school had to ride a bus to Bates High School in Annapolis, the only high school in Anne Arundel County for black pupils. Few changes had been made to the Magothy School since it opened in 1926, except for the addition of a third room in 1946, but the Johnsontown community supported the school faithfully.[360]

The Supreme Court decision on integration resulted in the closing of Magothy Elementary School near Mt. Zion Church in the mid-1950s. During the transition, older black residents remember community meetings where white speakers said that the black schools had wells and therefore did not need indoor plumbing. At public hearings, black parents refused the promise of a new four-room school and demanded the same facilities available to white children.[361] Thereafter black children on the peninsula attended the Jacobsville Elementary School.

Aware of the need to unify in order to improve their community, Sherman Bouyer, John Coats, George Caldwell, Sr., and the Rev. Charles Pearman (grandfather of Judge Clayton Greene, who was born and reared in Freetown) organized the Freetown Improvement Association in 1954.[362] The Association petitioned the Board of Education for an adequate school building, instructional materials equal to those available in schools for white students, and an equal teacher-pupil ratio. Anne Arundel County had built schools to serve the growing communities of Lake Shore in 1953 and Pasadena and Riviera Beach in 1955. Remodeling Lake Shore Elementary followed in 1958, and children in Freetown finally attended a new elementary school in 1959.

Churches on the peninsula also were growing. In 1954 members of the venerable Magothy Methodist Church began to raise funds for an education

---

[360]"Discovering Our School Communities," Magothy Elementary School.
[361]Louis P. Brown.
[362]*The Sun*, September 29, 1996.

building and bought almost three acres behind the church for an outdoor chapel. The stone pulpit and benches in the woodland, an inspiring place for worship, were the inspiration of the pastor, Ernest R. Twigg. The Men's Club did most of the construction, and the congregation began to hold 8:30 a.m. worship services there on Sundays during the summer. Soon thereafter the congregation began a long-term ministry to the deaf. Members sponsored a weekday kindergarten in 1957, laid the cornerstone for their education building that year, and established a library in 1958.[363] Mount Carmel Methodist Church built a large addition to their education building in 1955.

Reflecting the growth of the western end of the peninsula, in rapid succession Pasadena Methodist Church built a parsonage in 1954, bought property on Ritchie Highway south of their old church in 1956, welcomed their first full-time pastor in 1957, consecrated their new brick church on Ritchie Highway in 1958, and broke ground for a Fellowship Hall in 1962. By 1968 the church had 1302 members and 1003 registered in their Sunday School.[364] Also in the village of Pasadena, the Assembly of God made a major addition to their building in 1961.

Episcopal and Baptist churches came to the peninsula in 1958. In May St. Andrews Episcopal Church on Tick Neck Road opened its doors, and Lake Shore Baptist Church began as a mission of Grace Baptist Church at Sunset Beach. The congregation met at Lake Shore Elementary School before building their own church in 1959. After becoming independent in 1963, they moved to their present home in 1964 and remodeled their former church to use as a parsonage. When they built a parsonage in 1970, the old building became the Sunday School.

As further evidence of the community's growth, the Pasadena Post Office advanced to first class on July 12, 1958, and Riviera Beach became the first area to qualify for city delivery on May 16, 1959. City delivery meant

---

[363]James B. Calvert; Pritchett, "History of Magothy Methodist Church," pp.9-10, 30.
[364]Brown and Heckman, "History of Pasadena Methodist Church."

door to door mail delivery in government-owned vehicles, replacing private cars that stopped at mailboxes on property lines. Riviera Beach became a classified branch on December 4, 1961, but Lake Shore, established as a rural branch in 1952, was not named a classified branch until 1969.[365]

Among the new businesses in the fifties were drive-ins, places where people could order food and eat in their cars for the first time. Young people especially enjoyed this novelty. Brookwood Farms (on the northwestern tip of the peninsula where Mountain Road now leaves the Ritchie Highway) was the first to sell ice cream and milkshakes to young men lucky enough to have a car and a date. Another Brookwood Farms store soon opened on Fort Smallwood Road opposite the present Community United Methodist Church. In the 1960s, it became Lee's Drive-In.

With no pharmacy nearer than Glen Burnie, in 1954 Dr. Maurice Cummings and Bob Baxter opened Village Drugs at 2932 Mountain Road. They supplied the community with prescriptions, health and beauty aids, greeting cards, school supplies, boxed candy, and photo service, while their soda fountain offered sodas, sundaes, milkshakes, and hot and cold sandwiches. Hours were nine a.m. through ten p.m. seven days as week, with free home delivery. In 1969 Bob Baxter bought the store and changed its name to Bob's Village Drugs. He sold the business in 1986, but it continues as the Pasadena Pharmacy. One employee, Charlotte Smith, began to work at Village Drugs in 1957 and still is employed by its successor in 2000.

Dr. McLarity opened the Lake Shore Pharmacy at 4530 Mountain Road about 1955. Village Drugs bought that building and operated a pharmacy there until 1968. For part of that time, the building housed a postal substation. In 1969 Bob Baxter bought this building also and renovated it to serve as the Lake Shore Branch Post Office until the new Pasadena Post Office on Mountain Road opened. In 1989 the building was renovated

---

[365]Edward C. Seipp, Pasadena postmaster, 1947-1972.

Village Drugs, 2932 Mountain Road. Two additions were made to the original store on the left, built in 1954, before it became the Pasadena Pharmacy in 1986.
Collection of Robert Baxter

Lake Shore Pharmacy, 4530 Mountain Road, built in 1965.
Collection of Robert Baxter

again to meet the specifications for a day care center called "All God's Children."[366]

Businesses that were active during the fifties, in addition to older firms, included Fred Jones' Garage in Green Haven, George (Bud) Meidel's welding business on Old Annapolis Road, George Schmidt's stone work and sea walls, Evard's Lumber Company at Green Haven, and Barlen Motors on Mountain Road.[367] William Klug died in 1952, and Klug's added a modern Esso Station in 1954. Lewis Frazetti remembers opening a barber shop with two chairs in Riviera Beach in 1956. This shop has six chairs today, though it no longer offers one dollar haircuts. In 1959 Sam and Marie Angel Durner sold Angel's store to Andrew Godwin. Though he planned to change its name, customers insisted that the store was called Angel's.

Continuing to grow steadily, the Chairs bus line offered fifteen round trips to Baltimore daily in 1956. William Chairs owned ten modern buses, including Fords and Marmon-Herringtons. He sold the Lake Shore Bus Company to the Baltimore and Annapolis Railroad Company in 1960. After 1973, the Mass Transportation Administration continued this service as Route 17.[368]

While many businesses prospered, most of the beach resorts were in trouble. When the Bay Bridge opened in the early fifties, former beach patrons could reach the ocean in a few hours. Others had their own pools, free of the new worry about water pollution. Families could choose among many diversions, and a trip to the beach was no longer anticipated with excitement. Marginal business owners depended on slot machine revenue and risked losing their independence when slot machine distributors held notes or liens on their restaurants, taverns, and resorts.[369]

After searching for a location for radio transmission equipment to be used for ship-to-shore calls, the Chesapeake and Potomac Telephone Company bought three acres on the Bodkin peninsula on April 11,1955.

---

[366]Robert Baxter.
[367]Receipts in Schramm Collection.
[368]White, "Bus Service," *Anne Arundel History Notes*, 11, no.3. p.2.
[369]WJZ-TV (channel 13) editorial, 1960.

At that time, they acquired a cemetery rich in history. The Company honored their agreement to maintain the cemetery, resetting the tombstones and building a fence around 21 marked graves. Trevor Kiessling states that "the burials in Bodkin Neck Cemetery cover the most important fifty years of the history of the peninsula, from 1822 to 1872." Buried there are Captain John Gray, born in 1771, and members of the Cook, Dunbar, Welch, and Rockhold families.[370] With new technology for ship-to-shore calls, the transmission tower is no longer needed and the future of this cemetery where founders of the community rest is in doubt.

The Riviera Beach Volunteer Fire Company continued to grow in the 1950s and received many citations and awards. They added a third engine in 1954, and, by the late 1950s, a new rescue truck and the first fire truck in the United States to convert to diesel fuel. After winning several state championships, in 1964 their six-man Rescue Squad, led by Captain Edwin Raynor, won an international competition in Florida. Edwin Raynor Boulevard is named for this Riviera Beach fire chief who died after having a heart attack while fighting a fire.[371]

During the 1950s, while the population of Anne Arundel County grew by 75 percent, the county commissioners struggled to manage growth without long-range plans for zoning, better roads, proper sewage disposal, and relieving overcrowded schools. Citizens groups protested decisions made behind closed doors and worked to replace the commissioner form of government with charter government and a trained county business manager. Businessmen on the peninsula recall that getting permits to build or expand during the fifties was difficult without "passing money" to the right person.

By 1958 the Grand Jury reported that "the extent to which gambling has been permitted to flourish in Anne Arundel County is a matter of grave concern to many citizens of this county." Slot machine owners,

---

[370]Kiessling, "Bodkin Neck: Gateway to the Patapsco," pp. 2,3,21, Appendix I.
[371]History of the Riviera Beach Volunteer Fire Company; Gladys Rowens.

including those who had machines in taverns, restaurants, resorts, and grocery stores on the peninsula, were taking at least ten or fifteen million dollars a year from Anne Arundel County's economy without providing products, services, or capital improvements. The syndicate, as the license holders were called, was spending large sums to support candidates for public offices. In the 1958 county election, they contributed at least $50,000 to candidates who voted to keep them in business. Concerned citizens knew that ending the increasing power of the syndicate and replacing the outdated county commissioners system with charter government would be a hard-fought struggle.[372]

---

[372]Grand Jury Report, p.10, in the Kirkley Committee Report, pp.11-12; Kirkley Committee Report, pp.10-11. This estimate doubtless was conservative. As the *Washington Post* reported on April 26, 1960, "profits are jealously guarded secrets." Estimates ran as high as fifty million dollars annually, according to the *Arundel Observer*, June 25, 1959.

Meeting and Solving Challenges

The 1960 Census clearly shows the tremendous growth of the Third Election District of Anne Arundel County, including the Pasadena peninsula. In 1940 the population of the District had been 10,938; in 1950 it had increased to 26,319, making it the most populous district for the first time; by 1960 population had more than doubled again, reaching 58,992. Of this total, 54,637 people in the Third District were white and 4,355 or 7.4 per cent were non-white. Estimates of projected population growth were 98,000 in 1970; 142,000 in 1980; and 218,000 in 1990. The old County Commissioner form of government was not prepared to handle such rapid expansion.

A major problem was the increasing influence of gambling interests on the economic and political life of the community. In 1960 the Citizens Committee of Anne Arundel County presented a petition with 5,000 signatures to the state legislature, asking for a referendum to let the people decide whether gambling should be legal. This proposal divided the community when owners of stores, restaurants, taverns, and resorts circulated petitions against a referendum. Attached to those petitions was an erroneous statement that taxes would be increased by forty cents on the dollar without slot machine revenue. Fliers carrying messages like "Save Your Home" and "Protest Higher Taxes" urged people to sign petitions against a referendum.[373]

The *Sun* and WJZ-TV supported the proposal for a referendum, citing the Kirkley Committee Report's claim that gambling had attracted professional racketeers to the county and that the eleven slot machine license holders' tremendous influence over elected officials retarded the county's economic growth. During 1961, three of the eleven slot machine license holders were in court charged with assault on a restaurant owner with a lead pipe, firing shots inside a restaurant, and using force to repossess a restaurant the license holder had sold. Many voters did not want these men to have influence over elected office holders.[374]

After a hearing on February 28 for about 300 citizens in favor of a referendum on legalized gambling, a separate hearing was planned for opponents. An ad in the *Evening Capital* called on fraternal organizations, fire companies, and tavern and restaurant owners to attend because the referendum "would abolish all coin-operated machines that mean so much to your business or your organization. Your livelihood is at stake."[375] Though the referendum asked only for a vote on the issue of legalized gambling, taverns on the Pasadena peninsula and elsewhere closed from six until ten p.m. on March 2, 1961, "to protest higher taxes." Slot machine owners provided 32 buses to take over one thousand people to the State House to oppose a referendum. The proposal for a referendum failed. *The Sun* reported attempted bribery of public officials, reprisals against legislators who had supported the referendum, and the "appalling control" slot machine owners had over legislators.[376]

---

[373]Kirkley Committee Report, p.16; Supplement, "Events Since May 1960," pp.1-2.
[374]Kirkley Committee Report, pp.3-5, 10-11; Supplement, pp.3-4.
[375]*Evening Capital*, March 1, 1961.
[376]Kirkley Report Supplement, p.2; *The Sun*, April 17, 1961.

Despite widespread concern about unprecedented growth and the power of gambling interests, life on the peninsula continued to be pleasant. When Raymond F. Benton retired from the postal service in 1960 after having served residents faithfully for forty-one years, the entire community joined in honoring him at a surprise testimonial dinner. More than one hundred people came to the Lake Shore Volunteer Fire Department Hall where William Stallings of the Lake Shore Rotary Club presented a gift and Edward C. Seipp, postmaster, gave him a framed certificate of recognition from the United States Post Office.[377]

A bequest that saved *Hancock's Resolution* for future generations benefitted the community at this time. When John Henry (Harry) Hancock died in 1962, his generosity and foresight provided that the old stone house called *Hancock's Resolution* and ten acres of surrounding land would be given to an appropriate historical society to be chosen by his executors. Built about 1783, this one and one-half-story native sandstone house with a gambrel roof is a rare example of an 18th century stone dwelling. Since Harry Hancock and his sister, Mary Adeline (Mamie), had lived in their family home all their lives without modernizing it in any way, the house and grounds offered an ideal opportunity for study and for use as an historical site. In 1964 Historic Annapolis took title to the property.[378]

Two new schools brought changes in the mid-sixties. The 1964 Jacobsville Elementary School that replaced the 1926 building housed more than 800 pupils in 24 classrooms. It was located across Mountain Road and farther east than the old school. Though this was a modern school at that time, former pupils remember large classes and no art or music rooms. Art teachers wheeled a cart filled with supplies from one classroom to another. Girls wore dresses and dress shoes to classes, but they carried tennis shoes and wore shorts under their dresses on the two days a week that they had gym classes.[379]

---

[377]*Maryland Gazette*, November 3, 1960.
[378]Donna Ware, "A Self-Guiding Brochure."
[379]Debbie Smigovsky.

A seven- passenger 1915 Paige touring car at Hancock's Resolution in 1965.
Collection of Charles H. Calvert

When Northeast Senior High opened at Duvall Highway and Fort Smallwood Road in 1964, young people no longer needed to leave the peninsula to attend high school. Northeast not only became the first senior high school to serve the Pasadena peninsula but also the first air conditioned school in the county system. Built at a cost of three and one-half million dollars on a 35-acre site, the school had a capacity of 2,000 and an auditorium that seated 1,000 people. In addition to 39 classrooms, the new building contained an administrative suite, conference rooms, laboratories, counseling rooms, a student publications workroom, a cafeteria, a large and a small gymnasium, a health clinic, a library with study carrels, and two large teaching alcoves connected to the auditorium.[380]

[380] *Evening Capital*, September 23, 1964.

Two new churches also reflect the growth of population on the peninsula. The Chesapeake Christian Center Church of God on Tick Neck Road began as the Pasadena Church of God in 1963. Today they emphasize a strong youth ministry. Members of the Galilee Lutheran Church met in Lake Shore Elementary School before they built their church on Mountain Road in 1964.

When worshipers at the Community Methodist church in Riviera Beach outgrew their pink church, the congregation built a stone church with a classroom wing on Fort Smallwood Road. On Easter Sunday of 1963, 691 people attended their first worship service in their new home. The former sanctuary became a fellowship hall when the congregation added a large sanctuary in 1993. This church cherishes its traditional commitment to service to the community and response to human needs.[381]

Some changes to the business community came during the sixties. In 1963, after the death of John Wilson, Senior, his son John operated Wilson's service station. As the community grew, he remodeled the building and added bays, providing more space for inspection and repairs. This business has given many local young people their first jobs. Norman Huffman, who started to work there at the age of sixteen, is still employed at the station decades later.[382]

In 1968 Les Rizzo bought the old Hillman store on Mountain Road at Hog Neck Road and began to operate it as Pastore's Italian Grocery. Les and Marge Rizzo and their family lived over the store. They had only two employees, but they stocked shelves with many types of olives, seventeen kinds of cheese, rigatoni, manicotti, and linguine, as well as lasagne and spaghetti. Their local customers did not know what to do with these foods, but the Rizzos taught them how to use them. Marge Rizzo sold home-made pizza kits years before other stores carried pizzas. In addition, Italian families came to Pastore's from as far away as Brooklyn and An-

---

[381]Gleim, "History of Community Methodist Church."
[382]*Maryland Gazette*, July 18, 1998.

The Three B's Bakery, already a landmark in the sixties.

Collection of Laura Wiegmann

napolis. The Rizzos treated their customers like members of their family. When they brought their baby home from the hospital, their parking lot was jammed with people waiting to see her.[383]

The building of Route 100 in 1964 proved to be a mixed blessing. Though it cut like a knife slash across the peninsula and enabled traffic to move quickly toward the end of Mountain Road, it encouraged development near the tip of the peninsula. Eventually, severe traffic congestion resulted as construction continued along a dead-end route, creating a nearly insoluble problem.

Citizen groups awaited the November 3, 1964, election eagerly because they had been working for years to replace county commissioner government with more efficient charter government. A Charter Committee headed by retired Judge Benjamin Michaelson spent six months writing a proposed charter that provided for the end of local laws made at closed meetings, a merit system, long-range planning, and responsible government. The proposal passed in 1964 and took effect in 1965, the beginning of a period of transition. After voters adopted the charter, the Magnolia Democratic Club disbanded. Also in 1964, with wide support from citizen groups throughout Maryland, a state-wide effort to abolish legalized gambling in Southern Maryland succeeded.

With the change of administration in Anne Arundel County came an increased awareness of the importance of conserving open space. The County purchased Lake Waterford Park in 1965 and opened it to the public as the county's first park in 1966. Located at the intersection of Pasadena Road and Waterford Road (State Route 648), this land had been the site of the old Magothy Mill and successive water-powered gristmills. The 68-acre tract included a twelve-acre lake. When the Maryland Historical Trust reviewed the property, they identified a fieldstone foundation for a mill, millstones, and other artifacts. Since that time, the county has

---

[383] *The Sun*, September 6, 1987.

developed the site, stocking the lake with catfish, bluegill, bass, and trout, and providing tennis and basketball courts, ball fields, and picnic areas.[384]

Lake Waterford Park became the home of the Pasadena Chargers football team, known first as the Pasadena Crusaders. In 1968 Kenneth Bohn, Sr. and Loren Van Brackel started the Greater Pasadena Touchdown Club with the goal of providing a football program for boys eight to sixteen years old. Using their own funds at first, they eventually fielded six teams, from a 75-pound clinic team to a 140-pound county team. The program was open to all at no charge. Many people gave time and funding to make this effort a success. By 1974 over 250 boys and 50 cheerleaders were registered. Some boys have gone on to All-County high school football and others have played NCAA college football. In addition to physical conditioning and developing skills as players, participants learned character, fair play, teamwork, and respect for others. The Touchdown Club has dedicated its fieldhouse to the memory of Kenneth Bohn, Sr.[385]

When the George Fox Buccaneers football club faced difficulties in 1963, Ed Heaphy and other parents met to reorganize as the Buccaneers Northeast Pigskin Club. The Buccaneers added basketball that year and Cheerleaders in 1964. John MacIsaac started wrestling a few years later. In addition to the established Buccaneers and Little League in Riviera Beach, parents met in 1967 to draw up a charter and by-laws for the Riviera Beach Girls' Softball League.[386]

The Lake Shore Athletic Association formed in 1962 and eventually added Spartans basketball and football to their Little League program. In 1966 the Lake Shore Democratic Club helped the teams by paying for equipment and uniforms. During the next year, the Looper family gave the baseball teams the use of a tract of land on North Shore Drive. Looper Field was their home until 1994 when they moved to Woods Road. In 1967 or 1968, Lake Shore Little League became Lake Shore Youth Base-

---

[384] *Maryland Gazette*, May 4, 1967; The Sun, April 8, 1979.
[385] Jeanne Bohn.
[386] Joe Brockmeyer; Robert Boyd; Brent Lounge.

Lake Waterford before the dam was built in 1991.
Photo: Blue Moon Aerial Photography

ball when they affiliated with Pony Baseball and played by Pony rules instead of Williamsport rules. Also in 1967, Gus Serio sponsored a handicapped league that played at Downs Park.[387]

Beginning in 1958, residents of the peninsula could enjoy another type of recreation at the Shore Drive-In on the south side of Mountain Road not far from Armiger Drive where Sagamore Road is now. Floyd T. Necessary, who had been a coal miner, managed the Drive-In for Ritz Enterprises and showed first-run moving pictures there. In addition to a parking lot for 500 cars, the Drive-In offered a playground for children and a snack bar where the Necessary family sold hot dogs, hamburgers, soft drinks, and popcorn. In addition to hired help, Tommy, Patricia, and Sharon Necessary worked in the kitchen, snack bar, and box office and kept the playground and parking lot clean.

When a popular movie was showing, traffic backed up as far as Schramm's farm while cars waited in line to enter the parking lot for the first or second show. People still remember when a Disney movie, "That Darned Cat," caused a monumental traffic jam. Everyone wanted to leave as soon as the movie ended, but this was impossible on summer weekends when Mountain Road was crowded with people returning from the beaches. Then Mr. Necessary or one of his children would operate a red light that stopped cars on Mountain Road long enough for twenty or thirty cars at a time to leave the Drive-In. The business closed in 1973 when the cost of renting first-run movies became too high to make a profit.[388]

Despite much evidence of growth, the Pasadena community remained as neighborly and supportive as ever. When Al Klingelhoefer was injured seriously in a car accident in 1965, his friends in the Lake Shore Rotary Club knew that he was concerned about his tobacco crop. They cultivated the young plants, and the Riviera Beach Volunteer Fire Company used their pumper to fill the tank on his planter to water the tobacco. When it

---

[387]Gretchen Smith.
[388]Sharon Necessary Ranagan.

Maud Weaver, cashier, and Floyd Necessary, manager, in the snack bar at the Shore Drive-In theater, 1959.
Collection of Sharon Necessary Ranagan

flowered, his friends sold the crop in the field.[389] After his death, his family leased the Klingelhoefer farm for use as a riding stable.

Also during the mid-sixties, the Green Haven community united to oppose the sale of their public wharf to a local businessman. At a hearing, a spokesman for the Army Engineers joined Robert Christian and other community leaders in asking the county to disapprove the sale.[390] Though many county-owned landings once used by local residents have been sold, the Green Haven community fought successfully to retain their wharf.

On land that originally had been a part of Green Haven, Chesapeake Homes developed a 70-acre community called Havenwood. Havenwood began as an experimental housing project built under the Equity Down Payment (EDP) plan that allowed original owners to do finishing work on their homes and receive credit toward their down payments. Despite initial skepticism, this proved to be an excellent plan. Harry Magaha, who bought the third house in the development in August of 1964, recalls that the area (from 214th to 220th streets) was woods with just a trail to his home. By 1966 homeowners formed the Havenwood Community Association that sponsored Christmas parties into the seventies. Smaller adjacent communities like Green Haven Forest joined the Association and were collectively called Havenwood. Now all are a part of the Green Haven Improvement Association.[391]

Memories of the 1960s are as varied as the people who are remembering. Growing up near Magothy Bridge, Debbie Smigovsky recalls her family catching rockfish two or three feet long and neighborhood boys selling a dozen freshly-caught crabs to neighbors for a dollar. Near Waterford was Frank and Regina's, later John's Place, with a cement floor and pool tables, a popular spot for young people. Families drove to the Safeway at Severna Park for groceries before Lauer's Super Thrift opened. For general

---

[389] James B. Calvert; Charles H. Calvert; Henry Schmidt.
[390] Marie Christian.
[391] Harry Magaha; Tom Caines.

shopping, the nearest store was Grant's and the nearest drug store was Read's, both in Severna Park. For her, these were the good old days.[392]

Robert H. Burgess returned to Rock Creek in 1966 to find his former peaceful anchorage filled by piers. Instead of forests where wildlife roamed, in Wall Cove he saw a shipyard, marine railway, slips, and covered boat storage. He recalled anchoring in the quiet cove near a spring that supplied clear water. In the sixties, the area reminded him of the scene along "our highways, which have been bulldozed and cluttered by indiscriminate building." To him, the changes were tragic.[393]

Whether development of the peninsula was considered a gain or a loss depended on the beholder, but residents generally agreed that they benefitted from charter government after 1965 and adoption of a comprehensive zoning plan in 1968. Though these changes did not solve the problem of rapid growth, they did slow the rate of growth. Haphazard expansion ended and ramshackle sheds and trailers disappeared. Applicants for permits to build had to attend hearings that sometimes lasted for eight hours, but now there was a fair process to follow. As the sixties ended, more efficient government was assured.

---

[392]Debbie Smigovsky.
[393]Robert H. Burgess, "I Remember Rock Creek," *The Sun*, July 24, 1966.

Progress During the Seventies

Though residents of the peninsula were proud of the advances they made in many areas during the seventies, they were aware of water pollution as a major problem. During the early sixties, local fishermen could catch quantities of bass and trout, and a day's fishing in the Chesapeake Bay would yield enough white perch for the whole neighborhood to enjoy a fish fry. Families had crabbed off their piers, using hand lines and chicken necks or fish heads to catch three bushels of crabs in a day.[394] Water pollution ended these activities in the seventies.

Older residents recalled the clear blue-green waters of the creeks and rivers when vacationers washed their sheets in the Magothy. But boaters who were not thinking of environmental damage flushed waste and dumped beer bottles and other trash into the rivers and creeks. Much more serious was industrial waste that polluted the rivers and the Chesapeake Bay. After pollution killed underwater vegetation, the wide white sand beaches became victims of resulting erosion.

---

[394]Debbie Smigovsky.

Despite this problem, the seventies brought positive changes to the Pasadena peninsula. John Mason, manager of Kurtz's Beach, remembers one store in the area during the fifties, almost no one living there during the winter, few schools, no sidewalks, and no banks until Maryland National opened a local branch. In contrast, during the seventies planned development produced more tax dollars and resulted in better schools, libraries, sidewalks, improved roads, and businesses where residents could find a wide variety of goods and services. Furthermore, upwardly mobile new residents became an asset to the community.[395]

Among the changes in 1971 were a fine library and professional archaeological excavation at *Hancock's Resolution*. When the Riviera Beach Library opened in 1971, it replaced a small library on Fort Smallwood Road that had served the community since 1964. The 1971 archaeological study at *Hancock's Resolution* concentrated on the quarter acre surrounding the house and revealed new information about that site.[396]

The Riviera Beach Volunteer Fire Company recorded forty years of service to the community in 1971. A tragedy had occurred the previous year when several firefighters were injured and John Balcer lost his life in an accident as the company responded to a fire. Despite this loss, they continued to purchase new equipment and were one of the first four companies in the county to have a floodlight unit. By 1979 they acquired a 36-foot Coast Guard boat that they converted for fire fighting and rescue operations. They soon added a second vessel to their marine division and then a 3,500-gallon tanker, built with donated equipment and the labor of members.[397]

The Fort Smallwood Optimists received their charter in 1972 and immediately began to carry out their motto, "Friends of Youth." Members from a wide area still work with sports teams, send a youth to the Freedom Foundation each year, give scholarships to local high school

---

[395]John Mason.
[396]Donna Ware, "Self-Guided Tour."
[397]"History of the Riviera Beach Volunteer Fire Company."

graduates, and honor an outstanding boy or girl at each of the local high schools on Youth Appreciation Day. Women have been full members of the Optimists organization since 1972.[398]

Sports remained a major interest during the seventies when St. Jane Frances Catholic Church sponsored soccer for boys and girls of all denominations on their playing field. In 1972 the Havenwood Little League formed and the Pasadena Clinic League branched from the Riviera Beach Little League. Also in 1972, Andrew Gray and Robert Hall, members of the sponsoring Optimists, founded the Fort Smallwood Baseball League. At the eastern end of the peninsula, the Lake Shore Athletic Association's activities included Youth Baseball, Girls Softball, Pasadena Soccer Club, and Mountain Road Soccer League.[399]

Riviera Beach Little League team, the Mud Hens, c. 1970.
Schramm Collection

[398]Rosemarie Billing-Briggs.
[399]Robert Boyd; Brent Lounge; Rosemarie Billing-Briggs.

The Buccaneers football team, 1971.
Photo: Ed Vinson

The Little League Opening Day Parade crossing Stony Creek bridge, 1970.
Photo: Ed Vinson

Out at Second, Riviera Beach Little League baseball, 1970.
Photo: Ed Vinson

Head First into Third, Riviera Beach Little League baseball, 1970.
Photo: Ed Vinson

In 1972 the Patapsco River Power Squadron, which had been based in Baltimore since 1917, moved to Riviera Beach. With Louis Doetsch as commander, in 1973 they rebuilt an old building to serve as their headquarters. Originally adults benefitted from their program that included seamanship, piloting, and celestial navigation. Since training now is mandatory before young people can operate a boat, volunteers from the Patapsco River Power Squadron teach a basic boating course for novices under the supervision of the Department of Natural Resources. Graduates receive a certificate qualifying them to operate a boat legally.[400]

New schools, as well as Lake Shore's promotion to the status of a classified post office in 1969, reflect the rapid growth of the Pasadena peninsula at this time. When the federal government gave the 28-acre former Nike battery site to the Board of Education, the Board requested $440,000 in the county capital budget for Fort Smallwood Elementary School. But the funding was denied, despite the efforts of the local Parent-Teachers Association. In 1966 the principal, Cornelia Heptinstal, supervised pupils attending classes at the old Jacobsville School and in the Magothy Church Hall. The following year, despite the continuing protests of parents, their children were housed in the former Nike administration building and a barracks-like building a quarter of a mile away, near the missile silos.[401]

Without funding in the budget, the Board of Education ordered furnishings for the school, but the County Commissioners stopped deliveries by getting an injunction. Then the Circuit Court ruled that $29,000 could be transferred to the school from the capital budget. The County Council appealed the Circuit Court decision and passed a resolution forcing the Board of Education to sue the county government to obtain those funds. The School Board responded by filing suit against the county for funds that, they believed, had been illegally deleted from the budget.[402]

---

[400]Louis Doetsch.
[401]*The Sun*, August 22, 1967; Cornelia Anderson Heptinstal.
[402]*The Sun*, August 22, 1967.

Fort Smallwood Elementary School opened with makeshift furniture from other schools. The principal, Helen Becker, recalls having the first three grades in the barracks, which was divided into classrooms, and grades four, five, and six, as well as the office, cafeteria, and library, in the administration building. In order to conform with the building code requirements for safety, the Board of Education built steps to the windows in the classrooms, and pupils climbed from the windows when they had a fire drill. Food had to be transported from the cafeteria to the second building, and the younger children rode in a small bus from the barracks to the big school bus that stopped at the main building. After the parents realized that they had lost their struggle for a new school, they rallied to build playgrounds for both buildings and provided equipment and extras that the school lacked.[403]

Bodkin Elementary School opened in 1970 and Sunset Elementary in 1971. Riviera Beach Elementary School was renovated the same year. By 1973 High Point Elementary School was so crowded that the Board of Education tore down the original eight classrooms in order to build a completely new school behind the old school. The principal, Eileen Zindell, recalls that children attended classes in double sessions in the 1957 addition to the old school until February 22, 1975, when the new school opened and the 1957 building was demolished.[404]

In 1976 the Board of Education built Chesapeake Middle School and Chesapeake Senior High on the property of George Jenkins and John Ellison, despite community protests that the complex was too near the tip of the peninsula. Its location has complicated traffic problems there ever since. In 1977 Fort Smallwood School at Poplar Ridge replaced the school at the Nike battery site, which became the service department for Anne Arundel County Board of Education vehicles.

---

[403]Helen Becker.
[404]Eileen Zindell.

Chesapeake Senior High School, built in 1976.
Photo: Blue Moon Aerial Photography

Residents of the peninsula also saw changes to roads and churches. To relieve traffic, in the late seventies the county constructed the first phase of what later became Edwin Raynor Boulevard to connect Magothy Bridge Road with Mountain Road. After a new congregation worshiped in a rented building for three years, in 1973 they built the Magothy Seventh Day Adventist Church near Magothy Beach Road and State Route 100. In 1979 they changed their name to Pasadena Seventh Day Adventist Church. The Mt. Carmel congregation added a narthex, choir room, and air conditioning to their church and reconsecrated it on May 15, 1977.

In 1974 a group of women organized the Long Point Garden Club. Members still meet monthly at Long Point Hall, but today they represent many adjacent communities. Their projects encourage beautifying neighborhoods, as well as conserving nature's plant resources[405].

In an effort to speak with a united voice, communities along Mountain Road joined to form the Greater Mountain Road Council in 1975. With the support of activist Shirley Murphy, in 1980 the organization expanded to include the entire peninsula and became the Greater Pasadena Council, an umbrella association for forty neighborhoods. Representatives of many more communities continue to meet monthly to discuss civic issues like zoning, roads, schools, and the environment for the benefit of all.[406]

New commercial ventures during the seventies were too numerous to list. Two that are thriving today are Lauer's Super Thrift and Locust Lodge, an assisted living facility. In 1974 Lauer's filled a need in an area where there were few stores after Matusky's closed in 1970. The Lauer stores at Chesterfield Plaza and Riviera Plaza offer meats, produce, a bakery, a deli, and even video rentals. About 1972 Elizabeth Frisino was among the first to provide assisted living for the elderly when she transformed her Riviera Beach hotel into a facility for seniors. After she retired at 85, her niece, Dolores Rocklin, became manager. Locust Lodge is licensed for twenty residents. A smaller building houses patients with Alzheimer's who need special care.[407]

An old business faced and overcame difficulty at this time. Andrew Godwin's daughter and son-in-law, Joyce and Tom Clocker, had been the owners and managers of Angel's store since 1971. In the fall of 1976 a fire that destroyed the store shocked the community, but Tom and Joyce Clocker rebuilt and reopened in March 1977. Since that time, they have enlarged the new Angel's store twice.[408]

---

[405]Katherine Haines.
[406]Carolyn Roeding; Joseph Foran.
[407]Madden, "Locust Lodge," Riviera Beach Improvement Association Newsletter, November 1994.
[408]*Maryland Gazette*, May 20, 1998.

Angel's Store when Andrew Godwin bought it from Marvin and Marie Angel Durner, 1959.
Collection of Joyce Clocker

Fire also threatened another venerable institution. After rebuilding four piers and repaving the parking lot, members of the Maryland Yacht Club were enjoying a Labor Day cruise to St. Michaels in 1975 when they received news that their clubhouse had burned to the ground during the night. Even their trophies won during the previous fifty years had melted. Despite an insurance settlement, in 1976 the Club signed a twenty-year mortgage in order to build a new clubhouse and bathhouse at a cost of $250,000. The crowning of the Queen of the Chesapeake continued each June. Yacht Clubs including Ventnor, Bodkin, and White Rocks, as well as clubs outside the area, choose a princess to compete for this coveted title.[409]

The Chesapeake Woman's Club, organized and federated in 1977, promotes the welfare of residents of the Pasadena peninsula. Their public service includes working for a branch library in Lake Shore where they serve as volunteers. Their annual fashion show and luncheon raises funds that enable the club to support the Youth Art Fund, Save the Bay, and

---

[409]Fink, "Our History," Maryland Yacht Club, p.23.

displaced homemakers. Members also help high school students in need of support. Recently the club received a first place award for community service in statewide competition.[410]

In 1977 Anne Arundel County acquired 231 acres adjacent to Pinehurst for a county park at a cost of nearly two million dollars. Owned in colonial times by Charles Carroll of Carrollton, this property later belonged to Henry Dunbar. August Schmidt farmed 150 of those acres from 1887 until 1913. A Baltimorean, H. R. Mayo Thom, bought the property he called Rocky Beach Farm in 1913 as a summer home. He remodeled and enlarged the farmhouse to twenty rooms and installed a generator to provide electricity. His family's many guests enjoyed the formal Victorian garden, a gazebo, a bathhouse on the waterfront, and seven cottages to

The garden side of the Thom house as it appeared in the 1920s.
Collection of Downs Park , Rick Holt, Superintendent

[410]Joan Valenti.

house relatives and friends. Later these cottages were rented to summer vacationers. The Bishop family of Baltimore became the next owners in 1937. Thousands of people now enjoy this property as Downs Park.[411]

The seventies were a time of many advances that resulted from available tax dollars, a result of more efficient charter government. Residents of the peninsula enjoyed more and better schools, a second library, and a splendid new park, as the Greater Pasadena Council worked for the common good of all communities on the peninsula. Yet rapid population growth continued to cause problems.

---

[411]Marie Angel Durner, "Early History of Downs Park," *Anne Arundel History Notes*, vol.15, no.2 (January 1984):2, based on Richard Holt's research on Rocky Beach Farm.

Living in a Crowded Eden

The problems of water pollution and shore erosion grew worse during the early 1980s, and residents became increasingly aware of the damage that their priceless creeks and rivers had suffered. They could fish all day near the mouth of the Magothy and not catch anything. In 1908 Folger McKinsey had celebrated Magothy beaches, "the white length of them . . . curving and wonderful . . . blue waters rimming them . . . wild lilies brimming them . . . round the green vistas of oak and of pine." In August of 1984, a headline announced "Sewage Closes Rock Creek," while in June the newspaper reported, "Officials Take Tour of the 'Dead' Magothy River," quoting a biologist who said, "I think the river is shot. There's just too much development going on."[412]

Help for the rivers and creeks came in 1984 when the General Assembly passed the Critical Areas Act designating all land within 1,000 feet of the Chesapeake Bay and its tidal tributaries as a Critical Area. Water quality and marine life there would be protected by regulations. The Critical

---

[412] *The Sun*, July 22, 1908; *Maryland Gazette*, August 8 and June 23, 1984.

Area Commission also restricted building within a Limited Development Area or cutting trees and removing natural vegetation within a 100-foot buffer zone measured from the mean high water mark. In 1988 Anne Arundel County adopted similar regulations with provisions for enforcement and periodic revision thereafter. By this time, the Clean Water Act passed by Congress in the sixties had made some improvement in the condition of creeks and rivers. Nevertheless, a newspaper article called Rock Creek "a creek on the rocks." Residents said that the water began to turn color in 1978 and that pollution had "choked the life out of the creek."[413]

In contrast to this discouraging news, on July 2, 1982, the county opened Downs Park to the public. There residents could take advantage

Downs Park
Photo: Marion Warren

[413]*Maryland Gazette*, May 1, 1988.

of many recreational opportunities, as well as the natural beauty of 231 acres on the Chesapeake Bay. Visitors of all ages could enjoy picnicking, fishing, or hiking and biking trails. Active sports included tennis, basketball, handball, softball, volleyball, and pitching horseshoes. A children's play area, the shaded perimeter trail for joggers and bicyclists, and a nature trail offered a wide choice of activity. For quiet contemplation, others could seek one of the two bay overlooks or the restored Victorian Mother's Garden. In addition, patrons could rent pavilions or hire the Chesapeake Room for meetings.[414] At the Information Center, visitors with an interest in history could view the collection of artifacts and old photographs that Rick Holt, Park Superintendent, has assembled.

Population growth continued to bring improved roads. Magothy Bridge, built about 1920, was rebuilt in 1980, and a third lane was added to crowded Mountain Road about 1983. The county completed the second section of Edwin Raynor Boulevard north of Mountain Road and dedicated it in memory of former Riviera Beach Fire Chief Edwin Raynor on May 25, 1986. In his memory, at the end of the dedication the fire company paraded its equipment along the length of the new highway, with Mrs. Edwin Raynor riding in the Rescue vehicle.[415]

By the mid-eighties the peninsula's oldest park, Lake Waterford, hosted 100,000 visitors a year. In 1984 a $400,000 building program made possible four tennis courts, two baseball fields, improved trails, and picnic pavilions. Deborah Yeater became the first full-time superintendent in 1987.[416] In 1988 the community joined in planning a playground to be funded and built by volunteers. Designed by children from High Point, Pasadena, and Folger McKinsey schools and funded in part through the children's "Pennies from Heaven" drive, the playground was financed as well by dances, raffles, and contributions from fraternal organizations and businesses. Eighteen months of planning ended in five days of intensive

---

[414]Downs Park brochure, Department of Recreation and Parks.
[415]Betty Raynor.
[416]*Maryland Gazette*, June 16, 1984 and April 23, 1988.

A 1983 reunion of young people who grew up in Green Haven. In the background is the Green Haven Volunteer Fire Company's firehouse.
Photo: George Kelch

construction when an open field became a playground, a dream achieved through the joint efforts of a community known for support of its children.[417]

Young people on the peninsula continued to be involved in team sports. By the early eighties, the Buccaneer teams, Riviera Beach and Havenwood Little Leagues, the St. Jane Soccer League, and the Pasadena Clinic League had affiliated with the Riviera Beach Recreational Council. By 1984 Lake Shore Girls Softball, Youth Baseball, Fort Smallwood Optimists Baseball League, the Pasadena Soccer League, and the Mountain Road Soccer Club affiliated with the Lake Shore Recreational Council where Richard Hare served thirteen years as president of the Council until Tom Owen succeeded him. In 1985 the Mountain Road Wrestlers began as the Chesapeake Cubs.

---

[417]*Maryland Gazette*, April 23 and August 17, 1988; May 10, 1989.

Not affiliated with the councils but quite active were the Pasadena Chargers and the Riviera Beach and Havenwood Girls Softball teams.

With strong support from the community, the Recreational Council successfully petitioned the county for funding for a playing field; later the county provided for construction of the Lake Shore Athletic Complex. The complex consisted of fields where boys and girls from seven to fifteen years of age played baseball, soccer, lacrosse, and girls field hockey. In 1984, when the Coca-Cola Company sponsored Youth Olympics, Coach Richard Hare recalls that Lake Shore won a bronze medal in soccer in mid-Atlantic regional competition.[418]

During the eighties, families also supported new churches that joined those already serving the peninsula. The Emmanuel Lutheran Church congregation at Orchard Beach moved across Stony Creek to its present location on Fort Smallwood Road in 1982. There they built a sanctuary, offices, a kitchen, a multi-purpose room, and a library. The fine stained glass windows from the former building add to the beauty of the present sanctuary. In only two years they paid off their debt and added a nursery wing to the church. In 1997 they dedicated their Friendship Hall and additional space for Christian education. Also in 1982, the former Chelsea Beach Community Church became Chelsea Beach Lutheran Church, a mission of Emmanuel.[419]

Two more churches at opposite ends of the peninsula reflected the area's growth. Our Lady of the Chesapeake became the second Roman Catholic Church in the area when the congregation built a church across from Bodkin School in 1983. They had met at the school when they were a mission of St. Jane Frances Church in Riviera Beach. Now they are planning to build a parish hall. In the village of Pasadena, members of the Gethsemane Church of God in Christ had been holding services in the home of their founding pastor, Dr. Raymond Showell, since

---

[418]Richard Hare; Tom Owen.
[419]Emmanuel Church Directory; Nancy Quasney.

1982. In 1985 the congregation moved to a building on Chestnut Street that originally had been the Pasadena Methodist Church and later became a daycare center.

In 1985, just as members of Mt. Carmel Methodist Church were making an effort to have the ninety-year-old Bodkin School that served as their church hall recognized as an historic site, a three-alarm fire of suspicious origin destroyed the unique building. Designed and built with twin towers by Jefferson Monroe Cook in 1895, in 1926 the school became the property of the church where it was used for Sunday School classes, meetings, and social events. The community mourned the loss of a building that had significant architectural and historical importance.[420]

Fire destroys the Mt. Carmel Methodist Church hall, formerly Bodkin School, 1985.
Sun photo, Collection of Anne Arundel County Division of Planning

[420]*The Sun*, December 16, 1985; *Capital*, December 16, 1985.

With the concentration of population shifting eastward, in 1986 the Pasadena post office on Ritchie Highway closed, and an enlarged post office at Lake Shore became the main post office with Riviera Beach its only branch. People who live in the village of Pasadena now mail packages at Severna Park. In 1989 the Pasadena post office at Lake Shore celebrated its 75th birthday with exhibits, displays of old and new mail vehicles, guided tours, and a presentation by Emma Schramm who wrote a comprehensive history of the post office in 1985.[421]

At this time, owners of the many successful businesses on the peninsula had no way to discuss common interests and no unified voice. That situation ended when Edward Lauer, a local businessman, founded the Pasadena Business Association in 1986. He became the first president of an organization with 35 members. The group held bimonthly meetings, published a newsletter, communicated with legislators, funded scholarships, and planned annual social events. The PBA has grown steadily in size and in service to the community and its members.[422]

Local businesses continued to prosper despite changes. At Pastore's, Les and Marge Rizzo employed sixty people in 1984 when they chose a young employee, Bryan Metzbower, to be their partner. In 1987 they demolished their original building to make room behind it for a larger store that was part of a small mall. In September of 1991, Bryan and Sue Metzbower became the owners of Pastore's Italian grocery and deli. Klug's Esso station, the descendant of an old family business dating to about 1908, was demolished in 1989 and replaced by a WaWa convenience store and a Texaco station with William Klug's grandson John as one of the owners.[423]

Residents remember the addition of a drive-in window at McDonald's in Riviera Beach and the survival of Gino's near Lipin's Corner. The famous Mc Donald's "backwards" drive-in where the car's passenger side faced the service window caused an unaccompanied driver difficulty when

---

[421]*Maryland Gazette*, August 5, 1989. This history appears herein as Appendix A.

[422]Greater Pasadena Guidebook, 1993 Supplement to the *Maryland Gazette*, p.8.

[423]*Maryland Gazette*, September 19, 1987; *The Sun*, September 6, 1991; Pasadena Guide Book, 1993 Supplement to the *Maryland Gazette*, p.4.

he tried to reach his order. When Marriott bought the Gino's chain, many branches became Roy Rogers and others were closed; however, Marriott extended the contract of the Gino's on Baltimore and Annapolis Boulevard, making it the last survivor of a chain of 600 stores. Its main attraction was Kentucky Fried Chicken. Nowhere else near the peninsula could one buy a bucket of fried chicken. People came from as far as Catonsville to the last Gino's.[424]

Two events that were important to a water-oriented community occurred in 1987. Fire destroyed the Bodkin Yacht Club, a building that had stood on Main Creek since 1905. It had been a home and a tavern before the Bodkin Yacht Club bought it in 1962, after operating from Carbach's Marina on Main Creek. With the help of the Ladies Auxiliary, members raised funds so successfully that they were able to rebuild just eighteen months after the fire.[425]

A happier event was the beginning of the annual Parade of Boats, sponsored by the Marley Boat Club. Edwin Cheney, founder and commodore of the Boat Club, recalls that only three or four decorated boats paraded along the Patapsco shore and up and down Stony and Rock creeks on the second Saturday of December in 1987. Now Ventnor, White Rocks, and Amber Lighthouse clubs join Marley in a parade of ten or twelve boats. People along the parade route flash their outdoor lights to show their appreciation of the parade.[426]

Seven Foot Knoll, the first screwpile lighthouse in Maryland waters, had survived other Maryland screwpile lighthouses except the one at Thomas Point Shoal. The Coast Guard had automated the light and dispensed with keepers in 1948. In 1988 the Coast Guard's plan to abandon the Seven Foot Knoll Lighthouse or move it to Baltimore's Inner Harbor disturbed residents of Bayside Beach. They circulated a petition to delay the move, and Delegates Roy Huff and John Leopold questioned whether the decision to replace the light was irrevocable.

---

[424]Robert Reyes.
[425]*Maryland Gazette*, July 7, 1988.
[426]Edward Cheney.

The Coast Guard replied that they had no funds to maintain it in place, but donating it to Baltimore as a tourist attraction would preserve this historic screwpile lighthouse in a marine setting. Baltimore City allotted $75,000 for the project, supplemented by $50,000 from private sources, and proposed that it be named to the National Register of Historic Places. Further funding was needed to repair the framework and stabilize the structure.[427]

The Empire Construction Company spent months devising a plan for moving the lighthouse. On October 11, 1988, divers cut the iron pilings. Then a crane on a barge hoisted the 220-ton lighthouse and headed under the Key Bridge to the Baltimore harbor. When the lighthouse was dedicated, almost one hundred members of Thomas Steinhise's family attended the ceremony that recognized his heroic rescue of seamen during the hurricane of 1933.[428] Now the Living Classroom Foundation welcomes tourists to the Seven Foot Knoll Lighthouse at its new home. A modern tower-like steel structure with a beacon replaced the old lighthouse at Bodkin Point.

After four years of negotiation, in 1989 Anne Arundel County signed a 25-year agreement for the development of *Hancock's Resolution* near Bodkin Point as an historic park under the supervision of the Department of Recreation and Parks. Historic Annapolis Foundation, Incorporated, holds the title to the property. The County Executive, James Lighthizer, provided $150,000 in the county budget in 1989 for hiring a consultant to draw plans for restoration and taking steps toward development of the site.[429]

The Pasadena peninsula faced the last decade of the twentieth century with much to cherish: friendly people, community spirit, the natural beauty of the waterfront, and easy commuting to the city, but problems related to a tremendous rate of expansion remained as one residential community after another replaced what once had been productive farms.

---

[427]*The Sun*, July 18, 1988; Aug. 30, 1988; June 7, 1989; *Maryland Gazette*, July 20, 1988, Aug. 10, 1988.

[428]Holland, *Maryland Lighthouses*, p.176; The Sun, June 27, 1989; *Maryland Gazette*, April 25, 1990.

[429]*Maryland Gazette*, August 31, 1988; *Capital*, August 31, 1988.

Finding Solutions to Problems of Growth

The 1990 federal census showed a population of approximately 48,000 people on the Pasadena peninsula, with nearly 20,000 living on Tick Neck in communities like Riviera Beach, and Green Haven. The black population of the peninsula totaled about 1,160 (2 ½ percent).[430] In contrast to the days before World War II, only 11.6 percent of the population was engaged in farming or construction, while nearly 20 percent was engaged in trade and 25 percent provided services. Though the Pasadena Post Office had served 2,500 families on five routes in 1950, in 1993 there were 18,000 deliveries on 36 routes.[431]

As growth continued at a rapid rate, two-mile back-ups occurred as commuters tried to reach home from the point where State Route 100 merged into Mountain Road. From Lake Shore Plaza to the end of Mountain Road, people had to allow ten minutes for a break in traffic to enter the main road during commuting hours. Despite these traffic problems, older residents rejoiced in having better schools, better housing, more

---

[430]John Leocha, Assistant Anne Arundel County Demographer.
[431]Pasadena Guide Book, 1993 Supplement to the *Maryland Gazette*, 1993, p.12.

doctors, a wide choice of goods and services, and more business and career opportunities.

Water pollution, a problem of the eighties, remained a major concern in 1990, especially for beautiful Rock Creek that formerly had attracted thousands of excursionists every summer weekend. Now a foul odor came from its murky waters. Headlines in newspapers proclaimed: "Rock Creek Tributaries to Stay Closed for Another Year," "Troubled Tributary Focus of Clean-up," "Rock Creek Gets Budget Allocation for Dredging," and "Pasadena Developer Fined $15,000 for Polluting." Spokesmen for the community alleged that the county and state had destroyed wetlands and had been too lenient with developers on the peninsula, but they were especially indignant because the county's sewage pumping station at the head of Rock Creek was back-flushing sewage into the creek. A $150,000 dredging project had their ardent support.[432]

Though dredging began, it was stopped early in January of 1992. Newspaper headlines through July of that year tell the story: "Compromise May Save Rock Creek Plan," "Fate of Rock Creek Hangs in Balance," "Army Corps of Engineers Rejects Dredging Plan," "Rock Creek Gets $300,000 State Funds for Dredging," "Dredging Begins," and, at last, "Dredging Removes Odors from Rock Creek." Behind these headlines is the story of a community's struggle to save a priceless asset. Since the installation of an aerator that pumps oxygen into the water, there has been no fish kill and no contamination of the creek.[433]

News from the Magothy was encouraging. By the late 1980s, some recreational fishermen were reporting improved fishing in the Magothy and the Chesapeake Bay. The Magothy had been closed to fishing for yellow perch in September of 1983 as a result of a restoration project led by Hugh Gemignani, a biology professor at the Anne Arundel Community College. In the spring of 1992, yellow perch returned to the Magothy after

---

[432]*The Sun*, June 3, May 20, and June 24, 1990; *Maryland Gazette*, April 8, 1989.
[433]*Maryland Gazette*, January 25, February 5, 12, 15, and 26, April 8, July 8, all 1992; Louis Doetsch.

ten years' absence. By the fall of 1993, *The Sun* reported hope for a reinvigorated Magothy. In addition, as a result of federal legislation, industrial waste was no longer as serious a threat to the Patapsco and the Bay as it had been formerly. At Bodkin Point, a plan to level wetlands in 1993 aroused residents who successfully opposed major damage to a sensitive and critical area.

In the meantime, water had been leaking through the embankment at Lake Waterford and silt was settling in the lake. In 1991 an old pipe collapsed and flooding followed, with worse flooding feared. Despite community concern about preservation of the three-to-five-foot foundation of an early mill, replacing the 1925 dam meant the loss of that site. While constructing the new dam at a cost of 1.7 million dollars in 1992, workmen found nails that preservationists dated to the 1600s. The foundation stones from the old mill have been saved to make an historical marker.[434]

Plans for another green space were launched in 1991 when the county acquired 157 acres on Fort Smallwood Road for Anne Arundel County's second public golf course. This land, the former Klingelhoefer farm, had been used as a riding stable. The facility was to be named the James A. Moore Golf Course in memory of a local fireman who lost his life fighting a forest fire at Yellowstone National Park in 1988.[435]

A gain for historic preservation was William Mason's gift of the 150-year-old William Cook farmhouse to *Hancock's Resolution* in 1990. The house had two telescoping parts, the older being the one-and-one-half story section built in 1840. During the 1880s or 1890s, Henry Alfred Cook, son of William Henry Cook, added the two-story wing. This was the home of Rhoda Hancock who married Henry Alfred Cook in 1887. The last of their children to occupy the house were their elderly daughters, Matilda (Tillie) and Pansy Cook, who exemplified the manners of an

---

[434]Patricia Noue, "Lake Waterford Dam Repairs and Impact on the Environment"; *Maryland Gazette*, November 29, 1992.

[435]*The Sun*, September 6, 1991.

Home of Henry Alfred Cook and Rhoda Virginia Hancock Cook, now on the grounds of Hancock's Resolution. Collection of James B. Calvert

earlier era. A sign on their vegetable stand in the 1960s asked customers to "drop money in this drawer, please."[436]

After the death of the owners, the county moved the Victorian Cook home to *Hancock's Resolution* and renovated it to house the caretaker. Thus the place where Rhoda Hancock Cook had lived after her marriage began a new life at the site of her childhood home. Beginning in June 1989, work on the restoration of the old Hancock house continued with the addition of new joists and sills, reinforced floors, reshingled roof, re-pointed mortar, and freshly painted trim.[437]

A further gain for the community occurred when the Chesapeake Woman's Club was successful in their decade-long struggle for a library in

---

[436]Maryland Historical Trust Historic Sites Inventory AA-807; Blodwin Shipley Potee, "This Old House," *Anne Arundel History Notes*, vol.4, no.4 (July 1973):1.
[437]*Maryland Gazette*, July 18, 1990.

Lake Shore. By circulating a petition and collecting 4,500 signatures, they proved to officials that many people who lived in that area needed a library closer than the one ten miles away at Riviera Beach. With Councilman Carl (Dutch) Holland supporting the project, the County Council approved a $450,000 request to renovate four storefronts in the Long Point Mall to make space for the Mountain Road Branch Library. The 90,000 square foot facility cost 1.6 million dollars and opened in 1994 with 55,000 volumes and eight librarians.[438]

In 1995 the community felt pride when a native of Pasadena, Renee Rebstock Shanahan, became the only person in the history of the Miss Universe Pageants to hold all three state titles and to compete in all three nationally televised nationwide beauty contests. In 1987 Renee Rebstock won the title of Miss Maryland Teen; in 1992 she became Miss Maryland; and in 1995 Renee Shanahan was named Mrs. Maryland. Her husband, David Shanahan, held the titles of Mr. Maryland Teen in 1985 and Mr. Maryland in 1987, making the Shanahans the only couple ever to hold both sets of titles.[439]

Renee Rebstock Shanahan as Miss Maryland, with Governor Schaefer in 1992.
Collection of Helen Neisser

After the Green Haven and Powhatan Beach Volunteer Fire Companies had served

[438]*Maryland Gazette*, 1994.
[439]Helen Neisser.

the area faithfully for many years, they merged in 1994 to form the Armiger Volunteer Fire Company on Mountain Road at Solley Road. Robert (Robbie) Robinson served as the last president of the Green Haven Volunteer Fire Company and the first president of the Armiger Company. Three years later, the Lake Shore Volunteer Fire Company dedicated its new Cyclone II Pumper-Tanker to William G. Rothamel, a volunteer with the company for 53 years. Previously the Baltimore Area Girl Scouts had presented a certificate to Rothamel in appreciation of his dedication, competence, and long-term support of scouting at Camp Whippoorwill.

Historic preservation suffered a major loss in 1996 when the John Hanshaw House on Long Point Road near Mountain Road was demolished. The Hanshaw family owned this property from 1828 until 1877. The original log house was built between 1828 and 1850 and later was used as a summer kitchen. A late-19th -century addition made it an I-house with a central hall, typical of the homes of fairly affluent farmers. In 1924 the Chairs family, who owned the house at that time, added a dormer and a porch and shingled the exterior. Lois Chairs Jubb, who lived in this house as a child, remembers the fireplace "large enough to stand in" and the winding staircase on its right side.[440]

A new organization called Friends of Hancock's Resolution began to work on developing the educational potential of that site in 1997. The Friends authorized a conservation of historic buildings assessment, a Phase I archaeological survey, and an historical landscape evaluation, while The Lost Towns of Anne Arundel Project undertook an archaeological study of the eleven acres surrounding the house. With the support of County Executive John Gary, Anne Arundel County allotted $150,000 for preservation and restoration of *Hancock's Resolution* in 1998, and the state agreed to match that contribution.

---

[440]Maryland Historical Trust Historic Sites Inventory AA-1009; Lois Chairs Jubb.

James R. Morrison, president of the 116-member Friends of Hancock's Resolution, envisions the property as an educational experience for viewers. When they visit the restored buildings, they will see the kitchen as a center for living demonstrations and the store stocked to show its relationship with the oyster fleet. In October 1998, the county added twelve and a half adjacent acres to the property for a future farm park, visitors' center, and parking area.[441]

In 1997 residents of Lake Shore who were tired of taking their children to Baltimore for indoor soccer games formed the Lake Shore Arena Limited Partnership that designed a seven million dollar indoor arena to include three 200-by-85-foot air-conditioned rinks for use all year: an ice skating rink, a soccer rink, and a multi-purpose rink for soccer, ice skating, in-line skating, lacrosse, or hockey. A glass mezzanine for spectators, a pro shop, and two meeting rooms completed the plan. The Partnership signed a thirty-year agreement to lease land from the county at the Lake Shore Athletic Complex, planning to build near the intersection of State Route 100 and Mountain Road, with the main entrance off Magothy Beach Road.[442] Though this project has been delayed, proponents still hope to find the necessary funding.

Mountain Road had been adequate for almost two centuries, but commuters called it "an artery of frustration" and "an agonizing test of patience under stress" in the late nineties. Thomas Redmond, Pasadena's County Councilman, introduced a proposal to monitor traffic impact before permitting new subdivisions on roads that were the only access route along a peninsula. In December 1997, the Anne Arundel County Council considered this countywide bill that was the result of congestion on Mountain Road during rush hours. Residents of waterfront communities spoke in support of the proposal, but many developers opposed it.

---

[441]James R. Morrison, First annual meeting of Friends of Hancock's Resolution.
[442]*Maryland Gazette*, January 29, 1997, August 19, 1998.

Though the county already required a traffic study before building, proponents of the bill argued that the law had not been effective because county officials willingly negotiated exceptions. A county moratorium on new subdivisions also proved ineffective when the county issued 40 or 50 permits each year in already existing subdivisions. About 18,000 cars a day passed through the intersection of Mountain Road and State Route 100 in 1990; that number had increased to 23,000 by 1996. Supporters argued for passage of the bill that would end development on "jammed" roads. In response, County Executive John Gary suggested building a relief road on the narrow tip of the Pasadena peninsula.[443]

Despite concerns about traffic on Mountain Road, an old business continued to prosper there. In 1998 Angel's store celebrated its 75th anniversary and the retirement of Rosie O'Connell, who had served patrons for 38 years. At the age of 83, she recalled the many customers who had shared their joys and troubles with her. A second generation of the Clocker family, Walter and Andrew, now manage the store.[444]

In addition to the Schramm farm, which has undergone several changes over the decades, and Angel's and Pastore's (formerly Hillman's), which have changed management, two businesses survive from the 1930s. They are Wilson's service station, established in 1933 and owned by the son of the founder, and Kurtz's Beach, established in 1933, owned by Bonnie and Gus Kurtz, and operated by Kurtz's Ltd. (Bonnie Kurtz and her cousin, John Mason). Kurtz's now specializes in wedding receptions and other catered affairs. Surviving businesses from the 1940s include Louis Doetsch's Pasadena Yacht Yard and Tall Oaks Restaurant. Fran Dickson Koslowski Hasse celebrated the 50th anniversary of Tall Oaks in June of 1999.[445]

Changes have come at one of the oldest churches on the peninsula as well. Mount Zion United Methodist Church, founded in 1859, renovated

---

443 *Washington Post*, December 2, 1997.
444 *Maryland Gazette*, May 20, 1998.
445 *Maryland Gazette*, June 26, 1999.

their building in 1998. The congregation's multi-year fund raising effort made possible construction of a new fellowship hall, offices, kitchen facilities, rest rooms, an usher's room, a pastor's study, a sound system, and renovation of the sanctuary. The improvements will allow the church to expand its services to youth and seniors. The $750,000 project lasted six months and ended with a dedication and consecration service. Their five choirs add immeasurably to their worship services, and their annual week-long Magothy Camp Meeting is well-known over a wide area.[446]

The 138-year-old camp meeting takes place each year during the entire week that ends with Labor Day. Louis P. Brown remembers when people

Historic Mount Zion Church, renovated and enlarged in 1998.
Photo: Jon Armentrout

[446]*Maryland Gazette*, March or April, 1998.

arrived early because they knew that parking many cars from Baltimore, Washington, and surrounding counties would cause delays. Guest preachers, choirs, and bands came from as far as Delaware, Virginia, and southern Maryland to take part in worship services. Rosie Dailey, a long-time member, recalls the thousands who once came to camp meeting, but she says that the many hundreds who still attend feel the same spirit as before.[447]

The other old Methodist churches on the peninsula, Magothy and Mt. Carmel, remain active. In 1998 Magothy United Methodist Church dedicated a bronze tablet on the north side of Mountain Road where the church stood from 1794 until 1859. The memorial honors the church's founders and men like Dorsey Jacobs, who served as lay preacher and community leader for many years. Recently the century-old Mt. Carmel Church congregation has removed a structure between the original church and the hall to make space for a new sanctuary that will serve a growing community. They will preserve the historic original church on the grounds.

After twelve years of fund raising, Jenkins Memorial was ready to replace their 68-year-old sanctuary in 1999. The church had been holding three services each Sunday, with worshipers seated in the aisles. The $900,000 addition will double the size of the sanctuary and provide for stained glass windows, a pipe organ, and a 35-foot steeple. The former sanctuary will house Sunday School classes.[448]

While St. Jane Frances parochial school at Riviera Beach continued to serve over 600 children from pre-kindergarten through eighth grade, changes came at two local schools. The Jacobsville School that was built in 1963 (successor to the 1926 school) was demolished in 1998 to make way for a new elementary school with improved technology and without portable classrooms. In April teachers, students, and the entire community

---

[447]Rosie Dailey; Louis T. Brown.
[448]*Maryland Gazette*, February 10, 1999.

held a farewell party. Games, face-painting, and a silent auction occupied children and adults who crowded the halls to say goodbye and to express their appreciation of the old school. When pupils returned to fourteen classrooms at Riviera Beach Elementary School in the fall of 1999, they found the building thoroughly renovated and at last they had walls instead of open space classrooms. This project was the result of years of effort by parents who had pled for Board of Education funding.[449]

Though local schools have been integrated for decades, integrating the 2½ per cent of the population of the peninsula that is black into community activities has proceeded slowly. Many of the already small number of black residents left the peninsula when they found better jobs at shipyards and defense plants during World War II. Though older black residents say that their lives have improved greatly in recent decades, boat clubs, service associations, and business groups generally are not integrated. Often classes at local schools include only one or two children of color. Black parents believe that the best help they can give their children is to teach them that they can achieve. Their advice to young people is not to depend on quotas or affirmative action but to rely on their ability and work to succeed.[450]

Despite its rapid rate of growth, the Pasadena peninsula continued to attract new residents in great numbers. In 1981 the neighborhood called Chesterfield contained fifteen homes; in 1999, over 5,000 people lived in its 1,576 homes. The average price of a single-family home on the peninsula in 1996 was $146,135. Parents who had grown up on the peninsula often wanted their children to make their homes there too.[451]

Though the Schramms were reluctant to consider sale of their grandfather's farm, overwhelming estate taxes forced their decision to sell 180 acres to Koch Homes. Seven years after the sale, development began in 1999. Headlines and sub-heads in newspapers tell the story: "Old Turkey

---

[449]*Maryland Gazette*, April 29, 1998, February 10, 1999.
[450]Louis P. Brown.
[451]Carolyn Roeding, Greater Pasadena Council; *The Sun*, October 22, 1995.

Farm Lays Golden Egg," "Pasadena Tract Becomes Area's Hottest Housing Development," and "From the Farmhouse to the Townhouse." Bordered by Mountain Road, Catherine Avenue, and state routes 100 and 648, homes in Farmington Village, a community of 428 single-family homes and townhouses, have been selling rapidly, often to people who live nearby. The Schramms reserved 35 acres for their own home and remaining farm.[452] The Pasadena Business Association's new headquarters will stand on the site of the Schramm's old roadside stand.

Frequently throughout the nineties, communities fought zoning and environmental battles. People who loved their homes were willing to

A remnant of the Schramm farm amid new homes built on the former farm.
Photo: Blue Moon Aerial Photography

[452]*The Sun*, November 22, 1998; *Maryland Gazette*, February 10, 1999.

spend time, effort, and money when they believed that their neighborhoods were threatened. Controversy over expansion of a marina in 1997 led one community to file suit to oppose boat racks that were prohibited by a covenant. Public hearings were well-attended and discussion heated.[453] A proposal to close Woods Road to through traffic was quashed by activists who feared that the change would result in increased traffic congestion on Mountain Road. Strongly differing opinions about widening Mountain Road versus creating a bypass led to meetings where tempers flared when hundreds of people packed schools and community halls. In each case, controversy reflected residents' sincere interest in the future of their community.

Concern about halting development and relieving congestion on Mountain Road led to action. In 1997 the Mountain Road Preservation Committee, led by James Bilenki, Jr., formed to represent the area. Seventeen community associations belong to this organization. When many residents realized that development would occur as long as land was available, they supported the Magothy River Land Trust's proposal to reserve undeveloped land as green space. Delegate Joan Cadden lobbied for this concept and felt encouraged in 1998 when Maryland's Board of Public Works approved $155,525 in open space money to buy 14.85 acres adjacent to the Lake Shore Athletic Complex, including an environmentally sensitive stream.[454] At the turn of the century, the concept of reserved green space offered the best hope for the future of the peninsula.

---

[453]*The Sun*, April 15, 1998.
[454]*Maryland Gazette*, 1998.

Enjoying Life on the Peninsula

Despite problems caused by tremendous growth, the peninsula offers many opportunities for recreation. No longer do thousands of visitors crowd wide sand beaches, but residents now enjoy the area's parks, children have a wide choice of sports, and people use a variety of craft, from rowboats to yachts, to explore the creeks and rivers. The peninsula is the home of yacht clubs, sailing clubs, and dozens of teams that represent the area proudly.

There are many green spaces on the Pasadena peninsula. Lake Waterford Park, Downs Park, and the Lake Shore Athletic Complex are the largest, but smaller county-owned parks like Freetown, Havenwood, High Point, Jacobsville, Poplar Ridge, Rock Creek, and Sunset provide space for competitive sports and other activities. Baltimore's neglected Fort Smallwood Park is a beautiful site. Soon Tar Cove Park will be the site of a county golf course, and *Hancock's Resolution* will be the first educational park on the peninsula.

Lake Waterford Park offers a basketball court, tennis courts, a softball field, fishing in the lake, nature trails, and a playground for children. The Park is home to the Pasadena Chargers. Every spring boys and girls from age four to fifteen enjoy a fishing derby, and children under ten look forward to a Halloween celebration that ends with a hayride and to Easter week when they meet the Easter bunny on the nature trails and receive gifts and prizes.

Downs Park has developed varied opportunities for visitors, including a 1.8 mile Senior Exercise Trail with fifteen exercise stations, a Self-Guided Nature Trail with nine informative stations, and the Rocky Beach Farm Youth Group Camping Area. Mother's Garden is the setting for outdoor weddings, while craft fairs, an antique car show, bird club walks, and ranger-led tours attract many visitors. The Bay Concert Series presented each Sunday evening from Memorial Day through September is especially popular.[455] Today there are attractive alternatives to the lost white sand beaches.

There is a wealth of athletic talent on the Pasadena peninsula. Organizations provide opportunities for young people to participate in a wide variety of sports, and many adults give freely of their time to make these programs successful. The Riviera Beach (Northeast) and Lake Shore (Chesapeake) recreational associations are affiliated with the Anne Arundel County Department of Recreation and Parks. Representatives of the various teams make up the board of directors of each association. Most boys and girls participate primarily to enjoy recreation while learning sportsmanship, but the best players invest long hours of practice in order to excel in competition. These teams are feeders for Northeast, Chesapeake, and Mount St. Joe high schools.

The Pasadena Chargers practice and play football at Lake Waterford Park, with the support of the Chargers' Cheerleaders. One Chargers team won

---

[455]Down Park brochure, Anne Arundel County Department of Forests and Parks.

the county championship in their first year of competition. Since 1968 about 300 boys between the ages of six and fifteen have competed countywide. Tim Fogle played on their first team and has coached the Chargers since 1990. Each year during the nineties, one Chargers team has played for the county championship, and the 75-pound team won the championship every year from 1993 through 1998. The Chargers Cheerleaders usually place among the top four cheerleading teams in the county and have traveled as far as Myrtle Beach, South Carolina, in All-Star competition.[456]

The Chargers, Panthers, and Astros, as well as the Riviera Beach and Havenwood Girls Softball Leagues, are not affiliated with the Northeast Recreational Association; however, the Chargers, Panthers, and Astros are affiliated with the Anne Arundel County Department of Recreation and Parks and play in the county recreational association program. The Panthers, a new football team, formed in 1999. They have grown from 60 to about 100 players, ages seven through fifteen. They have no try-outs; everyone who comes has a chance to play. About 100 Panther Cheerleaders from age five through fifteen support the football team. Jerry Kerbe founded the Pasadena Saints baseball team in 1988. In recent years, the American Legion has sponsored this team for boys up to eighteen years of age. The Astros baseball team began in 2000. They field teams at two age levels, thirteen to fourteen and fifteen to sixteen.[457]

The Riviera Beach Girls Softball League, chartered in 1967, is the oldest in Maryland and one of the oldest girls' softball leagues on the East coast. Lee Espegren, who has worked with the League for 22 years, recalls that the team began when a woman sought an opportunity for her physically challenged granddaughter to enjoy sports. At first only a few girls played, and parents brought card tables to display baked goods that they sold to raise funds. Their playing field at the Riviera Beach School was small when Deana Park Lantz started the All-Stars team and arranged

---

[456]Tim Fogle.
[457]Chuck Yaruta; Lee Stepp, Joe Brockmeyer.

tournaments in 1976. After Anne Arundel County bought eight acres to make Rock Creek Park, they had four softball fields. Parents built a block structure to house lockers and a concession stand where they sold drinks and food, including crab cakes. Soon three or four hundred girls participated in intramural and Select traveling teams.[458]

The three age levels for competition in the Riviera Beach Girls Softball League are for girls ten years old and under, twelve and under, and sixteen and under. In addition to intramural competition, they have won fifteen state championships for different age levels since 1984 when statewide competition began. They hold six consecutive state championships in American Softball Association (ASA) competition and three in National Softball Association (NSA) competition. During the last six years, the Riviera Beach Girls Softball League recorded 256 wins to 25 losses. About 37 of these girls have earned softball scholarships to various colleges. Brent Lounge and Robert Boyd have managed or coached many championship teams.[459]

The Riviera Beach Spirit, their Select team, won Central Atlantic regional championships in 1982, 1986, 1988, 1997, and 1999. Thirteen Spirit teams have competed and placed as high as twelfth in national competitions as far away as Georgia, Colorado, Oklahoma, and Texas. In 2000 the twelve-and-under Spirit team won the ASA Central Atlantic Regional Championship and competed in the nationals. Head coach Joe Hart attributed their 34-5 record for the season to their dedication.[460]

The Havenwood Girls Softball League fields about 125 girls at five levels, beginning with coach-pitch training for four-to-eight-year-old girls and ending with High School Eligible from fifteen to nineteen years old. They have been playing recreational softball for nearly twenty years with George Fox Junior High as their home field. They play other north county teams, go to play-offs, and win some games, but their main goal is to give

---

[458]Lee Espegren.
[459]Brent Lounge; Robert Boyd.
[460]*Capital*, July 19, 2000.

THE RIVIERA BEACH GIRLS SOFTBALL LEAGUE

Riviera Beach Spirit team picture as National Champions, the 14 and under A team in Oklahoma, 1998.
Photo: Robert Boyd

1996 12 and under ASA tour in Florida: Ritual of spreading Rock Creek earth on home plate.
Photo: Robert Boyd

Batter Up!
Photo: Brent Lounge

Trophies won in five-year period, including Central Atlantic Regional Champions.
Photo: Brent Lounge

every girl a chance to play and to have fun. Unlike Little League, they have no geographic boundaries.[461]

The Anne Arundel County Department of Recreation and Parks is the umbrella organization for the Northeast Recreational Association, formerly the Riviera Beach Recreational Council, and the Chesapeake Recreational Association, formerly the Lake Shore Recreational Council. The Northeast Recreational Association includes Buccaneers Football, Buccaneers Boys and Girls Basketball, Buccaneers Cheerleaders, Buccaneers Wrestling, and Buccaneers Boys and Girls Lacrosse teams, as well as the Riviera Beach and Havenwood Little League teams, the St. Jane Frances Soccer League, the Pasadena Clinic League, and the adult soccer Attack League.

The Buccaneers Athletic Club Football League, founded in 1958, continues to field teams at six age and weight levels for boys from 65 to 140 pounds. Even the smallest boys have the finest equipment for their protection. Ed Heaphy was their director until 1969 when Ed Vinson succeeded him. In memory of his long service, Northeast High School annually awards the Ed Heaphy Memorial Trophy to an outstanding senior for athletic and academic achievement. The Buccaneers hold many conference and county championships. Their 1958, 1964, 1965, and 1992 teams recorded undefeated seasons; their 110- and 130-pound teams were county champions in 1964 and 1965; their 75-pound B team held the championship in 1992; and their 90-pound team won the county championship in 1994.[462]

The Buccaneers Cheerleaders started with four girls in 1964; now over 150 girls participate. They cheer for the football team during the fall season and then compete against other cheerleaders from fall through April. A Select group of serious athletes attends off-season cheerleading clinics, and six or eight of them became county champions in the fall of 1999.[463]

---

[461]Kathy Le Compte.
[462]Ed Vinson; Joe Brockmeyer.
[463]Kim Salyers.

The Buccaneers Basketball team has existed since 1963 and plays at age levels six to eight, eight to ten, eleven to twelve, and thirteen to fourteen. Girls and boys in the three older levels play in county competition. Between 1978 and 1985, the thirteen to fourteen-year-old players won county championships and tournaments and had a 9-1 season. Because so many Buccaneer players were on Varsity basketball teams at Chesapeake and Northeast high schools, their coach, Tom Caines, recalls being unable to cheer for either team when the two schools competed. Two of his former star players, Carlos Hall and Roger O'Dea, returned to coach for the Buccaneers.[464]

The Buccaneers Lacrosse teams field about 140 boys and 80 girls ranging in age from four to fourteen, playing at five age levels. The four to six-year-old Ankle Biters and the Clinic and Peewees, seven to ten years old, do not keep standings but simply have fun. The Midgets and Juniors, eleven to fourteen-years-old, play against other teams and are preparing to compete at the county level. They focus on basic skills and sportsmanship.[465]

The Buccaneers Wrestling teams have been successful at many levels since their founding in 1971 by John MacIsaac and Gil Haney. Gil Haney had wrestled for the Baltimore Y.M.C.A. before coaching the Buccaneers. Three members of his first team went on to become national champions. Gil Haney's sons, Tim and Ken, wrestled for the Buccaneers and coached in later years. Their current director and head coach is Mike Breen. About eighty wrestlers from age five through fifteen practice at Northeast High School from November until mid-March as often as three nights a week. After competing first in the County League, experienced boys progress to competition in the Maryland Junior Wrestling League, called the Beltway League. In 1999 two boys became state champions. The team's motto is, "Be humble winners and gracious losers."[466]

---

[464]Tom Caines.
[465]Chip and Kim Salyers.
[466]Mike Breen; Joe Brockmeyer.

Over one thousand boys and girls play on Buccaneer teams each year. In a family-oriented community, sports are a family activity. Both husbands and wives participate as coaches while their children compete. Sometimes three generations are involved with a team. Joe Brockmeyer, for example, played with the Buccaneers when his father was their treasurer. After playing football at Western Maryland College, he coaches Buccaneers football and Little League, and his three children play on Buccaneer teams. Throughout the peninsula, this is a familiar pattern as enthusiastic parents and dedicated coaches support several thousand players. Their only problem is a lack of enough indoor and outdoor playing fields.

For forty years John Gerwig was the manager of the Riviera Beach Little League, founded in 1953. The Riviera Beach Little League participates mainly in intramural competition, but outstanding players compete in All Stars District IV play-offs. Boys compete in seven divisions from T-ball through age 18. In recent years, the Riviera Beach 15-16 and 17-18-year-old players have won District IV championships, and the 13 and 14-year-old team held the District IV championship and played for the state championship in 1999. Little League teams like Riviera Beach and Havenwood that play under Williamsport rules can compete in structured tournaments that lead to a globally sanctioned Little League World Series.[467]

About 240 boys and girls from five to seventeen years old play in the Havenwood Little League. The boys' team has existed for 28 years and the girls' team about 24 years. Rigid boundaries separate them from the Riviera Beach Little League. During the regular season they play in intramural competition for each age level, and then some compete in invitational tournaments. The victors go on to the District IV All Star tournament. The Havenwood Little League team has progressed as far as the district finals that lead to state playoffs.[468]

---

[467]Joe Brockmeyer.
[468]Tom and Carol Caines.

As many as 830 boys and girls play soccer at Saint Jane Frances grounds in Riviera Beach. They have an intramural league, as well as a Select or travel team that held the county championship for three years between 1995 and 1998. Each year since the early seventies, the St Jane Frances Soccer League has offered anyone who ever played for the League a chance to compete for several $500 college scholarships. The Attack League, men over thirty years of age, play in county-wide competition in the Anne Arundel County Soccer League in the fall and the Anne Arundel Adult Soccer League in the spring.[469]

The Pasadena Clinic League, a non-competitive instructional league, offers an opportunity for five-to-eight-year-old children to participate in coach-pitch and kid-pitch softball, using a rubber ball. Founded in 1975 by John Swarthout and Tony and Kathy Reina, the Clinic League branched from the Riviera Beach Little League. Though it began with 52 children, three years later 300 participated, and nearly 500 are in the program now. Other organizations are copying this approach.[470]

The Lake Shore Recreational Council recently has been restructured as the Chesapeake Recreational Association with a nine-member Board. Their program includes the Anne Arundel Raiders football team and the Raiders Cheerleaders, the Fort Smallwood Optimist Baseball League, the Pasadena Soccer Club, Mountain Road Soccer Club, Mountain Road Chesapeake Youth Lacrosse, Lake Shore Athletic Association Girls Softball and Field Hockey, Lake Shore Athletic Association Basketball, Mountain Road Wrestling, and, most recently, the Pasadena Horse and Pony Association.[471]

In 1992 Carl Cicchetti started the Raiders with a football team. Raiders soccer, cheerleaders, and baseball followed by 1994. Four football teams, 72 boys from six to fifteen years old, compete. The ninety-pound team reached the county championship play-offs in 1998. The Raiders do not

---

[469]John Warner; Mark Van Denberghe.
[470]Ed Vinson; Joe Brockmeyer.
[471]Tom Owen

focus on winning but aim to enable boys and girls to enjoy playing and to grow at their own level. About 100 Raiders Cheerleaders from three to fifteen years old practice at five age levels. The three to five-year-old group does not compete and is not judged, though all receive ribbons. The Raiders Cheerleaders support their football team at home and away during the fall season and also participate in competitions.[472]

The Fort Smallwood Optimists Baseball League has been active since their founding in 1972. Between 200 and 300 boys and girls participate in the league. Children two to four years old play T-ball, while those seven and eight years old play coach-pitch. Boys and girls from 12 to 16 play at four age levels on travel teams. During 1998 and 1999, the 11-to-12-year-old team won a division championship, and the nine and ten-year-old players were runners-up in their division.[473]

The Mountain Road Soccer League includes about 800 boys and girls, beginning with 4½-year-old children in a development clinic and progressing through an intramural program for ages five through seven and county-wide competition in the Anne Arundel Youth Soccer Organization for ages eight through fifteen. The Mountain Road League has travel teams only when players in the same age bracket excel. In 2000 two girls' and one boys' teams are playing in the Baltimore Beltway League and the Maryland State Youth soccer competition. The Pasadena Soccer Club is smaller, but it concentrates on the Select level and fields travel teams.[474]

The Mountain Road Cobras, the boys' lacrosse team and the Pasadena Shore Shots, the girls' lacrosse team, combined in 2000 as the Chesapeake Youth Lacrosse Association in order to strengthen their program. They have over 200 players from age six to fourteen. Though they have been playing lacrosse at Lake Shore for only five years, in 1999 the girls won the B-level tournament and the Division B title in an undefeated season. These girls will represent the area in a national tournament in 2000.[475]

---

[472]Carl Cicchetti; Cathy Davis.
[473]Mark Ryer; Rosemarie Billing-Briggs; Philip Laumann.
[474]Roy Jackson.
[475]Debbie Hutchinson; Nancy Schrumm.

Beginning with one team about 1958, a 24-member staff now directs over 700 boys who are members of 55 Lake Shore Youth Baseball teams. They range from five to sixteen years old, playing at six age levels. Because they play by Pony rather than Williamsport rules, they have no geographic boundaries. They field intramural teams and travel teams at 11 to 12, 13 to 14, and 15 to 16 year-old levels. In 1999 the 11 and 12-year-old travel team won the Chesapeake Baseball Association championship. The group raises funds to update equipment and uniforms every year. With the help of sponsors, they are adding a batting cage at a cost of $20,000 in 2000. They hope to start a handicapped baseball league in 2001.[476]

The Lake Shore Athletic Association Girls Softball began as a small group in the 1970s and grew to about 250 players by 1982. Bill Henderson, their current director, has worked with the teams since that time. Now almost 400 girls from ages 4 to 18 play at six levels, beginning with T-ball. Intramural teams compete to enjoy sports, but the travel teams work hard to excel and qualify for out-of-state competition each year. They play against the best available competition sixty to seventy-five times a year. Like the Riviera Beach Girls softball teams, Lake Shore teams are among the best in the state and East Coast and are nationally recognized. They play and win in National Softball Association and American Softball Association-sponsored tournaments. Coached by Jim Parsons in 1992, they won a national championship in Texas. They have qualified as high as seventh nationally since then. Colleges seek their team members; in 1997 six of the twelve girls on the Lake Shore softball team received college scholarships.[477]

Tracy Crane, who played field hockey at Chesapeake High School and at college, now coaches at Chesapeake. Feeling the lack of a feeder system for field hockey, in 1994 she organized a two-week camp to teach the game while having fun. Though she began with only forty girls, 125

---

[476]George Green
[477]Bill Henderson; Tom Leonardo; Richard Hare.

Lake Shore baseball team at the complex on Woods Road, 1998.

Collection of Dale Courville, Manager (back row, right)

Matt Gunther explaining the fine points to James Anderson at bat.

Photo: Jim Anderson

attended her sixth camp in 1999. Two years ago, she started teams that play during the fall season at Peewee, Midget, and Junior levels, ages eight to fourteen. Two Peewee teams hold county championships. Five Select teams played within the county in 1999; in 2000 she hopes to field nine teams. Older girls who play on her Chesapeake High School team coach her field hockey teams, making possible a ratio of two coaches to every ten girls. Her aim is to enable team members to have fun and to enjoy being physically fit.[478]

Lake Shore Athletic Association Basketball began about ten years ago. Tom De Leonardo's program includes 500 boys and girls from age six to seventeen playing in intramural and county competition. The intramural teams play to have fun. Those who are serious about giving time to the sport have that opportunity. Every year from three to five Lake Shore basketball teams win championships. Their Cheerleaders are called the Lake Shore Spartans.[479]

Since 1994, Bruce Dulski and Bob Burns have coached the Mountain Road Wrestlers, founded as the Chesapeake Cubs in 1985. From only thirteen boys in 1989, the group has grown to seventy boys from age five to fifteen who wrestle at various weight levels. As part of the Anne Arundel County Wrestling League, they have won six county championships in eleven years. In 2000 they placed third in the Maryland State Tournament, the highest of any team in this county.[480]

Playing in these programs often leads to earning places on high school teams. Al Grau, Director of Athletics at Chesapeake High School, maintains a Sports Wall of Fame in the school cafeteria. There everyone can see plaques honoring the Athlete of the Year, All-American champions, individual state championships, and team championships. Chesapeake High School claimed state championships in wrestling for 1981 and 2000; gymnastics for 1982; track and field for 1987; softball for 1988,

---

[478]Tracy Crane.
[479]Tom De Leonardo.
[480]Bob Burns.

1990, 1991, 1992, and 1993; baseball for 1997; and boys' soccer for 1998.[481]

Under the direction of Roger Stitt, who has spent thirty-one years coaching, teaching, and directing athletics, Northeast High School offers a full sports program. Their baseball team holds three state and eight regional championships; both the boys' and the girls' basketball teams have won a regional championship; the football team claims five county championships; the boys' soccer team has won two regional championships, while the girls' soccer team holds two county championships; the girls' volleyball team claims three regional and four county championships; the girls' cross-country distance running team has won two regional championships; the girls' indoor track team claims two championships; the boys' indoor track team holds one regional championship; and the wrestling teams claims two county, two state, and three regional championships, as well as thirteen individual champions.

Head coach Harry Lentz , with assistant coach Al Kohlhafer, took baseball at Northeast to a new level in 1991 when their Little League veterans recorded a 24 to 0 undefeated season and received a Number One rating from a well-known sports magazine. The Northeast girls' softball team holds a Maryland record, nine state championships, and fourteen regional championships. They set a public school single season state record for 24 wins in 1999 and were 44-7 for the preceding two seasons. Two squads of cheerleaders support the Northeast High School teams. Though the numbers vary from year to year, about twenty per cent of the annual athletic awards go to black athletes, who make up less than five per cent of the school population.[482]

Boating remains a favorite recreation for many individuals and organized groups. The Maryland Yacht Club, founded in Baltimore in 1908, has been active at the Fairview site on Rock Creek since 1945 and is the

---

[481]Al Grau.
[482]Roger Stitt.

oldest club in the area. The Bodkin Yacht Club cherishes its history since 1957. Former members of the Ventnor Yacht Club have moved their boats to the Maryland Yacht Club, the Pasadena Yacht Yard, and other locations. The White Rocks Yacht Club, founded in the 1960s at the site of Brown's Grove, also remains active.[483]

The Magothy Sailing Association, a consortium of sailing clubs, and the Potapskut Sailing Association sponsor frequent sailing races and other activities. The Potapskut Sailing Association was founded by Joshua Rogers at Rock Creek. Their first commodore was Marshall Duer. Members moved to Blackhole Creek in 1946, built their clubhouse in 1947,

A sailboat race on the Magothy River under dark clouds, 1999.
Photo: Walter Kramme

---

[483]Louis Doetsch.

and hold regattas, races, and sailing competitions each summer.[484] Membership in these clubs is by invitation. Each club has a loyal following.

In addition to warm weather boating events, throughout the nineties the Marley Boat Club's Parade of Boats has been a festive holiday event on the second Saturday of December. By 1999 residents along the Patapsco River and Rock, Stony, and Bodkin creeks viewed nineteen decoratively lighted boats, and many people planned parties along the route to share the spectacle with their guests.[485]

Though homeowners on the peninsula may sometimes worry about traffic, environmental stress, or other problems of growth, many recreational activities help to divert their attention from these concerns.

A spinnaker race on the Patapsco beyond Rock Point.
Photo: Mary Johnson

[484]Taylor, *My River Speaks*, p.188.
[485]Edward H. Chaney, Jr.

Moving into the New Millennium

Residents of the Pasadena peninsula faced the new millennium with some unsolved problems but with hope for the future. Traffic congestion on Mountain Road, the lack of enforcement of a moratorium on building, the need for funds for reserved green space, and the critical importance of preserving ancient wetlands were the chief concerns. These were balanced by a thriving business community and neighborhoods well-served by churches, schools, libraries, fire companies, and the Magothy Health Center.

Despite a one-year moratorium on building on Mountain Road, development continued in 1999. The County Council voted on March 15th for a temporary extension of the moratorium on new subdivisions there. Developers attempted to derail the bill, but Pasadena's representative on the County Council, Shirley Murphy, sponsor of the bill that continued the moratorium, argued, "This is a failed road. It cannot take any more growth now."[486]

[486]*Capital*, March 16, 1999.

Carolyn Roeding, president of the Greater Pasadena Council, called the adequate facilities law a joke because developers could evade it simply by securing waivers. Though the area had already reached the critical point, new subdivisions continued to be approved, despite the law that requires enough infrastructure to support new building. The twenty-four-house Wharf Creek and the nineteen-home Meadow Run developments were built after the first moratorium was in effect. When the moratorium ended suddenly in the fall of 1999, the local delegation to the General Assembly asked County Executive Janet Owens to introduce emergency legislation to extend it until June 30, 2000.[487]

Debate continued about whether to widen Mountain Road or build a bypass. Many business owners believed that widening the road would ruin their businesses. The Mountain Road Preservation Committee's suggestion, reversible turning lanes, proved to be at least a partial solution to traffic jams at commuting hours. This experiment began on July 12, 1999. A year later, the State Highway Administration reported that the average commuting time on the peninsula each morning had dropped by thirteen to twenty minutes without significant increase in accidents. "The reversible lanes have far exceeded our expectations," said Senator Philip C. Jimeno . "Ninety-five per cent of the comments we hear from constituents are positive."[488]

The concept of a Greenway had gained support since 1998 when Delegate Joan Cadden advocated preserving green space along the Magothy River watershed. During the summer of 1999, the District 31 delegation to the General Assembly announced plans for a Magothy River Greenway that would include a large tract known as the Looper property, Saybrooke Two, and a corner of the Angel-Durner land near Grey's bog.[489]

The Mountain Road Preservation Committee, The Magothy River Land Trust, Delegate Joan Cadden, and County Council member Shirley

---

[487]*Maryland Gazette*, February 10, 1999; March 17, 1999.
[488]*Maryland Gazette*, February 10, 1999; *Capital*, February 11, 2000.
[489]*Maryland Gazette*, February 10, 1999; *Capital*, September 1, 1999.

Water lillies in bloom on one of Hines Ponds.
Photo: Marion Warren

Osprey nest.
Photo: Mary Johnson

Murphy worked with community associations and other elected representatives to find funds to enable the county and state to acquire property within the greenway boundaries. As Delegate Cadden pointed out, failure to preserve and protect large tracts of forested land would allow the consequences of development to affect, not only rivers and creeks, but also the Chesapeake Bay.

When the project received $425,000 in Program Open Space funds, residents were encouraged, but the Magothy River Land Trust's application for more than seven million dollars from Maryland's Rural Legacy Fund was denied in 1999 on the grounds that the Pasadena peninsula was developed, not rural. Nevertheless, Delegate Cadden and Melvin Bender, president of the Magothy River Land Trust, were not discouraged. "We're all on the same page for the first time," said Senator Philip C. Jimeno. "There's never been a concrete plan before. With the Magothy River Greenway, there's a concrete plan, there's a realistic goal, and everybody is working toward that goal."[490]

In October of 1999, environmentalists discovered three bogs on the north shore of the Magothy that contain many rare plants. "Much of the vegetation there has existed at the site since before the last Ice Age 11,000 years ago. The north shore of the Magothy River has just the right mix of geology, hydrology, and soil to make this happen, and that is very rare," said Sally Horner, biology professor at Anne Arundel Community College. "These bogs need to be studied in depth immediately," added environmentalist Keith Underwood. "Bogs are the kidneys of the Chesapeake Bay. They cleanse the water before it goes to tidal waters of the bay."[491]

As the public became increasingly aware of the importance of fragile wetlands and endangered plants that grow in bogs, botanist Phil Sheridan found at Lake Waterford the only two known Maryland specimens of a rare variety of box huckleberry. One hundred colonies of this plant are

---

[490]*Capital*, September 1 and October 20, 1999.
[491]*Capital*, October 27, 1999; *The Sun*, October 12, 1999.

Mother duck with ducklings
Photo: Mary Johnson

Canada geese walking on ice
Photo: Mary Johnson

known worldwide. Hundreds once grew at Lake Waterford, but the Virginia-based Meadowview Biological Research Station found just twelve in 1987. In 1997 there were two.[492]

Delegate John R. Leopold requested state funding in 1999 for a study of the feasibility of preserving Gray's Bog and growing cranberries there. Cranberries would not be a new plant in local wetlands. In 1952 John Pumphrey of Green Haven recalled that he once gathered buckets full of cranberries each year. At the age of 73, he still donned his high-top boots and found enough berries to make cranberry sauce for himself and his friends at Christmas time. He believed that cranberries could be grown commercially here. However, James Bilenki, Jr., expressed misgivings: "It is one of the very few freshwater bogs on this side of the Bay," he said. "I am concerned that any type of disturbance would destroy the bog." Bogs near Marley Creek and Furnace Branch produced cranberries in abundance before 1910. A few remain near the Severn and the Magothy, but the growth of berries is sparse.[493]

In December 1999, state and local officials toured sites along the Magothy River that have been called "the "biodiversity hot spot" of the state. J.L. Hearn of the Maryland Department of the Environment declared, "These are some of the most important wetlands in the state.... We should protect them." In May 2000, the Department of the Environment again expressed concern about ecosystems that contain a host of rare plants. County Council representative, Shirley Murphy, is urging approval of a law to increase the buffer zone around the bogs from 25 to 100 feet. Keith Underwood, a wetlands expert who called the local bogs "globally unique," believes that a buffer zone alone might not protect them because owners could receive waivers to build inside the buffer zone.[494]

With the support of the Mountain Road Preservation Committee and the Magothy River Land Trust, Delegate Joan Cadden again urged the

---

[492]*Capital*, April 1999.

[493]*Capital*, October 30 and December 3, 1999; *The Sun*, December 28, 1952; Kelbaugh, "The Wild Cranberries of Anne Arundel County," *Anne Arundel History Notes*, vol.22, no.3, pp.5-6.

[494]*Capital*, December 3, 1999 and May 3, 2000.

Magothy River Greenway.
Photo: Blue Moon Aerial Photography

county and the state to purchase land for a greenway that would include bogs where ancient vegetation is now endangered. The efforts of preservationists have been successful. Anne Arundel County has designated 2.2 million dollars for this purpose in 1999 and 2000, and in October 2000 the federal government contributed 2.5 million in T21 funds. The state of Maryland also has budgeted up to two million dollars in Program Open Space money for purchase of land to protect bogs on the peninsula. With adequate funding available, activists are confident that purchase of the large Looper tract and other properties will occur soon.[495]

The future of the Magothy River Greenway is bright. The project now is a line item in the Maryland Department of Natural Resources budget,

---

[495]Delegate Joan Cadden.

which means that additional funding will be available each year. Delegate Joan Cadden points out that "we now have the ability to give people tax incentives for adding land to the protected greenway." Already some land owners are considering easements to provide that their land cannot be sold for development. Perhaps reserved land someday could reach from the Bodkin to the Magothy. This tremendous accomplishment has been made possible by citizens working through community associations, the Magothy River Land Trust led by Melvin Bender, the Mountain Road Preservation Committee led by James Bilenki, Jr., Delegate Joan Cadden, and the community's other elected representatives. When the Magothy River Greenway becomes a reality, it will reverse a pattern that began when the early settlers first cleared the peninsula's ancient forests.

Though agriculture had been the foundation of life on the Pasadena peninsula from the beginning of its recorded history until recent decades, in the late 1990s only two local farms produced any quantity of fruits or vegetables. Gordon Wirth and the Schramm family are the surviving farmers, but they depend on retail sales at roadside stands or farmers' markets. The Schramms moved their roadside stand from its familiar location on Mountain Road to a site nearer their home on Schramm Road in 2000.

Many community organizations represent families living in nearly 100 neighborhoods on the peninsula. By working together as the Greater Pasadena Council, they are able to speak with a united voice. When the Council expresses support of issues that are important to members, their representatives hear the voice of the people. (See Appendix B for a list of current neighborhoods that are part of the Greater Pasadena Council.)

The Pasadena Business Association now represents many successful businesses. Organized in 1986 to give business owners a unified voice, it has made many contributions to the community. From its beginning, the group has raised funds for scholarships. Since 1992 they have sponsored an annual Legislative Day in Annapolis where they meet with their representatives and discuss issues of interest to the community. Since 1993 the PBA has sponsored an annual Trade Show to showcase businesses to the public, and in 1995 the annual Pasadena Parade began. Throughout each year, the PBA gives funds to community causes. Beginning with 35 members, the association under the direction of Carol Cross now numbers 280. Serving an area that had been divided by local loyalties, the Pasadena Business Association has stimulated a unified community spirit. Their role includes service and promotion of the entire peninsula.

Today shoppers can buy almost anything they want or find almost any service they need at Chesterfield Plaza, Lake Shore Plaza, Pine Grove Village, Pastore's Plaza, Lauer's Riviera Beach, Festival at Pasadena, or Long Point Mall. Gone are the days of traveling to Baltimore for medical or dental procedures. Dry cleaners, florists, hairdressers, banks, and libraries are nearby.

Ed and Helen Lauer and Meg Millsap enjoying the annual PBA crab feast at Kurtz's Beach.
Photo: Laura Wiegmann

New opportunities exist for people of all ages. On May 9, 2000, the Anne Arundel County Department of Aging opened the Pasadena Senior Center in the Lake Shore Shopping Center. Two hundred older residents take advantage of the many activities offered there. Since more people use this Senior Center than any other in the county, Shirley Murphy has asked the county to enlarge the available space after only a few months of operation.[496]

In addition, County Council representative Shirley Murphy reported that the county is ready to break ground for the 36-hole Tar Cove Golf Course, scheduled for completion in 2001. When the golf course and the planned 170-home subdivision nearby are completed, she believes a new road connecting State Route 100 and Fort Smallwood Road will be necessary. Carolyn Roeding, president of the Greater Pasadena Council, agrees. The county budget now includes three million dollars to reconfigure the congested intersection of Hog Neck Road and Fort Smallwood Road. After the golf course is finished, the county will review adjacent roads.[497]

Residents were disappointed when the Department of Recreation and Parks canceled their lease with the Lake Shore Arena Limited Partnership in September of 2000. Plans for a 125,000-square-foot youth sports arena had been postponed for several years by difficulty in obtaining building and grading permits and a special zoning exemption. The county might build several multi-purpose athletic fields on this land, but supporters of the arena still hope that private funding for an indoor facility will become available in the future.[498]

Organizations that provide services for residents of the peninsula include volunteer fire departments, Scout troops, the Patapsco River Power Squadron, and various service clubs. The Rotary, Lions, Kiwanis, and Optimists serve their communities in many ways. The Lake Shore Rotary Club is the only one of 65 clubs in a district that includes Baltimore and

---

[496]County Council representative, Shirley Murphy.
[497]*Capital*, July 19, 2000.
[498]*Maryland Gazette*, September 20, 2000.

Washington that participates one hundred per cent in the Paul Harris Fellows Club. This means that every member has contributed generously to grants that fund humanitarian efforts in this country and worldwide. Members spend one day a week working at the Salvation Army headquarters and serve lunch there once a month. They also award scholarships to pupils at Chesapeake High School.[499] The other service clubs on the peninsula have similar programs.

The American Legion and the Veterans of Foreign Wars also serve the community. Pasadena Post 277 of the American Legion was located in

Robert Brown, District Governor of Rotary International, presenting a Rotary Foundation award to Larry Sanders, president of the Lake Shore Rotary Club, 2000.
Photo: James B. Calvert

---

[499]James B. Calvert.

The Kiwanis Club's motorized sleigh takes Santa to visit local schools.
Photo: John Wilson, Jr.

Riviera Beach but has moved nearer Marley. Members sponsor the Pasadena Saints baseball team and the Kool Kids, children of veterans in the Sun Valley neighborhood who provide help for the elderly with the Post's financial support. In addition, they observe Flag Day, hold memorial services for deceased veterans, and furnish and raise flags that form the Avenue of Flags at the Veterans Cemetery near Crownsville. The Richard Kirk American Legion Post represents older veterans on the peninsula. The Veterans of Foreign Wars Post 2462 on Bayside Beach Road and their auxiliary raise funds for medical needs of veterans and their families and support political action to advance veterans' causes.[500]

On March 21, 1999, the Friends of *Hancock's Resolution* opened the Hancock house to the public for the first time in thirty years. Volunteers

---

[500]Carroll Babka, American Legion Post Commander and Past Commander, Anne Arundel County; Rosemarie Billing-Briggs.

have spent hundreds of hours clearing the grounds in preparation for hosting visitors on Sundays between one and four p.m. from late March until late October. With funding from Anne Arundel County, a Maryland bond bill, and a grant from the Maryland Historical Trust, rebuilding of the summer kitchen and porch began in August of 2000. Restoration work on the house will be done with meticulous attention to detail. For example, a laboratory is analyzing an original mortar sample in order to replicate it in the restoration process.[501]

Though people elsewhere often are critical of schools, on the peninsula parents are their faithful supporters and give high priority to whatever is beneficial to their children. Parent-Teacher Associations are active at all local schools. In 1999 county officials announced that Bodkin Elementary School outscored every other school in the state on Maryland School Performance Assessment Program (MSPAP) tests. These tests are given to third, fifth, and eighth grade students. Bodkin's composite third and fifth grade scores on reading and writing were the highest among more than 800 Maryland schools. The principal, Rocco Serretti, credited a strong writing program, a dedicated staff, and committed students. Educators hope to use Bodkin's methods as a model for other county schools.[502]

Northeast Senior High School has about 1470 students and graduates about 330 seniors each year. Twenty per cent of the graduates attend a four-year college, and fifty per cent choose community college. Northeast graduates have been accepted at Carnegie Mellon, Holy Cross, Notre Dame, William and Mary, Drexel, Fordham, Georgetown, Hood, Loyola, Michigan State, Mt. Holyoke, Penn State, Radford, Randolph Macon, Rensselear, Roanoke, St. Mary's, Sweet Briar, Tufts, U.S. Coast Guard Academy, U.S. Naval Academy, University of Pennsylvania, University of Virginia, Virginia Polytechnic, Washington College, Western Maryland, and many other colleges and universities.[503]

---

[501]*Maryland Gazette*, March 20, 1999; August 2, 2000.
[502]*Capital*, December 2 and 6, 1999.
[503]Chris Conner.

Chesapeake High School enrolls 1830 students and graduated 367 in 2000. Seventy per cent of the graduating seniors continue their education. In addition to many of the colleges and universities named above, Chesapeake graduates have earned admission to American University, Bucknell, Bryn Mawr, Case Western Reserve, Duke, Emory, George Washington, Gettysburg, Goucher, Hood, Harvard, Johns Hopkins, Lehigh, M.I.T., Princeton, Perdue, Stanford, Swarthmore, Syracuse, Temple, Tulane, UCLA, University of Chicago, U.S. Military Academy, U.S. Air Force Academy, Villanova, Wilson, Yale, and many others. Chesapeake honored two National Merit scholars in 2000, and a Chesapeake High School student has had a perfect score of 1600 on the Scholastic Aptitude Tests (SAT). Chesapeake's Marching Bank ranked second among Group I marching bands at the Atlantic Coast Championship Competition in 1999.[504]

Churches always have been central to life on the Pasadena peninsula. Instead of the four Methodist churches that existed before 1900, today many denominations are represented: two Roman Catholic, three Lutheran, Episcopal, Baptist, six Methodist, two Church of God, Seventh Day Adventist, and independent Jenkins Memorial, all with active programs for adults, youth, and children.

The Magothy Health Center is still a lay health center, owned and operated by the community. Though the Health Department provides the professional staff, volunteers run a thrift shop that is open on Wednesday and Saturday, the chief source of funds used to maintain the building and grounds. Since a major renovation in 1979, further improvements were made and a clinical wing was added. Services include child health clinics, maternity clinics, home health care for patients confined to their homes, and visits to schools, with emphasis on prevention and early diagnosis of health problems. Since its founding in 1938, services have expanded

---

[504]Tess Johnson.

Magothy Health Center, organized in 1938 and still operated by the community.
Photo: Marion E. Warren

while support from the community and benefits to the community have been constant.[505]

Growth remains a problem on the peninsula despite hopes for adoption of a long-term growth plan and strict enforcement of the adequate facilities law. Ninety per cent of the shore line of the Magothy River is developed residentially. People who recall the peninsula before World War II share the memories of Jane Pumphrey Nes, who grew up near the Magothy River. She writes, "How could I have understood that my world would vanish? . . . . to ride horseback through the woods alone, to watch from the river bank nature's eternal predawn ballet as a blue heron woke and flew slowly across the reeds. . . . the honking of wild swans on cold winter

[505]"History of the Magothy Health Center, 1938-1980."

nights, their elegant forms silhouetted in the moonlight. . . . We still sail the rivers, moor in the creeks. . . . But it is different now. Rarely are we alone."

That tranquil world has been replaced forever by a rapidly expanding population. Despite the losses that accompany growth, residents of the peninsula see hopeful signs and are looking forward to progress in the new millennium. After decades of abuse, rivers and creeks are clearer, fish have returned, and some underwater vegetation is appearing. Endangered species like the peregrine falcon, the brown pelican, and the bald eagle are reported on the peninsula. Today most adults are conscious of the importance of protecting the environment, especially the critical wetlands. Children are the environment's best advocates, offering hope for the future. And neighborhoods remain friendly, unified by their loyalty to churches, schools, and community associations.

Despite the tremendous growth of the area, at the beginning of a new millennium people who live in nearly one hundred neighborhoods on the Pasadena peninsula remain neighborly and family-oriented. Newcomers and successive generations of natives choose to make their homes there because of the wide variety of housing options, the natural beauty of rivers and creeks, the vocational and cultural resources of a large city nearby, good schools with supportive parents, active churches with varied programs, extracurricular activities for youth, a choice of places to shop, career opportunities, and green spaces that offer recreation or peaceful contemplation. As in the past, strangers will feel the friendliness of the people and will join them in supporting schools, churches, and other local organizations and in struggling to balance human needs with the needs of the environment that gives the peninsula its special character.

Winter storm.
Photo: Mary Johnson

Stony Creek at Pine Haven.
Photo: Mary Johnson

Ducks in snow on frozen Stony Creek.
Photo: Wendy Harris

Sunrise on a foggy morning.
Photo: Mary Johnson

Appendix A

HISTORY OF THE PASADENA POST OFFICE AND ALL POST OFFICES THAT COVERED THIS SAME AREA

Emma M. Schramm
November 1, 1985

CONTENTS

PASADENA BOUNDARIES 1985

The boundaries of the area covered by Pasadena Post Office runs from Stoney Creek to Powhattan Beach, over to the intersection of Ritchie Highway and Mountain Road, south on Ritchie Highway to Earleigh Heights Road, out New Earleigh Heights Road to Magothy Beach Road until it runs into Magothy River, and everything north of the Magothy River. The area is made up of many small communities with a heavy concentration of beach properties. The areas to the immediate north of Stoney Creek have a Baltimore mailing address and are considered outside the sprawling area of Pasadena. Gibson Island is not considered part of Pasadena.

Map A shows what Pasadena in 1985 looks like on paper.

Map A

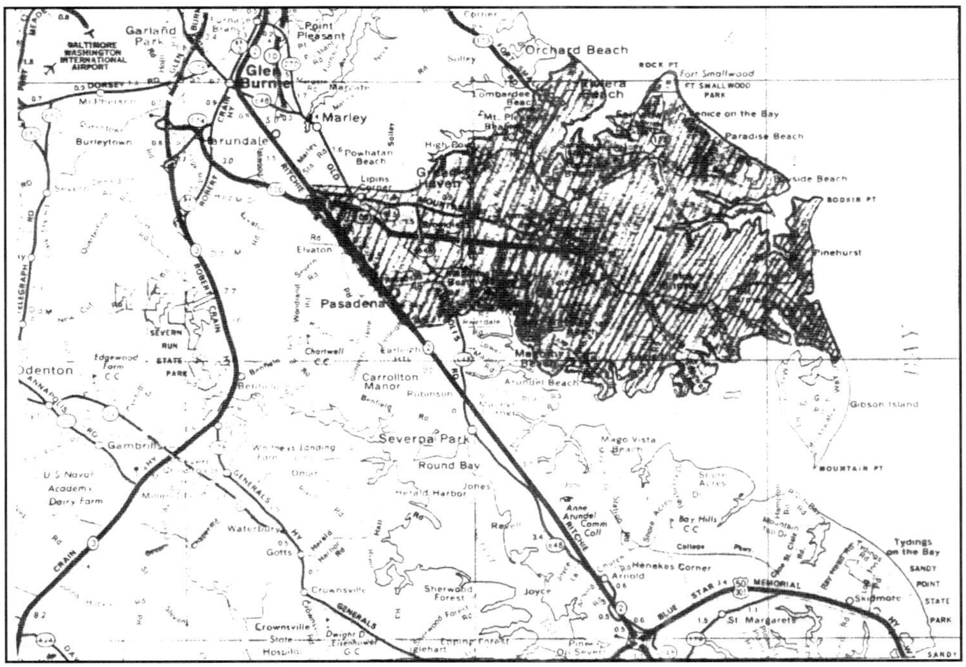

THE NAME OF PASADENA

The following is a quote from Hamill Kenny's *Origin and Meaning of the Indian Place Names of Maryland*, Waverly Press, Baltimore 1961—"Pasadena pae sa' dina].

A village near Earleigh Heights, Anne Arundel County (Gazetteer -MD 1941).

Fruit growers brought the Algonquian word, Pasadena, from Indiana to California in 1874. The BAE (Smithsonian) card index lists it as Ojibwa "a gap between mountains". Baraga (PtI, 1878) has Passadina "There is a low place between two mountains", a "valley".

There are no mountains near the Maryland village. Except for its being Algonquian, the name is entirely out of place in this county."

On August 13, 1888, the Southern Land and Silk Association of Baltimore City, Lizzie F. Baldy, President, purchased land in Anne Arundel Co.—Round Bay—Baldy Avenue and Pasadena Avenue, from Ida I. Carr. These same avenues are still there today, 1985.

This company also purchased land from William W. Brown and his wife. This was part of a tract of land known as Waterford and includes the present "town" of Pasadena.

This association planned to raise silkworms. It is believed that the wife of one of the men named the place Pasadena, after her former home in Pasadena, California.

FIRST POST OFFICE IN AREA—JOHNSON'S STORE

Map B shows the Pasadena area in 1860, and the name Pasadena is no where to be found. The only post office, for this area, on the map is Johnson's Store and Post Office, which appears to be at the location of Armiger Plaza or Mountain Road and Armiger Drive. The post office used to be in the building now known as the Eyeglass Menagerie, 2601 Mountain Road.

Map B

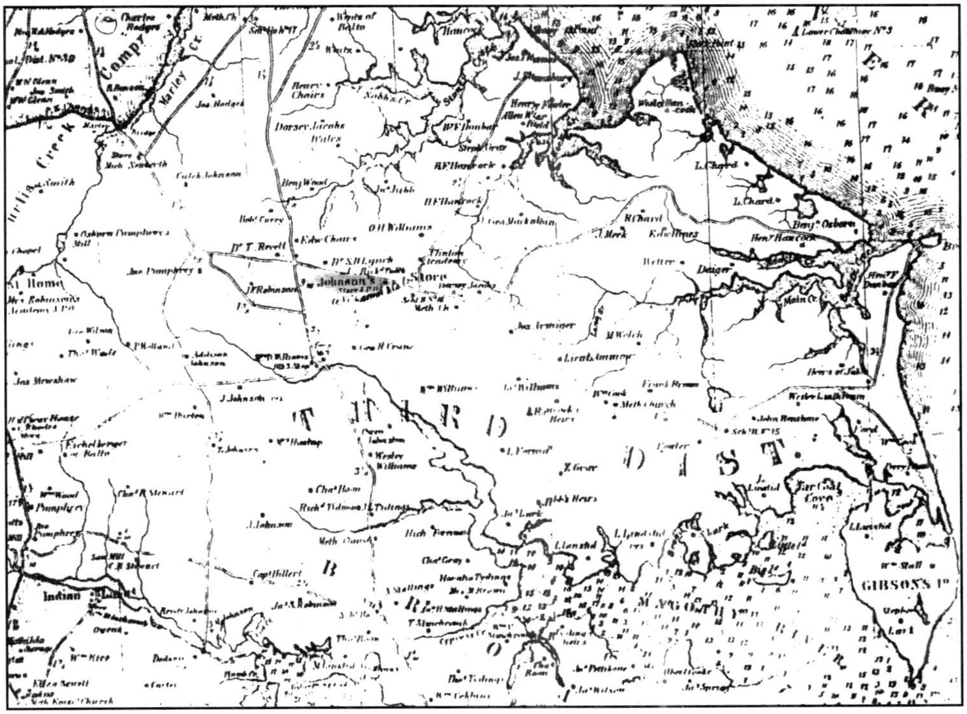

Johnson's Store is the only post office listed for this area in *"Postal Markings of Maryland, 1766—1855."*

According to the records at the national Archives in Washington, D.C. —Addison Johnson was postmaster in 1855 and Gerard S. Chesnut was postmaster in 1860. During the Civil War, the post office was discontinued (1863) and then reestablished the same year.

JACOBSVILLE

The name of the post office was changed from Johnson's Store to Jacobsville on September 20, 1872. I guess that the location was also moved to Jacobsville.

Map C from 1878 shows Jacobsville Post Office on the south side of Mountain Road at Hog Neck Road or the new Jacobsville School's property.

Members of the Jacobs family were postmasters from 1872 until 1888. Jacobsville Post Office was discontinued on March 17, 1888, and moved to Armiger.

On March 27, 1908, another post office by the name of Jacobsville was established with Emory W. McDaniel as postmaster. This office was discontinued on December 31, 1909, and moved to Elvaton.

Map C

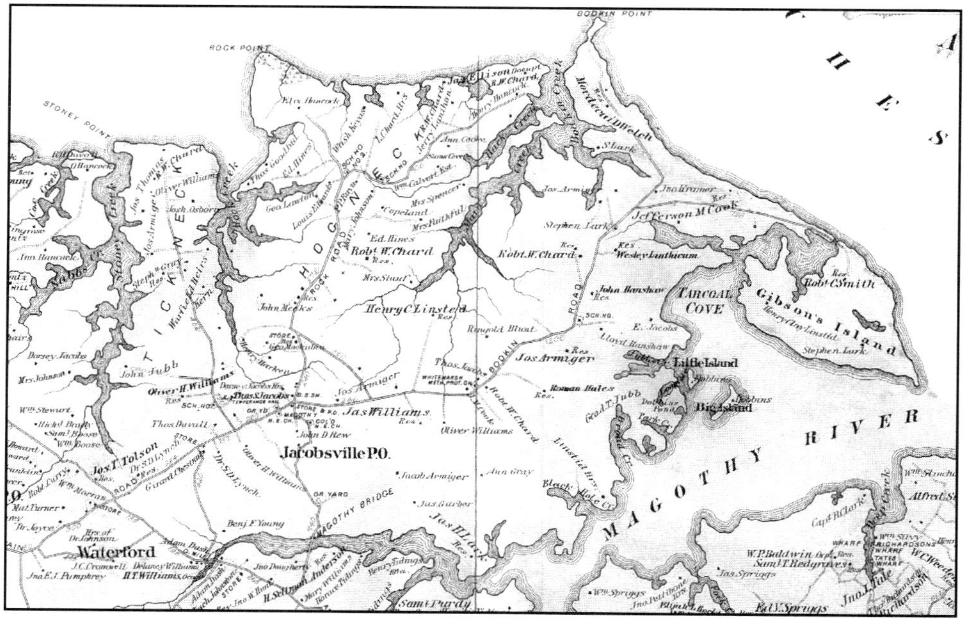

ARMIGER

On March 5, 1888, James S. Armiger applied for a new post office to be called Armiger. Charles H. Williams was to be the contractor to bring the mail three times a week. Mr. Armiger listed the nearest railroad stations as Johnson's Station (Elvaton) and Robinson Station. He estimated the population to be served at 1500.

Mr. James S. Armiger became postmaster on March 17, 1888. Jacobsville Post Office closed and moved to Armiger, which was then at Armiger Plaza again. This was the same location as the first post office of the area.

Mr. Thomas H. Benson became postmaster September 7, 1895. Mr. George Dauman became postmaster April 24, 1903.

In 1907, according to the records at the National Archives, Armiger Post Office moved 1-1/2 miles. It was still listed on Star Route 13238 which also served Maynard and Lake Shore. Mr. Benjamin A. Klug became postmaster November 25, 1907. Armiger Post Office was discontinued August 31, 1909, and moved to Elvaton.

Perhaps you are asking what is a star route. The Federal Government made contracts with private messengers for the delivery of mail to post offices that were difficult to reach by train or boat. This is why most of the forms in the National Archives on post offices ask nearest creek, river, and railroad station. Star routes became less important as railroads were built throughout the country. But when buses and automobiles became

popular and railroads stopped serving many places, the number of star routes increased. The routes are known as star route because post office records indicate such routes with three stars or asterisks—which stand for celerity, certainty, and security. Private messengers handled star routes.

The building which housed the Armiger Post Office also housed the first Armiger telephone exchange. In 1914, the C&P Telephone Company bought out the Rock Creek and Marley Telephone Company (exchange was in Klug's Store) and moved both to Schramm's farm.

MAYNARD

There was a post office called Maynard off of Fort Smallwood Road on Fairview Beach Road from May, 1888, to December 21, 1907, when it moved to Armiger. The postmasters were Edward W. Maynard (May 10, 1888), James M. Lockerman (December 12, 1899), Joseph R. Daniels (December 18, 1900), Henry D. Cook (November 16, 1901), William H. Windsor (June 8, 1903), and George H. Prescott (February 6, 1904).

LAKE SHORE

There was a Lake Shore Post Office in a store on the north side of Mountain Road, next to what is now the Lake Shore Fire House. It was listed as on the route from Myrtle (Glen Burnie) to Jacobsville. The postmasters were as follows: Orland J. Hales (1888), Charles G. Jacobs (1891), William D. Dorsey (1899), Herbert W. Moore (1912), and Sarah Sidle (1913). Lake Shore Post Office became part of Pasadena on February 15, 1916.

FROST - EARLEIGH HEIGHTS

There was a post office called Frost in 1887. This office was two miles south of Elvaton and two miles north of Robinson. Frost was changed to Earleigh Heights in 1892 and located 30 feet on the east side of the B&A Short Line. Since the present area of Pasadena includes the north side of Earleigh Heights Road, and Map D shows Earleigh Heights Post Office taking care of all of Earleigh Heights Road, it is certain that the present day (1985) Pasadena area includes some of what used to be Earleigh Heights Post Office area.

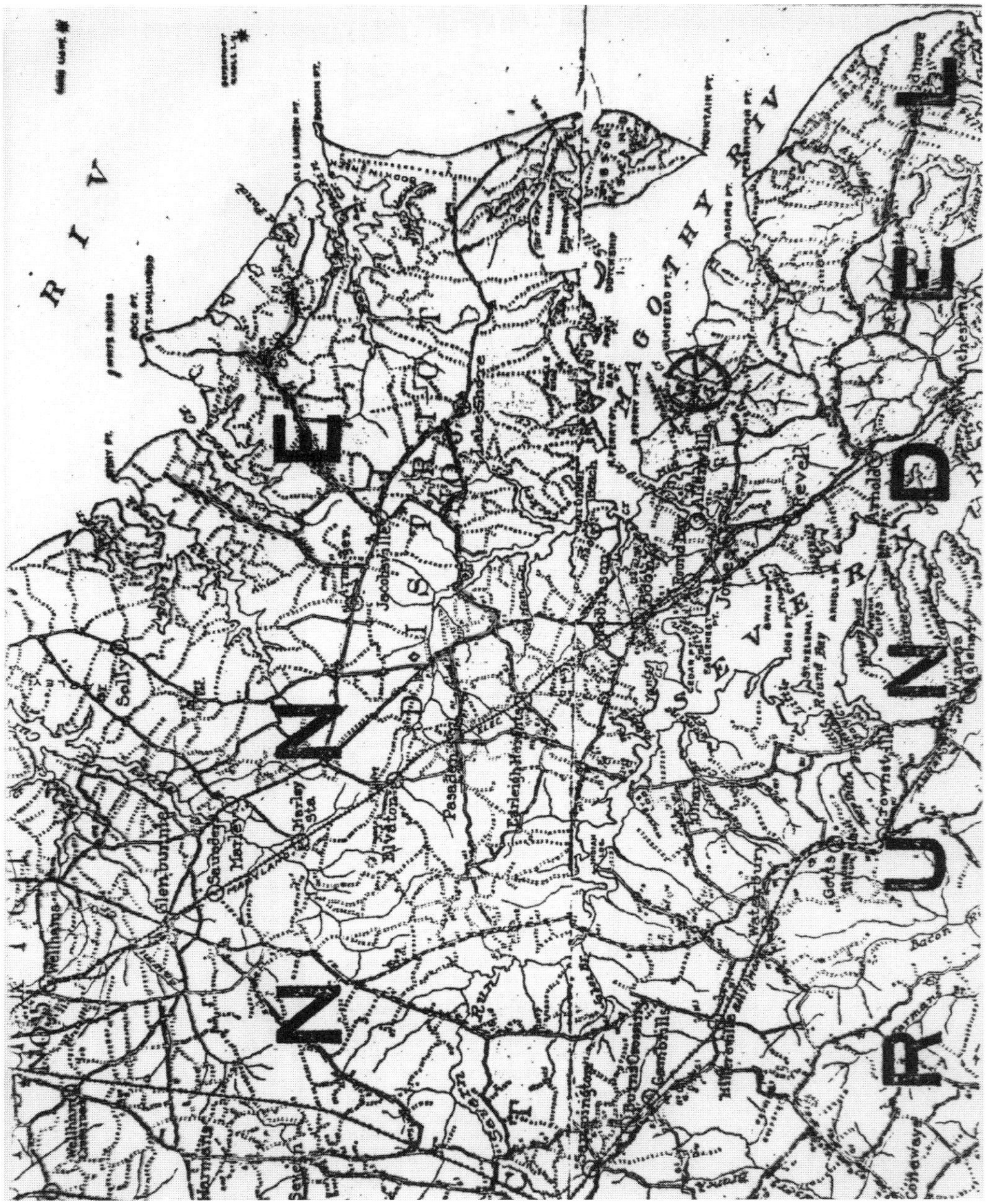
ANNE ARUNDEL
Pasadena
Jacobsville
Glenburnie
Arnold
Revell
Round Bay
Millersville
Severn
Marley
Elvaton
Selby

Map D

AMUSIA—NEW ALTONA

In 1917, Mr. T. L. Stine was postmaster of Amusia, 200 yards on the south side of the Rock Creek Steam Boat Company Wharf at Fairview Beach. This was the same location as the Maynard Post Office (1888—1907). On April 14, 1920, the name was changed from Amusia to New Altona.

The location was also changed from Fairview Beach to New Altona Beach on Stony Creek. It was served by the Stoney Creek Steam Boat Company with Baltimore as the source of supply. Mr. Stine estimated he would be serving 50 patrons and a great deal of transit in summer. There were to be no cancellations. On February 15, 1925, this post office became part of Glen Burnie.

MARLEY—SOLLEY

The other two post offices near the Pasadena area were Marley and Solley. I am not sure if they ever served part of the Pasadena area. The records at the National Archives only give the postmaster and the location—not the area covered by each post office.

ELVATON

One of the older post offices that most people remember is Elvaton. This post office was located near Elvaton Station. One record in the National Archives refers to it as Johnson's Station. The community which now bears the name Elvaton was at one time called Elvatown in honor of Dr. Johnson's wife, Elva.

The postmasters of Elvaton were: Clarence S. Johnson (January 19, 1889), Barbara Childs (May 4, 1893), Greenberry Sappington (January 24, 1896), Ellen Wade (May 25, 1898), Elzey Lee Wade (September 30, 1909), and Albert Clark (April 28, 1914).

As you can see on the following page, the records from the National Archives in Washington are not very clear and not complete. On the change of location in 1898, Ellen Wade would serve approximately 100 population which is quite different from the population served today.

A TIME LINE OF THE POST OFFICES OF THE 1985 PASADENA AREA

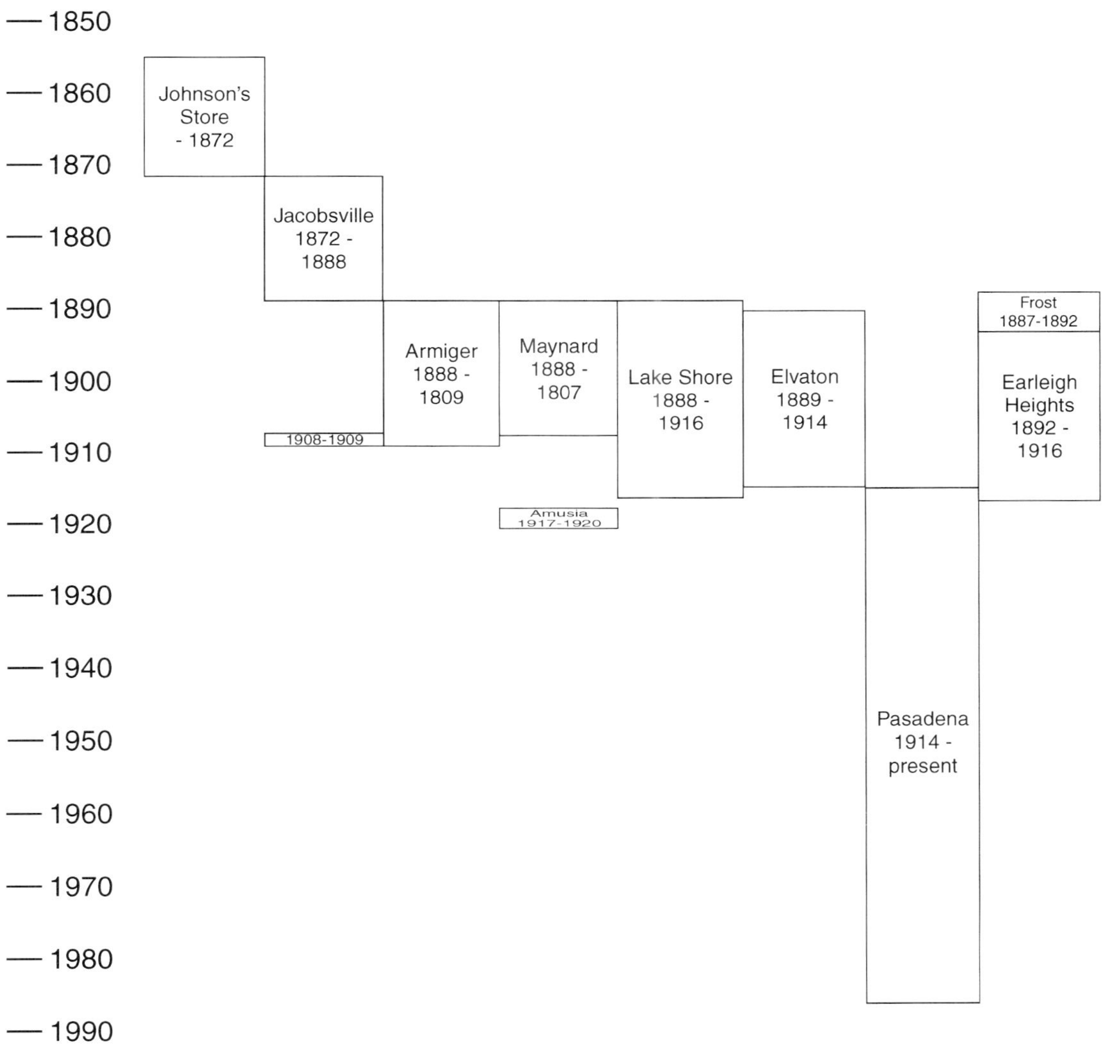

PASADENA

Finally, we get to Pasadena Post Office. On August 8, 1914, the name of the post office was changed from Elvaton to Pasadena. Mr. Albert B. Clark was postmaster and the location was 200 yards on the east side of the railroad.

Some of the other locations of the Pasadena Post Office are Mission and Light Streets, 200 feet west of Ritchie Highway, Pasadena Station Building, part of Clarence Johnson's Store, the building on the corner of Hamburg and Magnolia Streets (August 1949), and then to Ritchie Highway.

Before 1896, there was not rural free delivery of mail. Everyone had to go to the post office for all mail. Farmers' organizations were active in getting Congress to provide money for free delivery of mail to rural areas. In 1917, the service of rural free delivery was extended to most of the rural districts of the United States. I can't find any written information on the rural route carriers of Pasadena, Maryland. This is by word of mouth— Mr. Charles Boone delivered mail to the post offices only—some say. Other people say to individuals. Mr. Herbert Groh was a carrier from approximately 1914 until he entered the service for World War I. He was drowned in a seaplane accident off Cape May, New Jersey, on October 8, 1918. He was delivering mail for the Navy. Mr. Ernest Ruths, Sr. and then Mr. Jefferson Chairs delivered mail from approximately 1916 to July 23, 1919.

Mr. Raymond Benton became a rural carrier on July 23, 1919, and for 21 years, he delivered all the mail out of Pasadena Post Office by himself. During this period of time, a doctor had car trouble near Mr. Benton's home. Mr. Benton helped to get the car running and got gasoline over one hand. When he got home, it caught fire from the heat of the stove. He continued to deliver mail with only one good hand.

The line on Map D (1915) indicates the route taken by Mr. Herbert Groh. Please note mail was not delivered on every road. Sometimes several boxes would be together in a row. We seem to be going backwards with mail boxes grouped together in Chesterfield and Turf Valley.

Mr. Edward C. Seipp started the second route on June 1, 1940. So that means in forty-five years, Pasadena Post Office area has increased from two routes to a total of 32 routes—19 rural routes and 13 house-to-house deliveries.

THE POSTMASTERS FOR PASADENA

Albert Clark	August 8, 1914
James A. Winslow	Appointment Rescinded April 9, 1919
Vallonia B. Pratt	(Acting) June 6, 1919
James A. Winslow	November 1, 1919
Mrs. Hazel C. Winslow	December 16, 1925
Harold C. Winslow	March 18, 1926
John M. Appleton	(Acting) May 19, 1930
Clarence H. Chute	February 26, 1931
Edward C. Seipp	March 1, 1947
William Riddle	October 14, 1972

City delivery service was established May 16, 1959.

Riviera Beach Branch established as rural branch February, 1948. Changed to classified branch, December 4, 1961.

Green Haven Branch established as rural branch October 1, 1951.

Lake Shore Branch established as rural branch October, 1952. Changed to classified branch November 15, 1969.

Pasadena now has 68 people employed, 32 of whom are mail carriers. Of these 32, 19 are rural route and 13 are house-to-house delivery.

Pasadena now takes care of approximately 56,000 people with 14,116 mail boxes or stops.

There are 384 lock boxes at the main office, 320 at Riviera Beach, and 144 at Lake Shore, making a total of 848 lock boxes.

In this history, I have not included all the substations because there is not much information written on them.

MY SOURCES OF INFORMATION

Microfilms – National Archives, Washington, D.C.

N 841 – Roll 55

M 1126 – Roll 264

Copies of microfilms donated to Riviera Beach Library

History of Pasadena School—Social Studies Unit 1955–1956 Copy at Pasadena School.

Origin and Meaning of the Indian Place Names of Maryland, Hamill Kenny – Waverly Press 1961.

Postal Markings of Maryland, 1766-1856.

Maps included in this history:

Map A—Rand McNally, 1985 Baltimore with Metropolitan Baltimore-Washington, D.C.

Map B—Maryland State Archives Special Collections (Maps), 187 Martenet's Map of A.A. Co.

Map C—Maryland State Archives Special Collections (Maps), 297 Hopkins Atlas of A. A. Co., pp. 18-19 Third District, 1878

Map D—Rand McNally & Company Map of Anne Arundel and Prince Georges Counties, Maryland, 1915

Mr. William Riddle, Postmaster of Pasadena Post Office.

NOTES

Please forgive me if I made some mistakes, but I had some trouble reading some of the microfilm. The archives' records are not complete.

Many, many thanks to everyone that has helped me in some way. A special thanks to Catherine Wachter for typing this for me.

Emma Schramm

After I had finished my history of Pasadena Post Office. Mr. Phil Cook found this account written in a ledger his mother and sisters had kept:

"Herbert Groh gave the mail up in 1917. Mr. and Mrs. Ware carried it until September, then Ernest Ruth carried it to December, then Jeff Chaus carried it until July 1918, then old Mr. Ruth carried it until the last of October. Mr. Myers, the hotel keeper of Fairview took charge of it until the spring of 1919 when Mr. Duchmiller commenced carrying it. He carried it a few months. Then Mr. Benton from Pasadena took it.

Appendix B

COMMUNITY ASSOCIATIONS ON THE PASADENA PENINSULA

October 30, 2000

1. Armiger Community Association
2. Aspen Park Homeowners Association
3. Bahama Beach Community Association
4. Bar Harbor
5. Barrington Manor Community Association
6. Bayside Beach Community Association
7. Beacrane Community Association
8. Beauty Beach Community Association
9. Bell Forest Homeowners Association
10. Blossom Hills Community Association
11. Bodkin Pointe
12. Boulevard Park Association
13. Brittingham Community Association
14. Cedarwood Cove Community Association
15. Chandler Pointe Homeowners Association
16. Chasewood Run Civic Association
17. Chelsea Beach Resident Association
18. Chesterfield
19. Chestnut Hill Cove
20. Clearview Village Association
21. Clearwater Beach Community Association
22. Cottage Grove Community Association
23. Country Place Homeowners Association
24. Dales Homeowners Association
25. Deerfield Open Space Association

26. Eagle Hill Community Association
27. Elizabeth's Landing Community Association
28. Fairwood Association
29. Forest Glen Community Association
30. Freetown Community Association
31. Gibson Island Corporation
32. Greater Pasadena Council
33. Green Haven Community Association
34. Green Gables Association
35. Havenwood Community Association
36. High Point Improvement Association
37. Highpoint Community Association
38. Hunters Harbor Community Association
39. Lake Waterford Community Association
40. Laurel Acres Community Association
41. Lombardee Beach Community Association
42. Long Point Community Association
43. Luke Gardens Civic Association
44. Lyndale Community Association
45. Magothy Beach Community Association
46. Magothy Cove Homeowners Association
47. Magothy Estates Community Association
48. Magothy Forest Community Association
49. Magothy Forge Community Association
50. Magothy Park Beach

51. Mount Pleasant Beach
52. Middlebury Community Association
53. North Shore Association
54. Norwich Acres Association
55. Oak Hollow Community Association
56. Orchard Beach Community Association
57. Paradise Beach Community Association
58. Pekin Villa Community Association
59. Pine Grove Village
60. Pine Haven Improvement Association
61. Pinehurst/Bodkin Association
62. Poplar Ridge Community Association
63. Powhatan Beach Improvement
64. Queens Park Community Association
65. Race Point Homeowners Association
66. Riviera Isles Community Association
67. Riviera Beach Community Improvement
68. Rock Creek Surfside
69. Rock Hill Beach Community Association
70. Rock Creek Park Association
71. Rockview Beach Association
72. Rockwood Beach Community Association
73. Royal Beach Community Association
74. Saybrooke Homeowners Association
75. Sharonville Civic Association

76. Sillery Bay Association
77. Sillery Bay/Hunters Harbor Civic
78. Silver Sands Community Association
79. Solley Civic Association
80. Stone Haven Improvement Association
81. Stoneview Community Association
82. Stony Beach Community Association
83. Stoneybrooke Village Association
84. Sunset Beach Community Association
85. Sunset Knoll Community Association
86. Sun Valley Improvement and Recreation Association
87. Sylvan View Community Association
88. Venice on the Bay Civic Association
89. Ventnor Community Association
90. Water Oak Point Community Association
91. Water Oak Cove Association
92. Water Oak Forest Community Association
93. West Riverdale
94. Westridge Community Association
95. Wharf Creek Association
96. Whites Cove Community Association
97. Windemere Community Association
98. Woodbrooke Improvement Association
99. Woodholme Community Association

Original Sponsors

Angel's Food Market, Inc.

The Clocker Family, 4681 Mountain Road, Pasadena, MD 21122 / Ph: 410-255-6800 Fax: 410-255-3501

When Angel's Food Market first opened in 1923, Mountain Road was a country lane leading to weekend holidays at Pasadena beachfront communities. It was the place to stop for picnic supplies and cold drinks. When the Angel family sold it to Andrew Goodwin in 1959, the store had become the primary supermarket for the area. Mr. Goodwin's daughter and son-in-law, Joyce and Tom Clocker, bought the store in 1971. Their three sons, Tom, Andrew and Walt, have all managed the business and their children have begun working in the store.

Angel's is a much-loved store, but local residents are not the only shoppers. Salad lovers from all over make the trip to buy the famous cole slaw, macaroni and potato salads which are essential for every special occasion throughout the year. Now Angel's ready-to-serve meals, including Italian specialties, German sour beef and dumplings and Maryland crab soup, are earning the same reputation for quality and freshness. The homemade meals are available in individual portions as well as family-size meals.

With fresh produce, an in-store bakery, a large delicatessen, and quality meats and seafood, Angel's remains the principal supermarket for many people. The full line of beer, wine and liquor make Angel's truly a "one-stop" shopping destination.

It's also the place where neighbors meet one another and chat for a while in what many consider Pasadena's "Town Square." While quality, freshness and homemade food are priorities for the Clocker family, they all believe in this comfortable way of shopping. They say:

Angel's—where you are treated like a neighbor, not a number.

Constellation Power Source Generation, Inc.

1000 Brandon Shores Road, Baltimore, MD 21226 / Glenn Nilson Ph: 410-787-6475 Fax: 410-787-6529

THE POWER BEHIND PASADENA

For more than 40 years, the power behind Pasadena has risen tall along the shores of the Patapsco River. The stacks of the Brandon Shores and H. A. Wagner electric power plants are as much a part of the Pasadena landscape as seafood. And since the 1950s, those plants and the people behind them have provided the energy that has kept both Pasadena and Central Maryland moving, growing and improving. On July 1, 2000, these BGE plants were transferred to Constellation Power Source. Both companies are members of Constellation Energy Group. (NYSE: CEG)

Conceived in the first flush of economic and population growth after World War II, the first unit of the Herbert A. Wagner generating station began operating commercially on February 15, 1956. At the time it was the largest operating unit on BGE's system, generating enough electricity to supply 300,000 people. By 1972, Wagner's size had quadrupled to keep pace with the region's ever-growing demand for electricity.

While the economy slowed after the oil embargo of the mid-1970s, it bounced back in the 80s and 90s. To meet the new surge in demand for electricity, Brandon Shores Unit 1 began operation in May 1984 and Unit 2 in May 1991.

Today, Brandon Shores ranks as the cleanest coal-burning plant in Maryland. Both units were built to burn low-sulfur coal, making them at the outset an environmentally sound, reliable and low-cost source of electricity. Over the years, BGE, and now Constellation Power Source, have continued to install state-of-the-art environmental control equipment to reduce plant emissions further and produce cleaner air for the region.

More than 300 employees work at the plants, and many of them live and volunteer in the area. In fact, Constellation Energy Group is the largest corporate philanthropic contributor in the state and is actively involved in a multitude of civic, cultural, educational, environmental and health and welfare organizations throughout Anne Arundel County.

Constellation Power Source as BGE has had a long and proud association with Pasadena and is now looking ahead to the future. Maryland has joined the growing number of states that are deregulating their electric generation industry, giving customers their first opportunity to shop around for electricity. Constellation Power Source is well positioned to meet the wholesale energy needs of North America, and BGE prepared to continue safely and reliably delivering the electricity needed by 1.1 million consumers.

Situated on 375 acres along Pasadena's Ft. Smallwood Road, the Brandon Shores/H. A. Wagner Complex today generates enough power to meet the energy needs of 40% of the 2.6 million people living in Central Maryland.

Century 21 Volke Realty

Mark Volke / Karyn Volke, 4181 Mountain Road, Pasadena, MD 21122 / Ph: 410-437-1900 Fax: 410-437-1917
email: markvolke@realtor.com

As lifelong Pasadena residents, Karyn and Mark Volke love this area where they have worked with thousands of families and businesses through Century 21 Volke Realty. Founded 11 years ago, the business has grown through referrals and repeat business from many satisfied clients.

(Left to right) Karyn Keating Volke, Mark Volke, Sharon Adams, Henry Summey, and Debby Price.

"We started our business so people would have a homegrown Realtor who knows the community, is a part of the community and knows many of the residents," said Karyn. "All of our agents are full-time professionals living in this area, your neighbors."

Real estate is a natural outgrowth of the couple's love of people and their history of volunteerism. Mark has been a hurricane relief worker twice, served as church deacon, and held offices in various professional and community associations. His father, the Rev. Charles Volke, pastored Grace Baptist Church in Sunset Beach for 20 years. Mark graduated from Northeast High School and holds B. S. degrees in both business and marketing from Towson State University.

Karyn grew up in Pasadena and graduated from Northeast and Anne Arundel Community College. She has been involved in Laurel Acres-Whipoorwill Community Association and is a long-time school volunteer.

Mark and Karyn believe in the importance of family and community. Along with their three daughters, April, 13, Candace, 12, and Claire, 8, they enjoy local sports and are active in church activities.

Mark and Karyn are serious about their profession and each holds a GRI (Graduate of Realtors Institute) and CRS (Certified Residential Specialist) designation. They and their agents are experts in residential sales and listings, commercial and land sales, property management, buyer brokerage, HUD and VA foreclosures. As part of Century 21, the world's largest real estate firm, the small, personalized agency still has the advantages of nationwide advertising, research and relocation resources.

"To us, real estate is a counseling job; we don't sell anything," said Karyn, explaining the conviction she and Mark have about their profession. "We help people make good buying or selling decisions. We use our education, experience and resources to provide all the information they need. We get to know people and develop a trusting relationship, a friendship with our clients. Then we let them make the decisions."

Mark and Karyn believe Century 21 Volke Realty continues to attract clients because they are committed to supporting their clients throughout the life-changing experience of buying and selling real estate.

Cheshire Crab Restaurant and Pleasure Cove Marina

Jerry Herson, 1701 Poplar Ridge Road, Pasadena, MD 21122 / Restaurant: 410-360-2220 Marina: 410-437-6600
Fax: 410-437-6127 Web Site: www.pleasurecovemarina.com

The Cheshire Crab Restaurant and Pleasure Cove Marina have an impressive array of dining and marina services assembled by owner Jerry Herson. His goal is to be a neighborhood business affordable to every one.

"It is important to me that anyone can come here to eat, to store a boat, to get an engine replaced, to fuel up—whatever is needed—and know they are a welcome and important customer," says Jerry. "Our state-of-the-art travel lift can take care of the largest boat that can get down the Bodkin, but we want the runabout boater to feel that his business is appreciated, too."

The Cheshire Crab has a full-service bar separate from the restaurant. Over 75% of the 150 employees in the marina and restaurant are from Pasadena and Jerry wants the atmosphere to be one where families are comfortable having them work there. "We are a neighborhood, family-oriented place," said Jerry.

The Cheshire Crab serves a wide variety of meals including seafood, steak and Italian specialties, sandwiches and, of course, steamed to order crabs.

"We always try to have crabs, and bring them in daily year round ," said Jerry. "Our waterfront deck has become a popular crab-eating spot, and the Sunday brunch is a real favorite of our customers."

The deck overlooks the deep, calm harbor of Pleasure Cove Marina. Heavy-duty lifts take the boats out of the water and store them on shore on covered racks, keeping the boats free of the ravages of the water and protecting the environment.

Offering full marine repairs including entire engine replacements, parts, fuel and water taxi service on the Bodkin, Pleasure Cove Marina offers patrons of the Cheshire Crab Restaurant a discount on their fuel. There is also the Ship's Store filled with sundries for boaters.

Jerry Herson wants to become even more involved in the community and is currently planning a swimming pool and gymnasium which would be available to local high schools and offer low-cost memberships to the public year. It may possibly include a day spa and other amenities.

"There are not many reasonably priced facilities like this in this area," explained Jerry. "I believe we can offer a total recreation center that everybody can use. I want Pleasure Cove and Cheshire Crab to be the place where everybody can relax and have fun."

Chilltrol, Inc.

Dick Roeder, Jr., 152 Blades Lane, Glen Burnie, MD 21060 / Ph: 410-360-2700 Fax: 410-761-6313 email: chilltrol@aol.com

With professionalism as its hallmark, Chilltrol has become recognized for its highly trained and experienced staff as they install and service heating, air conditioning and refrigeration systems. "I actively recruit only the top HVAC (heating, ventilation, air conditioning) mechanics who can meet the standards we set for our team," explains Chilltrol President Dick Roeder, Jr. "People know when they call us, we will handle any problem that may occur. We have the experience, the manpower and the equipment."

Starting in his home garage 12 years ago, Dick has built his business into a fleet of 50 vehicles and a team of 78 employees. "We cover the entire state of Maryland and the surrounding areas," said Dick. "About forty- five percent of our work is custom residential, forty-five percent is commercial and ten percent is industrial."

Chilltrol's residential experts specialize in custom-built homes. Homeowners have come to rely on Chilltrol for distinctive systems, whether repairing or replacing systems in older homes or designing systems for new custom-built homes. Courtesy and cleanliness, along with expert performance, have been cited by homeowners as the reason to call Chilltrol.

Always working toward the goal of making his company the best in its field, Dick Roeder is expanding carefully. Now reaching the largest industrial and government customers, including the U.S. Naval Academy, Coca-Cola, and Hewlett Packard, all employees take pride in building the business as part of the Chilltrol team. "We can attract the highly trained and experienced HVAC professionals based on our employee compensation and bonus plans," explains Dick. "I want everyone to share in the success of our business."

Always on call, Chilltrol has a 24-hour operator who can dispatch a mechanic immediately to handle any problems. With a computerized sheetmetal shop, a fully staffed Service Department, and as the second largest Trane dealer in this area, Chilltrol continues to be first when commercial, industrial and residential customers need HVAC installation and repair service.

Edison Electric Company, Inc.

Mike Thompson, 200 Holsum Way, Glen Burnie, MD 21060 / Ph: 410-582-9777 Fax: 410-582-9616

If anything defines the opportunities that hard work and small business provide, it is the history of Edison Electric Company, Inc. Once a stockboy working for Edison founder John "Jack" R. Raap, Mike Thompson is now the owner and president of the company and has built the business into one of the largest electrical contractors in the area.

Edison Electric began as a one-man business in Jack's Sunset Beach home garage in 1967. After moving to Mountain Road a year later, Edison grew along with the Pasadena community around it. By 1981, Jack had made Edison a prominent force in the electrical field with 20 employees, including Mike Thompson. Though the recession of the 80s slowed business, Jack never laid off a single employee.

Mike had worked his way up to foreman, then president, when tragedy struck in 1990 with CEO Jack Raap's sudden passing. His wife, Rhonda, managed the company for two years before selling it to Mike. The business remained on Mountain Road until the rapid growth of the building industry forced it to relocate to a larger facility in Glen Burnie in 1997.

Now with 40 employees, Edison Electric Company, Inc. continues serving the Pasadena community and surrounding areas. Residential jobs as small as installing an outlet or dimmer switch or as large as rewiring an entire home are done expertly by qualified electricians. "People feel comfortable calling Edison because they know us, and their families know our families," said Mike. "And we always offer free estimates on any job."

Edison Electric also received the coveted "Sub Contractor of the Year Award" for the past seven years from both Ryan Homes and NV Homes. This recognition for expertise in new construction has made Edison's future growth a certainty.

"We are hoping to open additional locations throughout Maryland which will eventually allow for employee ownership," explained Mike. Jack Raap's legacy of loyalty and success continues on through Mike Thompson and Edison Electric Company, Inc.

GableSigns, Inc.

Paul and Matt Gable, 7440 Ft. Smallwood Road, Baltimore, MD 21226 / Ph: 410-255-6400 Fax: 410-437-5336
email: solutions@gablesigns.com Web: www,gablesigns.com

For almost twenty years, GableSigns has been making its mark throughout Pasadena and surrounding areas with its attractive signs and attention-getting graphics. Visit any business, school, church, community or shopping center and chances are you'll see a Gable sign.

From modest beginnings in their parents' backyard, owners Paul and Matt Gable have grown GableSigns, Inc. into a nationally recognized company known for quality designs and craftsmanship.

Paul, GableSigns' founder and president, quickly developed a reputation for his talent by winning a trophy in a school poster contest when he was eight. His first "paying" sign project came at the age of eleven for a local snowball vendor. "The pay was $7.00 and free snowballs for the summer. What a deal!" quips Paul. While at Chesapeake High School, Paul took graphic arts courses and began making a pitch to local businesses for his signs.

Upon graduation in 1980, Paul saw an opportunity to turn his passion into a career and began making signs in his parents' garage. As this backyard enterprise grew with new clients and a few part-time employees, his brother Matt started committing his after school hours to the company, joining on full-time after graduation in 1985. "Without a doubt, Matt's knowledge of the industry, his enthusiasm and his motivation have been a driving force behind the success of our company," Paul affirms.

Moving to a commercial building on Ft. Smallwood Road in 1986, GableSigns expanded its capabilities to include fabricated metal, plastic, electrical and neon signs. It was here the company grew steadily over the next 13 years as buildings and equipment were up-graded to meet the needs of customers and additional employees. "Because we started locally, many of our clients and employees live here in Pasadena," Matt comments. "We owe much of the credit for our company's success to them."

Today, GableSigns employs over 75 sign professionals and craftsmen, completing sign projects all over Maryland and surrounding areas. For some clients, their role has expanded to include shipping and installation all across the country. Regardless of the quantity or distance, the company stays focused on quality. Others agree as evidenced by the company's seventh consecutive design award granted by the United States Sign Council, an industry association with over 1,500 members.

This year, GableSigns moved to its newly constructed 40,000-square-foot state-of-the-art sign manufacturing facility. "The additional space and computerized sign-making equipment will enable us to provide better service, higher quality, and a nicer environment for our staff," Paul remarks.

Despite their growth and national recognition, Paul and Matt plan to keep their company firmly rooted in Pasadena. "It's a great place for our business," notes Paul. "And because it's our hometown, we take special pride in every project we do here."

J. B. Machine Parts and Supply, Inc. and J. B. Marine

Mike Jacobs, 8029 East Shore Road, Pasadena, MD 21122 / Ph: 410-437-9995 Toll Free: 888-437-9995
Fax: 410-360-1929 / email: web@jbmarine-machine.com

Long years of hard work and experience have produced the Up & Out Boat Lift, the most durable boat lift on the market. Manufactured by J.B. Marine, it meets the exacting standards of founder Dave Jacobs. While he was still working full time at Koppers Company, Dave Jacobs started doing automotive work in his back yard in the early 1960s. In 1973, that part-time business matured into a full-time industrial machine shop, J.B. Machine.

When his sons, Mike and Jamie, joined him in business, the company began to expand into manufacturing and installing boat lifts, adding J.B. Marine.

When J.B. Marine puts in a boat lift, the goal is perfection. "We always use extra heavy duty material and we never skimp in any area," explained Dave Jacobs. "We would rather make a smaller profit and give our customer the best value."

Now that Mike Jacobs has taken over the day-to-day business, he adheres to his father's philosophy. "We want to be the best," he says, "but we will never sacrifice the quality of our boat lift for any reason."

This dedication to quality has put J.B. Marine in demand throughout the East Coast. The company is now in the top ten of boat lift builders. "Customer satisfaction is big in this business," says Mike. "Most of our business has been word-of-mouth, and our reputation is widely known for excellence."

All manufacturing and assembly is done right at J.B. Marine in Pasadena. The company will move to larger quarters on Solley Road by the end of the year. J.B. Machine designs and manufactures parts and machinery for all types of businesses, and also repairs and maintains machinery.

"We are an industrial machine shop catering to the plastic, beverage, spice, recycling and computer industries," said Mike Jacobs, Dave's youngest son and president of the business "We repair and maintain machines that enable our customers to keep their worldwide businesses running smoothly."

J.B. Machine provides well-drilling equipment to a widespread area including southern and western Maryland, the Eastern Shore, and Virginia. J.B. Machine also has designed and manufactured a medical waste disposal system that can crush glass vials.

Shirley Jacobs, Dave's wife and business partner and the mother of Mike and Jamie, speaks with pride of her family and the business that has been a large part of their life. "Our business has survived all these years because of our strong belief in our family; we all work together."

In the photograph, left to right: Jamie, Mike, Dave, Shirley and Becky Jacobs

Jet Blast, Inc.

Tim Wilson, 6800 Ft. Smallwood Road, Baltimore, MD 21226 / Ph: 410-636-0730 Fax: 410-636-0819
Web: www.jetblast.com

Jet Blast was founded by its owner, Timothy Wilson, in February of 1979. With only $5,000 in capital and rented equipment, Tim began working out of his father's Pasadena garage. After Tim recruited a few of his fellow Northeast High School alumni, Jet Blast grew strong and fast. Tim soon moved Jet Blast to the much larger location on Ft. Smallwood Road. Led by Tim's management team, Ed Jefferson, Steve Jones, and Mike Mahon, Jet Blast's commitment to quality and excellence made it one of the industry's "Top Professionals." Named by *Inc. Magazine* as one of the Top 500 Fastest Growing Private Companies in the United States, Jet Blast has received numerous awards and industry recognition.

Over the past two decades, Jet Blast has provided services to some of the largest industrial, municipal and utility concerns on the East Coast, providing safe employment to hundreds of Pasadena residents.

Jet Blast, Inc. has harnessed the force of water under high pressure and turned it into the most powerful cleaning tool ever known to industry. Jet Blast technicians use specialized equipment operating at pressures up to 35,000 psi (enough to cut through six inches of steel or three feet of cement.) Additionally, Jet Blast maintains a fleet of the most technically advanced vacuum equipment with enough power to pick up a 10-pound brick. More important, however, is Jet Blast's commitment to quality and safety of its employees. All of Jet Blast's employees receive the most current technical training and use state-of-the-art safety equipment and procedures.

JET BLAST®

A proud member of the Pasadena Business Community since 1979

Koch Homes, Inc.

Richard E. Pezzullo, Jr., Director of Sales and Marketing, 2661 Riva Road, Suite 220, Annapolis, MD 21401
Ph: 410-573-5720 Fax: 410-573-5257 / Web: www.kochhomes.com

Quality homebuilding in Anne Arundel County has long been a tradition in the Koch family. It began in 1931 with Charles Koch purchasing 170 acres on the Magothy River for a private summer residence and future land development opportunity. The property was subsequently subdivided and developed into the community now known as "North Shore on the Magothy."

In 1951, Ross J. Koch started Bucher & Koch Realty Company, Inc., which focused primarily on custom building in North Shore and the surrounding Pasadena area. Over the next 25 years Ross Koch developed a reputation for exceeding industry standards for quality of construction and attention to detail. His son, Gary W. Koch, joined the firm in 1977 and Koch Homes, Inc. was founded a year later.

Koch Homes has become recognized as the premier homebuilder in Anne Arundel County as evidenced by numerous awards received for its outstanding achievements in residential development. It has been a five-time winner of the Anne Arundel County Award of Excellence, five-time winner of the Sales & Marketing Council Award, and two-time winner of the Land & Development Council Award.

Some of the communities developed by Koch Homes in the Pasadena area include Whippoorwill Estates, Sillery Bay Forest, Chandler Point, Saybrooke by the Lake, Blue Waters Farm, Meadow Run and most recently, Farmington Village.

Farmington Village, once a large part of the 200-acre historic Schramm farm, is currently being developed by Koch Homes. Farmington Village includes a wide variety of housing from affordable townhomes to luxury single family homes. Koch's reputation for quality, combined with amenities such as club house, pool and walking paths, has made it one of the fastest selling new developments in Anne Arundel County.

Farmington Village embodies the highest levels of standards for which Koch Homes has been recognized. A focus on a sense of arrival, relationship of home to land, and the feeling of an overall planned environment has made Farmington Village another award-winning community.

Kurtz's Beach, Ltd.

John Mason/Bonnie Kurtz, 2070 Kurtz Avenue, Pasadena, MD 21122 / Ph: 410-255-1280 Fax: 410-255-2062

Most of the beaches that drew city dwellers to Pasadena have disappeared, but Kurtz's Beach has done much more than survive. It is home to a flourishing catering business, Kurtz's Beach, Ltd., hosting hundreds of celebrations throughout the year from elegant weddings to summertime picnics and crab feasts.

With blue waters in the background, many brides have opted for an outdoor wedding in the waterfront gazebo. In cooler weather, the magnificent octagonal ballroom offers spectacular views, with a second hall available for larger crowds.

Outside, Bradford pear trees border the beach, and picnic tables stand under expansive, shady pavilions surrounded by lush shrubs and plants. In any season, Kurtz's presents a relaxing and lovely alternative to traditional catering halls. Only the food outshines the location.

"We are very particular about the freshness and quality of ingredients that we use for meals," says Master Chef John Mason, president of Kurtz Beach, Ltd., and a graduate of Baltimore International Culinary College. "Everything is prepared right here under close supervision of myself, my partner, Bonnie, and a dedicated staff of prep chefs."

Kurtz's serves good, basic meals like those found in your grandmother's kitchen, according to John, but presented with a flair that makes every event an occasion. Many corporations, large and small, entrust their picnics and parties to Kurtz's which provides not only the food, but entertainment as well. That can include DJ's, bands, kiddy rides, magicians, clowns, and even jousting for guests. Smaller groups enjoy Kurtz's on Multi-Picnic Days when two or three groups save costs by sharing the facilities.

John's first cousin, Bonnie Kurtz, is vice president of Kurtz's Beach, Ltd. She and her husband, Gus Kurtz, own the Kurtz Beach property. It was Gus' father and uncle, Gustave and Sam Kurtz, who founded the beach business in 1933. It went through several transformations until Bonnie and John formed a partnership to turn the former public beach into a site for private gatherings in the early 90s.

John and Bonnie share a love of catering, and both agree that their success can be attributed to the many members of their family who gather every week to lend a hand. "You will find mothers, fathers, aunts, uncles, brothers, sisters, nephews, nieces—even grandmothers—working everywhere, assuring that everything is as perfect as possible. Even staff members are related to somebody because they bring their families to work at Kurtz's too."

With rapidly increasing popularity, Kurtz's Beach, Ltd., has been offered seemingly golden opportunities to open other sites. John and Bonnie have rejected this idea because they would lose the personal touch and the family assistance, both a large part of the appeal and success of Kurtz's Beach, Ltd.

Kurtz's Beach with employee family.

Lauer's Supermarket and Bakery

Edward B. Lauer and Helen B. Lauer
Chesterfield Plaza, 8095-A Edwin Raynor Blvd., Pasadena, 21122 / Ph: 410-255-0070 Fax: 410-360-9574
Riviera Plaza, 8479 Ft. Smallwood Road, Riviera Beach, 21122 / Ph: 410-437-4800 Fax: 410-360-9609

**"Friendly, Fast and Fresh,
Serving You Is What We Do Best!"**

This motto sums up the core philosophy of Lauer's Grocery Stores, says founder and president, Ed Lauer. "Quality and freshness throughout our stores are always top priorities," he explains. "All of our employees understand how important it is that customers get only the best."

When Ed opened his first store on Mountain Road in 1974, his years of experience with Food Fair had prepared him for the long hours and hard work demanded by the grocery business. He closely managed all areas of the store, working side by side with store personnel to develop the Lauer way.

His wife, Helen, took a critical look at the produce department and decided to manage that area herself until it met her standards. She moved on to the bakery department, arriving at 2 a.m. each morning, until it too represented the above motto. Lauer's now has one of the finest and most complete lines of breads, pies and cakes, including custom orders.

A true family business, all five of the Lauer daughters worked at the store during their high school and college years. Two chose it as their career. Bernadette Snoops designed and installed the scanning system in the store in 1981, making it the first independent supermarket in Maryland to use the then-new technology. When the Riviera Beach location was purchased from Acme in 1982, daughter Babette Lauer Poyer joined the family business as did son-in-law Craig Snoops. Son-in-law Joseph Millsap joined the family business in January of 1991.

Lauer's has a family of employees too, many having worked in the stores 15 years or longer, including John Ferdock who celebrated his 25th year in 1999. A strong profit sharing plan and excellent benefits package engender employee loyalty and dedication to the business.

Education is dear to the heart of the Lauer family and "Lauer's Learning Ladder," a register tape redemption program open to all private and public schools, has provided thousands of dollars for a variety of educational tools. Strongly supporting the entire community, the store generously sponsors numerous sports teams and Downs Park concerts, proves food for church dinners and school functions, and gives discounts and direct donations to many worthy causes.

Now that both the Riviera Beach and Edwin Raynor Boulevard stores have been completely updated, the latest addition, the Lauer brand of customer commitment continues even stronger into the new millennium.

McCully-Polyniak Funeral Home, P.A.

Valerie Polyniak, 3204 Mountain Road, Pasadena, MD 21122 / Ph: 410-255-2381 Fax: 410-255-2604
Funeral Service, Pre-Planning and Pre-Financing, Cremation, Memorial Services

After 97 years of conducting funerals for over three generations in South Baltimore, Brooklyn, Pasadena and surrounding areas, McCully-Polyniak remains a family-owned, family-run business. "People have come to rely on our family, and trust our personal compassionate approach," said Valerie Polyniak, niece of Doris McCully and the late James L. McCully. Begun in South Baltimore by I. Few McCully, James' father, the family's philosophy has always been that of service, not business. "My uncle built this business on a man's word and a handshake. We consider everyone's financial situation and work with families during that intense time of bereavement."

With a degree in mortuary science including training in grief counseling, Valerie began working part-time with her aunt and uncle when she was 15. The relatively small number of funeral directors who are women include Doris McCully, also a licensed mortician, who served several terms on the State Licensing Board of Morticians. She and Valerie bring a special sensitivity at a time when it is most needed

"I always try to meet personally with the families," said Valerie. "Between Aunt Doris and myself, we do see everyone at all three locations to express our condolences. People always ask for Aunt Doris because of friendship and loyalty developed over the years."

Valerie is president of McCully-Polyniak Funeral Home, P.A., her Aunt Doris is vice president, and her husband John is secretary-treasurer as well as general manager of the entire operation.

Formerly in investment brokerage, John joined the firm in 1998. The couple has two children: Scott, 17, a senior at Mt. St. Joseph High School where he is an Honors student and vice president of his senior class, and Julie, 15, a sophomore at Chesapeake High School. A dancer since the age of 2, Julie is also active in the Galilee Lutheran Church Youth Group.

Valerie and John are raising their family in Pasadena, and are frequent Mountain Road travelers because of their business, community involvement and their children's activities. They keep the same hectic pace of most families today, but they never lose sight of the importance of their funeral service.

"After 30 years at our Mountain Road location, Pasadena families know they can rely on McCully-Polyniak to care for them as our friends and neighbors in their time of need," said Valerie.

"In this day of numerous corporate acquisitions, it brings us great pride to still be independently owned and operated. It is our hope to remain a family business for many years to come."

(Left to right) John and Valerie Polniak, Doris McCuly, Julie and Scott Polyniak.

Pastore's Italian Deli

Brian & Sue Metzbower, 3820 Mountain Road, Pasadena, MD 21122 / Ph: 410-255-8822 Fax: 410-255-8906

Pasadena's own Little Italy has stood at the corner of Mountain and Hog Neck roads for over 30 years. Although bright and modern, Pastore's Italian Deli still has the soul of the old, aromatic shops which had pasta-filled barrels and meats and cheeses hung from the ceiling.

Now shelves of packaged domestic and imported pasta in a multitude of shapes and cuts sit beside jars and cans of various olive oils, roasted peppers, pepperoncini, tomato pastes and sauces, ceci beans, pesto sauce, Italian tuna—everything to make the simplest or most exotic of Italian dishes.

The delicatessen boasts imported prosciutto, capacola, Genoa salami, mortadella and other musically-named meats as well as fresh Italian sausage links. Complementing them are fresh provolone, parmagianna, romano, fontinella and ricotta cheeses. Fresh mozzarella rests in water next to ricotta salada, marinated mushrooms, and homemade salads including pasta florentine and Greek pasta salad.

While Pastore's is a gourmet cook's dream, it is perfect for non-cooks too. Here you can purchase ready-made meals for two to 200. Homemade delicacies from simple sauce to trays of lasagna are ready for dinner. For larger crowds, Pastore's is known for its off-site catering, delivering hot meals and large sandwich platters with condiments included.

Pizza is everybody's favorite and Pastore's popular pizza kit has three crusts, Don Pepino sauce and a 9-ounce bag of specially blended grated pizza cheeses, all ready for your oven. Or you can have hot pizza delivered to you door seven days a week. Ordering one or more pizzas entitles your to delivery of anything else, from groceries to subs to meals. You can also dine in Pastore's comfortable cafe.

Pastore's has a great bakery filled with fresh bread and rolls, turnovers and doughnuts, and chunky chocolate cookies out of the oven every few hours. Refrigerated cases hold cannoli, tiramisu, cassata and rum cakes. It's a popular shopping spot during the holidays for buying pizzelle makers and cappuccino and espresso pots, as well as fine Italian candies and cookies.

Begun in 1966 by Les and Marge Rizzo, Pastore's has employed hundreds of Pasadena residents including Brian Metzbower when he was a teenager. He and his wife, Sue, became partners in 1984, then took full ownership when the Rizzo's retired in 1997. The children of both couples, Michella and Tina Rizzo, Jessica, Katie and Ashley Metzbower, have all worked in the business through the years.

Now employing 90 people, Pastore's is the first choice when there's a celebration, a wake, a business meeting or any event where delicious food and quick service is most important. Pastore's serves today's faster-paced society and still retains the personality and warmth of an old-time neighborhood shop.

Pastore's owners Brian and Sue Metzbower; daughter, Katie, left.

Phelps' Package Liquors, Inc.

Clifford R. Phelps, 4447 Mountain Road, Pasadena, MD 21122 / Ph: 410-255-0151 Fax: 360-8530

In 1928, Walter J. Phelps and his wife Mary purchased 25 acres of ground at Mountain and Woods roads. Walter was a descendant of that same Walter Phelps who moved his family to Anne Arundel County when he purchased a 100-acre farm at South River in 1673.

Like his ancestor, Walter J. Phelps was a farmer, but was better known for producing charcoal for a variety of Baltimore industries. Since 1895, he had been operating his coal business on Mountain Road near Solley Road on a farm belonging to his father-in-law, Dr. Elijah Joyce. Walter bought free standing timber in the area and employed a crew of men to cut it and construct "charcoal pits" on the property for the production of coal. He stockpiled large quantities of bagged charcoal which he transported to Baltimore by a two-horse wagon before he switched to a truck around 1918. Walter was listed in the Baltimore City Directory as owner of the Phelps Coal and Can Company as early as 1900.

Walter's son, Clifford A. Phelps, also worked in the family business of charcoal production and light farming on the family property. In 1935, Clifford A. Phelps married a Pasadena girl, Irene Brown, who helped in the family business. In 1937, Clifford A. and Irene had a son, Clifford R. Phelps. A year later, they opened a gasoline station at the corner of Mountain and Woods roads. In 1939, near the end of the era of charcoal burners in Anne Arundel County, Walter J. Phelps, the charcoal professional, passed away.

In 1947, the family's gasoline station was changed to a tavern which soon added a liquor store, becoming a tavern and liquor store combination. By 1956, farming in the Pasadena area was a disappearing occupation. It ended for the Phelps family in the same way that charcoal production had ended ten years earlier.

When Clifford A. Phelps passed away in 1971, the family business was continued by Clifford R. and his mother, Irene. In 1972, a son named Clifford M. was born to Clifford R. and his wife. By 1978 the tavern business had been discontinued and the liquor store enlarged. Cliff M. started in the family business at age 9, bagging all the store's ice. He now works in the liquor store and operates the family topsoil business, screening and delivering topsoil and fill dirt by the dumptruck load to homeowners in the area.

Redmond's Towing Service

Tom Redmond, 8224 Baltimore & Annapolis Boulevard, Pasadena, MD 21122 / Ph: 410-437-1111
Fax: 410-437-7432

Redmond's Towing Service has been known for providing quality service to the motoring public for the past 33 years. Begun by Tom Redmond when he was only 20 years old, the towing business has grown to include ten tow trucks, including wheel-lift and rollback trucks for specialty towing.

Although based in Pasadena, Redmond's Towing has accounts throughout Anne Arundel county and the state of Maryland.

Tom Redmond has traced roots back to 1675 when his ancestors first settled in Anne Arundel County. He was born in his grandmother's house on Solley Road and attended local schools.

A strong love of Pasadena turned him into a community and civic activist; he worked on legislative committees with the Maryland General Assembly for fifteen years. His commitment to the area was recognized when he was elected to represent this district on the Anne Arundel County Council.

Tom served two terms as president of the Towing and Recovery Professionals of Maryland, was president of the Maryland Auto & Truck Recyclers' Association, and was the president of the Pasadena Business Association for two years.

The Pasadena Business Association Thanksgiving Sharing and Caring Parade originated from Tom's idea that Pasadena should have its own parade. In November, 1996, he organized the first parade with the help of other PBA members. It was a huge success, and has become an annual event eagerly anticipated by the thousands who participate and line the parade route. Moreover, the parade helps collect tons of food which is distributed to needy families in the Pasadena community.

A life member of both the Anne Arundel County Historical Society and the Sierra Club, Tom was the first life member of Friends of Hancock's Resolution. He has worked many years for literacy, local youth sports and other environmental concerns.

Tom has seven children, Tom, Jr., Richard, Eric, Chad, Steven, Casey and William.

Tom Redmond with one of his signs that have welcomed motorists along Route 100 to Pasadena for over 25 years.

TeleRep Call Centers

Sandie and Don Olson, 14 Wellham Ave., Glen Burnie, MD 21061 / Ph: 410-761-2424 Fax: 410-761-3357
Web: www.telerep.com

When Sandie Olson decided the minimum wage she was being paid as an answering service operator was not enough, her husband, Don, a U. S. postal worker, encouraged her to start her own service. She took that challenge in 1975, beginning Arundel Telephone Secretaries, Inc. with only three small businesses that needed an answering service. As clients increased, Don joined her and they founded TeleRep Call Centers which now serves over 600 clients across the United States.

TeleRep is firmly committed to providing quality jobs for area residents. The corporate headquarters on Wellham Avenue in Glen Burnie has just been expanded to include all three floors that accommodate the almost 90 new employees who have joined the 60 already employed there.

All TeleRep operators are highly trained professionals using the latest technology. Sandie began in her basement with an old switchboard like the one used by Lily Tomlin's "Ernestine," but TeleRep now boasts the latest computerized phone systems. TeleRep's highly motivated Customer Service Representatives combined with state-of-the-art software allows TeleRep to represent businesses with maximum professionalism and integrity.

TeleRep still takes around-the-clock calls for plumbers, business reps and other service businesses, but it also fills the need for in-bound telemarketing and customer service. For example, the White House Historical Association catalog orders are all received and processed at TeleRep. Pizza Hut hired TeleRep to field all of their customer service calls from franchisees, while Pitney-Bowes uses TeleRep for customer service surveys.

The Internet is the next frontier for TeleRep, and Sandie and Don see exciting possibilities for their clients and their employees including televideo customer service.

Business success for Sandie and Don has helped their family grow closer. Evette is the sales manager, Amberly is the comptroller, and Heather is an employee trainer. Their son Wesley is 14, but he is already helping with the computers.

Almost family, Cynthia Blair-Smullin, a Pasadena native and company manager, has been with TeleRep for 20 years.

The Olsons attribute TeleRep's success to the dedication, loyalty and support of their associates and clients from Pasadena and surrounding areas.

The Olson family in TeleRep's computerized telephone center. *(Left to right)* Amberly, Sandie, Don, Heather, Wesley, and Evette.

The Bank of Glen Burnie

Joyce Cleveland, 8707 Ft. Smallwood Road, Pasadena, MD 21122 / Ph: 410-437-2070 Fax: 410-437-6432
Web: www.thebankofglenburnie.com

CELEBRATING 50 YEARS OF COMMUNITY BANKING

In the late 1940s, northern Anne Arundel County was experiencing tremendous growth. A group of local businessmen, concerned that banking services were not keeping pace with this growth, banded together and chartered The Bank of Glen Burnie. Founded as a locally-owned, independent community bank, The Bank of Glen Burnie opened its doors in August 1949. Since that day, business has been conducted on a first-name basis.

Today The Bank of Glen Burnie serves the commercial and retail banking needs of area residents with offices in Pasadena, Odenton, Crownsville, Severna Park, Severn, and Ferndale, in addition to two locations in Glen Burnie. Customers benefit from a comprehensive line of banking products and services, 24-hour telephone banking and a network of 11 ATMs.

The Riviera Beach Office—which celebrated its 25th Anniversary in 1998—is one of the Bank's most active branches.

"We know the retail and commercial needs of our customers because we are part of this community," said Joyce Cleveland, Assistant Vice President and Branch Manager. "Our staff, directors, and stockholders live and work in these neighborhoods. You are going to meet us in the grocery store, at church and on the ball fields with our children. This is what community banking is all about."

The Bank of Glen Burnie's great strength and stability have been built on a commitment to personalized customer service, strong leadership and local decision-making. In the face of emerging technologies and overwhelming industry changes, these attributes have withstood the test of time.

The Bank of Glen Burnie pledges to carry on the tradition of community banking and is ready to meet the challenges of providing a new decade of service to all its valued customers, old and new.

Tom Clocker of Angel's Food Market with Joyce Cleveland, vice president of The Bank of Glen Burnie and Riviera Beach branch manager.

W. Ray Huff & Associates, Inc.

W. Ray Huff, 8349 Ritchie Highway, Pasadena, MD 21122 / Ph: 410-647-1111 Fax: 410-544-5735
Web: www.Huffinsurance.com

W. Ray Huff & Associates, Inc. is now insuring its third generation of clients, providing all types of insurance including health, life, auto and casualty.

"We do little advertising because the majority of our business is referrals from satisfied customers," said Ray Huff, founder and president of the agency. "We believe in service after the sale. We explain updated coverage for current policies, let clients know about changes, help process claims, and make sure the claims are paid."

Ray became a licensed independent agent in 1960, starting out in his home garage, then moving to Glen Burnie and eventually building his Pasadena office in 1967.

"I really like helping people," he said. "We have helped many, many small businesses over the years and I can honestly say that some of our commercial work saved businesses from failure."

An affable man, Ray's love of people brought him success not only in business but in the community, too. He was a respected member of the Maryland House of Delegates for eight years and served on the boards of many civic groups such as the YMCA.

His daughter, Nancy Huff Nicklow, a Salisbury University business graduate, has worked in the agency since she was a teenager. A licensed agent since 1994, Nancy is now office manager as well as manager of personal lines insurance.

Faith Vanskiver, agency vice president and commercial lines manager, has been with the company for 27 years. "I really enjoy the work, Ray is a great employer, and I plan to stay in the business."

All three agents agree that education about insurance is an important tool for financial stability and success. W. Ray Huff & Associates, Inc. now has a web site, www.HuffInsurance.com, which provides information on the many kinds of insurance and the various companies represented by the agency, along with general consumer advice.

"We find that people are unaware of things such as Motor Vehicle Administration rules regarding turning in tags when auto insurance is discontinued for any reason," said Ray. "We want them to have quick access to information and answers to their questions."

All W. Ray Huff & Associates, Inc. agents adhere to the philosophy embraced by Ray over the years. "We give people the facts, sell them what they need, not what we want to sell, and don't worry about commissions," explained Ray. "Then we don't forget about them. That's why we're serving the same families now: Grandparents who bought from us almost 40 years ago, their children and their grandchildren."

(Left to right) Nancy Huff Nicklow, W. Ray Huff, and Faith Vanskiver.

New Sponsors

Cityline Business Park

Mike Agro, Sr., 6407 Ft. Smallwood Road, Baltimore, MD 21226 / Ph: 410-354-3900 Fax: 410-354-3901
email: citylnbpk@aol.com

With a strategic location providing immediate access to the Baltimore-Washington metropolitan area and the entire Eastern seaboard, Cityline Business Park has become a much sought after address for both large and small businesses. Located on Fort Smallwood Road at the Baltimore city line, this small industrial park is only one block from I-695.

Cityline bears little resemblance to the typical mammoth industrial park since it is truly a "Mom and Pop" type operation. Owners Maureen and Mike Agro began Cityline in 1982 when they mortgaged their home to purchase their first Fort Smallwood Road lot and build two small buildings. One housed Agro Motors, Inc., a used truck and equipment business, and the other was leased.

To meet the demand for commercial rentals, they have continued to buy almost the entire block and build a variety of small shops and larger buildings. Some tenants are single owners who once worked out of their homes, and others are large national companies. The mixture of products and services offered at Cityline include auto and boat mechanics, small manufacturers of industrial and fiber optics peripherals, environmental service companies, trucking companies, contractors, a banking service company, a roofer, and Cookie's Cityline Diner.

There is seldom a vacancy in the current buildings, but development of the ten-acre facility has accelerated since the Agro's son, Mike, Jr., joined Cityline full-time. A large two-story, two-garage building was recently completed, a striking contrast to the much smaller 800 square foot shops that were Cityline's beginnings.

"We can adjust our space and build to the requirements of almost any business," said Mike Agro, Sr. "Every business needs this type of location with quick access to Baltimore, to Pasadena and to the entire state."

The family is available to all of the tenants every day in the Agro Motors, Inc., office at Cityline. Unlike large industrial parks, there is no management or leasing company; the family handles everything from negotiating rents to construction, maintenance and repair. Regardless of the size or nature of the business, Cityline tenants appreciate the hands-on operation and stay for many years.

The Agro's two daughters, Amy, an OSHA safety specialist, and Katy, a retail sales manager, have occasionally worked in the business. With the birth in June 2000 of Sam Agro, the son of Mike Jr. and his wife, Tracy, who also have a daughter, Taylor Osborne, the Agro family is growing.

Cityline Business Park's future also includes growth as the Agros meet the expansion requirements of current tenants and the space requirements of new tenants through construction of custom-built facilities.

County National Bank

Lois Simpson, Manager, 4001 Mountain Road, Pasadena, MD 21122 / Ph: 410-360-5900 Fax: 410-360-5903
Web Site: www.countynational.com

It's a step back in time to a friendlier, more polite era when County National bank tellers greet you by name. With thousands of customers, it would seem an impossible job to remember so many names. However, County National makes it a policy to be a neighborhood bank and customers are always the top priority.

"We live in this community and patronize the businesses here," explained Lois Simpson, Manager of the Pasadena branch of County National Bank. "That means we have a connection with many people and we know their names because they are our friends and neighbors."

Old-fashioned courtesy is the standard at County National, but state-of-the-art technology provides all customers, business and personal, with the same quality banking services as the larger, less personal banks. Convenient lobby and drive-up teller hours, 24-hour telephone banking, ATM/debit cards, absolutely free checking, competitive interest rates, cost effective business checking and loans are examples of County National's services.

County National first opened its doors at the Mountain Road location in 1996 after its organization by local business leaders. Known for integrity and community involvement, the founding officers of County National were Jan W. Clark, President and CEO, John G. Warner, Executive Vice President, and Henry L. Hein, Chairman of the Board, with other prominent county leaders serving on the Board of Directors.

Customers appreciate the pleasant atmosphere where tellers and managers who know and care about them address their needs and concerns.

"Those people at County National are great," said Dave Jacobs of J. B. Machine. "They listen to you and believe in their customers because they know them and their business."

Lois Simpson and other County National associates take active roles within the community with full support of the Bank's board. "Community service and support of our schools and civic associations are important roles for everyone at County National Bank, including officers, directors and employees," said Lois.

With two other locations in Glen Burnie and Odenton, County National plans to grow while remaining an independent community bank focused on its customers' needs.

Maher's Florist

Winnie Maher, 8095C Edwin Raynor Boulevard, Pasadena, MD 21122 / Ph: 410-255-8181 Fax: 410-255-8192
email: winsblooms@aol.com

Winnie Maher and her husband, Skip, mortgaged their home 23 years ago so Winnie could open Maher's Florist. In the beginning, Skip would leave his fulltime Department of Defense job each day and make deliveries from the shop. "He has always been my right hand and worked along with me as the business grew," said Winnie. She also credits her sister, Lil, with helping her in those early days.

Now she has the pleasure of both daughters working with her. Kim Wharton is the manager and head designer at the Edwin Raynor Boulevard shop, and Kristin Fontz works in the shop on holidays and heads up the limousine service offered by Maher's Florist.

Winnie left her Pasadena business in the capable hands of her daughters in 1992 when she accompanied Skip to an overseas assignment in England. She opened a flower shop there, introducing her English customers to American floristry while her American customers enjoyed having her arrange flowers from all over the world.

Maher's sells cut flowers, floral arrangements for all occasions, wedding flowers, and funeral arrangements. For the bereaved, Maher's offers comfort by creating unique designs reflecting a hobby or interest of the deceased. Maher's is also a full-service gift shop carrying candy, fruit baskets, themed baskets, gifts like "Beanie Babies", and home décor. Winnie recently completed a course in balloon design and now creates arches and other patterns for wedding receptions, proms, and special events.

Brides have always looked to Maher's for full service wedding planning including trained bridal consultants, floral arrangements, tuxedo and formal wear rental, and personalized invitations. In 1998, Maher's added a 1995 white Lincoln limousine that is in demand for weddings and many other occasions. Maher's is becoming a strong force in the transportation business and, along with limousine service, plans to provide VIP and passenger

sedans for the Baltimore-Washington area.

Open seven days a week, Maher's holds membership in all of the major wire services and can send flowers anywhere in the world.

Although Maher's plans continued growth, it will always remain a family owned business in Pasadena. Today, all members of the Maher family, including the grandchildren Nikki, 11, Josh, 10, and Thayne, 7, meet at the florist shop to work and to celebrate holidays.

Skip and Winnie were childhood sweethearts in Pasadena. They grew up in Pine Grove Village, played at Cottage Grove, attended Glen Burnie High School, and worked at the Acme Market. Youthful memories include walking home together after Winnie won "Miss Congeniality" at a carnival at the Riviera Beach Fire Department.

"We have grown along with Pasadena," said Winnie, "and our loyal Pasadena customers and friends are a big part of our success."

McDonald's

Barbara & Bob Houck, 8500 Ft. Smallwood Road, Pasadena, MD 21122 / Ph: 410-437-0000 Fax: 410-437-0312

Long-time Pasadena residents recall the anticipation following news that the Golden Arches were coming to town. Since the 1977 opening of McDonald's of Riviera Beach, an entire generation has been regular customers, and hundreds of young students had their first job "under the arches."

In 1982, Barbara and Bob Houck became owner/operators of the restaurant. They are charter members of the Pasadena Business Association and have been continually involved in the community.

The managers and crew of McDonald's of Riviera Beach are known for their friendly spirit and outstanding customer service. At the heart of the restaurant are long-time employees Carolyn Burkentine, Marie Noonan, Jean Vandenhuerk, and Emma Kaiser who were honored at the 20th anniversary celebration of the Riviera Beach restaurant in 1997.

Area seniors gather at "The Beach McDonald's" for morning chats and weekly bingo. Families with school age children greatly enjoy "Principal's Night" when teachers and administrators take over making french fries and serving customers. The restaurant donates a portion of sales to the schools.

In the summer of 1994, Barbara and Bob Houck were given the opportunity to open another McDonald's in the Pasadena area. A ground-breaking celebration in November opened McDonald's Lake Shore with great fanfare. From the beginning, it has been one of the most successful restaurants in the region.

Community relations representative Carolyn Burkentine organizes fun festivals at which talented local performers entertain. Movies, games, and drawings are popular crowd pleasers. The festival raises generous funds to support the local Ronald McDonald Children's Charities. The restaurant is also an annual patron of the Downs Park Concert Series.

Restaurant manager, Thomas Graves, provides strong leadership and lively encouragement to his crew. Everyone focuses on customer needs and serving with a smile. The restaurant's motto: "Keep that drive thru rollin'!"

McDonald's of Lake Shore

The Schmidt Farm

Henry A. Schmidt, 8328 Schmidt's Lane, Pasadena, MD 21122 / Ph: 410-255-7969

Pasadena is full of new communities and families just moving into the area, but the spirit of the peninsula is nurtured by earlier residents like the Schmidt family. Henry Alfred Schmidt, owner of the Schmidt Farm and the Mountain Road Airport, is proud that his grandchildren are the fifth generation on his father's side of the family and the twelfth generation on his mother's side who have lived in Anne Arundel County.

"My family has lived here continuously beginning with my grandfather, Augustus Carl Ferdinand Schmidt, who had his first farm at Pinehurst in 1883," said Henry. "My mother, Grace Adaline Cook Schmidt, was descended from the Hancocks who first settled in Maryland in 1664. After living on the Severn river for several generations, the Hancocks bought land on the Pasadena peninsula in 1766."

Henry's father, William John Martin Schmidt, started the Schmidt family farm on Mountain Road in 1920, growing fruits and vegetables. Along with the Schmidts, four other families lived there year round, working the fields. But during picking season, about ten more families came from Baltimore to harvest the crops.

"They were Polish families," said Henry. "The husbands were stevedores who would come down on the weekends. The mothers and children would work in the fields all morning, then crab and fish and swim in the creek, and they would have outdoor barbecue dinners in the evening."

Produce from the Schmidt Farm supplied Camp Milbur, Camp Whipoorwill, Cottage Grove Park and The Gibson Island Club. Schmidt's produce stand, still on Mountain Road at the entrance to the farm, was a favorite stop for families coming to the Pasadena beaches. "That stand was built in 1927 from stones plowed out of the fields," explained Henry. "It was active until 1967 when I stopped farming fulltime."

The 146-acre farm is now home to three generations of Schmidts: Henry, his son and daughter and their spouses, and their three children. About 20 acres of the farm also includes the Mountain Road Airport. Newcomers zipping down Mountain Road amid busy traffic seldom realize there is an airport nearby. Built in 1950, it replaced Whip's Field and was the only airport in the area to accommodate light aircraft at that time.

The Schmidt Farm remains an oasis of history and resistance to development in Pasadena. Schmidt grandchildren and their friends and classmates often play there just as Henry and his brother and cousins did long ago.

Many people wonder what the future will hold for the Schmidt Farm. "As my son says, we plan on doing the same thing we've done for the past 80 years," said Henry. "Our family plans on enjoying this farm."

Wilson's Bus Service, Inc.

Gail Hyser, 4413, Mountain Road, Pasadena, MD 21122 / Ph: 410-255-1047 Fax: 410-255-4826

When those big yellow buses go rolling down the streets of Pasadena carrying our most precious resource, our school children, safety is the primary concern for Wilson's Bus Service, Inc. With 40 years experience driving for Anne Arundel County schools, Wilson's has shuttled tens of thousands of children spanning several generations.

"The standard was set when my Dad, John Wilson, Jr., began the bus company in 1961," says Gail Hyser, president of Wilson's Bus Service. "But we never rest on our excellent safety record. Our drivers are all given rigorous interviews and training, and we continually evaluate our drivers' performance. We have ongoing driver training and drug and alcohol testing and awareness programs."

Wilson's services both Chesapeake and Northeast High Schools and their feeder elementary and middle schools. Along with daily school transportation, the company drives children on field trips and to athletic events out of the Pasadena area. The company has 37 employees including drivers, attendants, mechanics and office staff.

Wilson's Bus Service proudly points out that 95% of its employees are Pasadena residents, and are driving their families, friends and neighbors in their own communities. "We have this additional assurance of familiar faces for our children," said Gail. "Many of our employees have been with the company for over 25 years."

This loyalty is a hallmark of the Wilson Family. John Wilson, Sr., began Wilson's gas station in 1934, and it has been at its present location on Mountain Road since 1937. When John, Jr., took over after his father's death, he remodeled and enlarged the station, and it provided the first employment for many young men.

As Pasadena grew, John, Jr., decided to open another company, Wilson's Bus Service, beginning with one bus in 1961, which he drove. The company was incorporated in 1970, and now has 30 buses which all meet the stringent federal, state and local government safety specifications.

John and his wife, Diana, ran the company until 1997 when they retired. Now their daughter, Gail, steers the company forward. She was always involved in the company, painting mud flaps on the buses as a child. Gail began working as a driver for the company 18 years ago. Long involved with the National School Transportation Association, she received the prestigious Gold Merit Award in areas of safety, driver training, safety maintenance, and supervisory service.

Gail believes her job as president of Wilson's Bus Service, Inc., is to provide the safest ride possible for school children. "When they're on our buses, we feel like they are our children," she says. "Our drivers always call them 'my kids.' Wilson's cares about all of the children as if each of them was our own child, and our goal is to make their bus ride a safe and happy part of the school day."

Patrons

THE BAY

Delta Trash
J. Ben Poe III

Gibson Island Country School
A Classic education for boys and girls since 1956, pre-K through 5.

James Anderson, CPA
Anderson, Davis & Associates, CPA, PA

THE RIVER

Senator Alfred J. Lipin (retired) and Mrs. Irene H. Lipin

THE CREEK

Emily J. Anderson
James J. Anderson, Jr.
Mary Sandra "Sandy" Anderson
Rose K. Mason
Mr. & Mrs. William N. Mason, Jr.
Janine & Matthew Thomas
James R. King, Jr.
Gil & Pat Willey
Debbie, Travis, & Kristen Romano
Frank Loane, Sr. and Linda Loane
Frank Loane, Jr. and Julie, Chelsea, Emily Loane
Bill Loane and Karen Loane
Ruth Poe
Mr. And Mrs. John B. Poe, Jr.
Thomas Poe
J. Ben Poe
Sharon Poe
Christopher Jacob Poe
Allison Hunter Poe
Jeremy Marlin Poe

Jason Poe
Melissa Poe
My Friend "Duke" Poe
Jan and Barbara Clark
Albert and Catherine Thyr
David & Shirley Jacobs
Bruce & Darlene Follin & Family
The Zeh Family
David Jacobs II & Family
Jamie & Gail Jacobs & Family
Michael & Rebecca Jacobs & Family
Steve & Dawn Kemp & Family
John and Lois Harman Simpson
Heather Kaye Myers
Walter Stanley and Virginia Harman
Cayce Simpson
Dr. Elijah Joyce (1826-1908), great grandfather of Clifford R. Phelps
Dr. Elijah Joyce practiced medicine on Mountain Road from 1868 to 1898
Irene S. Phelps, wife of the late Clifford A. Phelps (1907-1971)
Clifford M. Phelps—son of Clifford R. Phelps—son of Clifford A. Phelps
Clifford R. Phelps and wife, Sally Ann, Mountain Road, Pasadena, MD
Berry Griebel, Steward Edwards, Angus & Ella Griebel-Edwards
Bill, Wendy and Amber Harris

IN MEMORY OF

James W. Anderson
George & Eather (Boots) Elliott
James (Jack) Jacobs
Ray Werner—father of Darlene and Kimberly
Eloise M. Wade
Walter J. Phelps (1870-1939), father of Clifford A. Phelps

Bibliography

BOOKS

Bradford, James C., editor. *Anne Arundel County, Maryland: A Bicentennial History*. Annapolis, Md: Annapolis and Anne Arundel County Bicentennial Committee, 1977. See "Land and People" by Jane McWilliams, pp.1-11.

Burgess, Robert H. *This Was Chesapeake Bay*. Cambridge, Md.: Cornell Maritime Press, 1963.

Burgess, Robert H. and H. Graham Wood. *Steamboats Out of Baltimore*. Cambridge, Md.: Tidewater Publishers, 1968.

Clark, William Bullock. *Maryland Geological Survey: The Geology of Anne Arundel County*. Baltimore: Johns Hopkins University Press, 1917.

DAR Patriot Index. Washington: National Society of the Daughters of the American Revolution, 1966.

Ennis, Robert B. *Maryland: A Description of Its Lands, Products, and Industries*. Baltimore: George W. King Printing Company, 1910.

Fields, Barbara J. *Slavery and Freedom on the Middle Ground: Maryland During the Nineteenth Century*. New Haven: Yale University Press, 1985.

Gillespie, C. Richard. *The James Adams Floating Theatre*. Centreville, Md.: Tidewater Publishers, 1991.

Hartzell, Daniel D. *Marylanders in the Confederacy*. Silver Spring, Md.: Family Line Publication, 1986.

Holland, F. Ross. *Maryland Lighthouses of the Chesapeake Bay*. Crownsville, Md., Maryland Historical Trust Press, and Colton's Point, Md.: The Friends of St. Clement's Island Museum, Inc., 1997.

Keith, Robert C. *Baltimore Harbor: A Picture History*. Baltimore: Johns Hopkins University Press, 1991.

Kelly, Jacques. *Anne Arundel County: A Pictorial History*. Norfolk: The Donning Company, 1989.

Kenny, Hamill. *The Placenames of Maryland, Their Origin and Meaning.* Baltimore: Maryland Historical Society, 1984.

Lord, Walter. *The Dawn's Early Light*. New York: W.W. Norton and Company, 1972.

Marine, William H. *The British Invasion of Maryland, 1812-1815*. Baltimore: Society of the War of 1812 in Maryland, 1913.

Matthews, Edward B. *The Counties of Maryland: Their Origin and Boundaries and Election Districts.* Maryland Geological Survey, Vol. VI, Part V. Baltimore: Johns Hopkins University Press, 1907.

Mumford, Willard R. *Strawberries, Peas, and Beans: Truck Farming in Anne Arundel County*. Linthicum, Md.: Anne Arundel County Historical Society, 2000.

Nelker, Gladys. *Town Neck Hundred of Anne Arundel County*. Westminster, Md.: Family Line Publication, 1990.

Newman, Harry Wright. *Maryland Military Records*. Washington: published by the author, 1938.

Ramage, Kenneth, editor. *Lyman Shotshell Handbook*, second edition. Middlefield, Connecticut: Lyman Publishing Company, 1976.

Riley, Elihu S. *A History of Anne Arundel County in Maryland*. Annapolis: Charles G. Feldmeyer, 1905.

Smith, Captain John. *The General Historie of Virginia, New England, and the Summer Isles*. Volume I, Second and Third Books, from the London edition of 1629. Richmond: Franklin Press, 1819.

Steuart, Rieman. *A History of the Maryland Line in the Revolutionary War, 1775-1783.* Towson, Md.: Society of the Cincinnati of Maryland, 1969.

Taylor, Marianne. *My River Speaks: The History and Lore of the Magothy River*. Arnold, Md: Bay Media Press, Inc., 1998.

Travers, Paul J. *The Patapsco: Baltimore's River of History*. Centreville, Md.: Tidewater Publishing Company, 1990.

Ware, Donna M. *The Historical Properties of Anne Arundel County*. Annapolis: A project of the Environmental and Special Projects Division, Office of Planning and Zoning, Anne Arundel County, 1990.

Warfield, Joshua Dorsey. *The Founders of Anne Arundel and Howard Counties, Maryland*. Baltimore: Kohn and Pollock, 1905.

Wright, F. Edward. *Maryland Militia: War of 1812*. Vol. 4, Anne Arundel and Calvert Counties. Silver Spring, Md.: Family Line Publication, 1981.

PUBLISHED ARTICLES

Benson, Robert Louis. "Historical Survey of the Natural Resources of Anne Arundel County." *Anne Arundel County History Notes,* vol. 23, no.1 (October 1991):11-13.

Blaisdell, Gail R. "Bloomer Girls Have Vanished." *Maryland Living*, July 7, 1968:4.

Cole, Merle T. "Army Air Defense Installations in Anne Arundel County, 1950-1973." *Anne Arundel County History Notes,* vol.15, no.1 (Oct. 1983):5-6.

Cole, "Fort Smallwood's Military Mission." *Anne Arundel County History Notes,* vol.25, no. 3 (April 1994):1,6-7,9-10.

Cunningham, Isabel Shipley. "Anne Arundel's Famous Green-Meat Cantaloupes." *Anne Arundel County History Notes,* vol.27, no.4 (July 1996):3,4,8-10.

Durner, Marie Angel. "Early Days on Mountain Road." *Anne Arundel County History Notes*, vol.16, no.3 (April 1985):1-2.

Durner, "Early History of Downs Park," *Anne Arundel County History Notes*, vol.15, no.2 (January 1984):2. (Based on Richard Holt's account of life on Rocky Beach Farm, 1913-37)

Durner, "Tom Stallings' Blacksmith Shop," *Anne Arundel County History Notes*, vol.8, no.2 (January 1997):3. (Based on recollections of his son, William C. Stallings)

Guhne, Joani, "In 1890 McBee House Was One of Four in Pasadena," *Times-Voice,* November 20, 1980.

Gould, Robert F. "Eminent Chemists of Maryland." *Maryland Historical Magazine,* vol.80, no.1 (Spring 1985):19.

Kelbaugh, Jack. "By Water, Road, and Rail: The Early Railroads of Northern Anne Arundel County." *Anne Arundel County History Notes*, Part III, vol.23, no.3 (April 1992):1,6,10-14; Part IV, vol. 23, no.4 (July 1992):3,7,9-11.

Kelbaugh, "The Wild Cranberries of Anne Arundel County." *Anne Arundel County History Notes*, vol.22, no.3 (April 1991):5-6.

McLaughlin, Dr. Randall M., "Memories of the Anne Arundel Years," *Anne Arundel County History Notes*, vol.28. no.4 (July 1997):15.

Mellin, Jack. "Green Haven Advertising Brochures." *Anne Arundel County History Notes,* vol.22, no.2 (Jan.1991):9.

Potee, Blodwin Shipley, "Bugeyes, Docks, and Wharves." *Anne Arundel County History Notes*, vol.16, no.2 (Jan. 1985):1.

Potee, "The Squire's Tin House." *Anne Arundel County History Notes,* vol.6, no.3 (April 1975):1.

Potee, "This Old House." *Anne Arundel County History Notes*, vol.6, no.3 (July 1973):1.

Robinson, John M. "The History of Pinehurst." *Anne Arundel County History Notes*, Part I, vol. 21 (January 1990):4; Part II, vol.21, no.4 (July 1990):1-2,7-8.

Slanker, Harold E., Jr. "The J.F. Johnson Lumber Company." *Anne Arundel County History Notes,* vol.24, no.4 (July 1992):2.

Smith, Middleton. "A Graphic Summary of American Agriculture." Yearbook of the Department of Agriculture, 1915. Washington: Government Printing Office, 1916.

Stearnes, Richard E. "Some Indian Village Sites of Tidewater Maryland." *Proceedings of the Natural History Society of Maryland,* no.9 (July 1942):6-8.

Waite, Merton B. "Fruit Growing." Yearbook of the Department of Agriculture 1905. Washington: Government Printing Office, 1906.

White, Roger B. "All Ashore for Fairview Park." *Anne Arundel County History Notes,* vol.12, no.2 (Jan. 1981):1-2.

White, "Bus Service to Anne Arundel County: 1910-1980." *Anne Arundel County History Notes,* vol.11, no.3 (April 1980):1-3.

White, "Saturday Night at the Dance Halls." *Anne Arundel County History Notes*, Part I, vol.20, no.4 (July 1989):4-9; Part II, vol.21, no.1 (October 1989):1-6.

NEWSPAPERS AND NEWSLETTERS

The Anne Arundel Advocate, Green Haven, 1924.

Arundel Observer, Glen Burnie, Maryland, 1959.

Bayside Beach News, Issue 2,1997; Issue 4, 1998.

Evening Capital, Annapolis, 1884-1890, 1919, 1961, 1964.

Capital, Annapolis, Maryland, 1999-2000.

The Green Haven Hash, 1937, 1939.

Maryland Gazette, Annapolis, 1903, 1935-1941, 1962, 1967, 1977, 1984-1993, 1997-1999. See also the 1993 supplement to the *Maryland Gazette*, "The Pasadena Guide Book."

Maryland Republican, Annapolis, 1871, 1878, 1886.

The Sun, Baltimore, 1852, 1862, 1864, 1884, 1890, 1894, 1908, 1910, 1923, 1943, 1944, 1953, 1961, 1964-1967, 1979, 1985-1999.

Washington Post, Washington, D.C., 1960, 1997.

GOVERNMENT AND MILITARY RECORDS

Act Relating to Public Roads in Anne Arundel County. Jan.3, 1800. (Liber J.G., No.3, f.350)

Agricultural Schedules of the Federal Census, 1850, Anne Arundel County (Microfilm 5164-1, State Archives)

Archives of Maryland, Vol.19:69. Proceedings of the House of Delegates, 1694.

Baltimore County Tax List, 1699-1707 (when the peninsula was part of Baltimore County).

Census of 1790, Heads of Families at the First Census of the United States: Maryland. Washington: Government Printing Office, 1907.

Census, Anne Arundel County, Maryland, 1850. Pasadena, Maryland: Anne Arundel County Genealogical Society, 1991. Compiled by John W. Powell.

Census, Book 3, Third and Fifth Districts, Anne Arundel County, 1860. See pages130-157 for residents of the community called Johnson's Store.

Census of the Unites States for 1910, with Supplement for Maryland. Washington: Government Printing Office, 1913.

Civil War Enrollment Records, Anne Arundel County, Third District, 1862. (The Enrollment Officer's hand-written records are in this marble-back school notebook.)

Federal Direct Tax, 1798. Maryland State Papers.

Muster Rolls and Other Records of Maryland Troops in the American Revolution. Archives of Maryland, vol. 18. Baltimore: Maryland Historical Society, 1900.

Oaths of Fidelity, 1777-1781, Red Book 22, pp. 27, 27.1, Maryland State Archives.

Revolutionary Records: Army Accounts paid by the State of Maryland to Continental Troops. Drawer 50, Maryland State Archives.

Slave Schedules of the 1860 Federal Census, Anne Arundel County (Microfilm 7202, Maryland State Archives)

REPORTS

Conservation Commission of Maryland, Report for 1908-1909. Baltimore, 1909, pp.95-96.

Glaser, John D. Petrology and Origin of Potomac and Magothy Sediments. Maryland Geological Survey Report no.11, 1969, pp.62-64.

Maryland Agricultural Experiment Station Bulletin A-E, Annual Report, 1888-1891, p.5; Bulletin no.33, April 1895, pp. 118-119,126; Bulletin no.116, March 1907, p.251. College Park: Maryland Agricultural College.

Maryland and Its Advantages for Immigrants. Baltimore: The State Bureau of Immigration, 1911, p.25.

Maryland State Bureau of Immigration, Annual Report 1907, p.16. (M305, Maryland State Archives)

Maryland Historical Trust, Archaeological Sites Inventory. 18 AN-760, Wishing Rock; 18 AN-949, Canal at Pinehurst.

Maryland Historical Trust, Historic Sites Inventory. AA-21, Lake Shore Homestead (Williams); AA-128, Johnson's Store; AA-730, Locust Lodge; AA-807, Cook Farm; AA-897, Fort Smallwood; AA-898, Fort Smallwood Park; AA-923, Bodkin School; AA-931, Seven Foot Knoll Lighthouse; AA-1009, Hanshaw House; AA-1043, Magothy Church; AA-1044, Mt. Zion Church; AA-2050, Sons of Temperance Lodge.

Maryland, Its Resources, Industries, and Institutions. Johns Hopkins University Report, Baltimore, 1893, pp.159, 171.

Report of the Public Schools of Maryland. Report of the State Board of Education to the General Assembly. Annapolis, 1865, 1868, 1869, 1873, 1876, 1877, 1881, 1884, 1886; Baltimore, 1888, 1891, 1892, 1896, 1908, 1912; Annapolis, 1916; Baltimore, 1920.

Statistics of Fruits and Vegetables, Yearbook of the Department of Agriculture 1925. Washington: Government Printing Office, 1926, p. 936.

Walker, Mark. Plantation in Suburbia: An Integrated Approach to Hancock's Resolution, Anne Arundel County, Maryland. The Lost Towns of Anne Arundel Project, PACE, Annapolis, Maryland, 1998.

Wright, Russell. Hancock's Resolution, An Historic Structure. Report on the Hancock Family Farm, Anne Arundel County, Maryland. Vol.1, Existing Conditions. Warren, Rhode Island: Prepared for Historic Annapolis, Inc., 1980.

Zambala, Dennis, Executive Director, Baltimore Museum of Industry. "Seven-Foot Knoll Lighthouse." Maryland Historic Trust Historic Sites Inventory AA-931, August 1987.

UNPUBLISHED MATERIAL

Brief histories of churches, fire departments, service clubs, and the Magothy Health Center are available through those organizations and are not included here.

Barnes, John A. Letter to Henry A. Hancock, Bodkin Creek. April 15, 1861. Edwin T. Calvert Collection.

Behm, Carl. "The Grachur Story: 1912-1992."

Brown, Hazel and Bettie Heckman. "History of Pasadena Methodist Church." 1962.

Calvert, Edwin T. "Hancock's Resolution," Historic Annapolis pamphlet. October, 1965.

Corey, Arthur T. "The Coreys of Bodkin Creek." Fort Collins, Colorado, 1990.

"Discovering Our School Communities." Anne Arundel County School Histories of Freetown, High Point, Jacobsville, Magothy, Pasadena, and Riviera Beach. 1952.

Fink, Harold E. "Our History," Special Edition of the Maryland Yacht Club *Kedge Anchor*. Fairview, Pasadena, 1980.

Hein, Bertha S. and Ruth E. Bollman. "A Church, Its People, Its Community." May, 1964. An account of Magothy Methodist Church and related history

"History of Camp Whippoorwill" (1928-1951). William G. Rothamel Collection.

Jachowski, Martha and John Mogey. "Pinehurst on the Bay/Bodkin." 1994.

Kiessling, Trevor A., Jr. "Bodkin Neck: The Gateway to the Patapsco." 1979. A valuable source of information about this area.

Kirkley, Charles F. "Report of the Committee to Study the Effects of Legalized Gambling in Anne Arundel County." May 1960. See also "Events Since May 1960," a brief supplement to the Kirkley report. 1961.

"Lake Shore Volunteer Fire Company Dedication." May 4, 1947. John Williams Collection. (Contains interesting 1940s photographs)

Lopez, Joseph Osia. "Capture, Escape, and Recapture of Joseph Osia Lopez." No date. James B. Calvert Collection.

Madden, Charles. "Locust Lodge, A Landmark,." Riviera Beach Community Association Newsletter. November 1994.

McGrain, John W. "The Molinography of Anne Arundel County." One of three articles bound as *Water Power: A Composite*. Undated.

Noue, Patricia. "Lake Waterford Park: Lake Waterford Dam Repair and Impact on the Environment." 1993.

124th Anniversary of Mount Zion United Methodist Church. 1983. James B. Calvert Collection. A brief history of Mt. Zion Church.

Potee, Blodwin Shipley. "The History of Mt. Carmel United Methodist Church, 1884-1979."

Pritchett, Virginia Aten. "A History of Magothy Methodist Church, 1777-1960." (A second printing includes Helen Coggins' additions, extending the history to 1977.)

Schell, Rev. Edwin C., Executive Secretary of the Methodist Historical Society of the Baltimore Conference of the United Methodist Church. Notes taken from the minutes of the Methodist Protestant Church Conferences and the *Baltimore Methodist*, *Washington Christian Advocate*, and *Methodist Protestant* newspapers. 1830-1939. Invaluable research and the only source of the early history of White March Church at Lake Shore.

Schramm, Emma M. "History of the Pasadena Post Office and All Other Post Offices That Covered This Same Area." November 1985. (See Appendix A for a reprint.)

Schramm, Emma M. "Sixty Years in Anne Arundel County: The Schramm Farm, 1910-1970."

Steponaitis, Laurie Cameron. "A Survey of Artifact Collections from the Patuxent River Drainage, Maryland." Maryland Historical Trust Monograph Series No.1. 1980.

Ware, Donna M. "A Self-Guiding Brochure for Hancock's Resolution."

Index

NOTE TO RESEARCHERS: For names not listed individually, see Taxpayers, 1696; Oath of Fidelity, signers; Census of 1790; Militiamen, War of 1812; Landowners; Slaveowners; Civil War, and Hopkins Atlas, patrons.

Sun Valley
Lipins Cor.
Silver Sands
Altoona Beach
Pine Haven
Olde Mill
Green Haven
177
100
607
648
2
POWHATAN
BEACH RD
MOUNTAIN RD
OUTING AVE
EAST SHORE
DUVALL HWY.
TICK NECK RD
RAYNOR BLVD
Armiger
ROAD
Jacob
HOWARD RD
SOLLEY
LOCUST DR
FRANCIS RD
HECKINGER RD
ELVATON RD
B & A
RITCHIE HWY.
LONGHILL RD
WATERFORD RD
OBRECHT RD
WOOD RD
BROOK
DOGWOOD RD
TRAIL
WOODLAND
PASADENA RD
LAKE WATERFORD PARK
Chartwell
KINDER PARK
KINDER RD
CHARTWELL C.C.
ANDREWS
CATHERINE
Pasadena
HARLEM RD
ULMAN BRIDGE
EDWIN
MAGOTHY BRIDGE ROAD
EARLEIGH RD
JUMPERS HOLE RD
HEIGHTS
TRUCK HOUSE
ANNAPOLIS RD
Riverdale
BEACH
WOODS ROAD
EVERGREEN RD
PARK
Robinson RD
MAGOTHY RD
Chelsea Beach
Cattail Cr.
WALDO RD
LAKE SHORE
SEVERNA PARK
SEVERN RIVER
ARUNDEL BEACH RD
Maceys Corner
Cape Arthur
MCKINSEY RD
CYPRESS RD
Sunrise Beach
Cedar Point
Eaglenest Point
Herald Harbor
FERRY PT RD
Blackhole Cr.
SHADY
EAGLE
North Ferry Point
Cypress Cr.
Mago Vista Beach
Manhattan Beach
Mill Cr.
MAGO VISTA RD
Kyle Point
Little Round Bay
Long Point
St. Helena I.
Swan Point
South Ferry Point
Rock Point
MAGOTHY
BROAD WATER RD
ANNE ARUNDEL COMMUNITY COLLEGE
COLLEGE
GOVERNOR
Rugby Hall Estates
Aisquith Cr.
GLEN OBAN
Sherwood Forest
FOREST
Brewer Point
Brewer Cr.
COACHWAY
Clements
Belvedere Heights
Bayberry
ACRES
SHORE
BAY HILLS
JOYCE